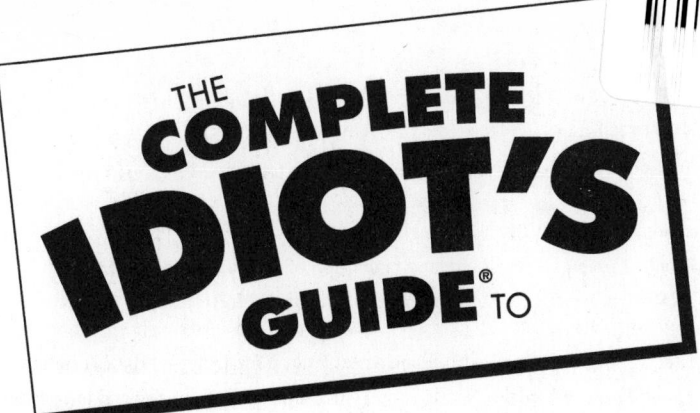

THE COMPLETE IDIOT'S GUIDE TO

Starting and Running a Thrift Store

by Ravel Buckley with Carol Costa

ALPHA

A member of Penguin Group (USA) Inc.

ALPHA BOOKS

Published by the Penguin Group

Penguin Group (USA) Inc., 375 Hudson Street, New York, New York 10014, USA

Penguin Group (Canada), 90 Eglinton Avenue East, Suite 700, Toronto, Ontario M4P 2Y3, Canada (a division of Pearson Penguin Canada Inc.)

Penguin Books Ltd., 80 Strand, London WC2R 0RL, England

Penguin Ireland, 25 St. Stephen's Green, Dublin 2, Ireland (a division of Penguin Books Ltd.)

Penguin Group (Australia), 250 Camberwell Road, Camberwell, Victoria 3124, Australia (a division of Pearson Australia Group Pty. Ltd.)

Penguin Books India Pvt. Ltd., 11 Community Centre, Panchsheel Park, New Delhi—110 017, India

Penguin Group (NZ), 67 Apollo Drive, Rosedale, North Shore, Auckland 1311, New Zealand (a division of Pearson New Zealand Ltd.)

Penguin Books (South Africa) (Pty.) Ltd., 24 Sturdee Avenue, Rosebank, Johannesburg 2196, South Africa

Penguin Books Ltd., Registered Offices: 80 Strand, London WC2R 0RL, England

Copyright © 2010 by Ravel Buckley and Carol Costa

International Standard Book Number: 978-1-59257-952-5
Library of Congress Catalog Card Number: 2009930702

12 11 10   8 7 6 5 4 3 2 1

Interpretation of the printing code: The rightmost number of the first series of numbers is the year of the book's printing; the rightmost number of the second series of numbers is the number of the book's printing. For example, a printing code of 10-1 shows that the first printing occurred in 2010.

Printed in the United States of America

Note: This publication contains the opinions and ideas of its authors. It is intended to provide helpful and informative material on the subject matter covered. It is sold with the understanding that the authors and publisher are not engaged in rendering professional services in the book. If the reader requires personal assistance or advice, a competent professional should be consulted.

The authors and publisher specifically disclaim any responsibility for any liability, loss, or risk, personal or otherwise, which is incurred as a consequence, directly or indirectly, of the use and application of any of the contents of this book.

Most Alpha books are available at special quantity discounts for bulk purchases for sales promotions, premiums, fundraising, or educational use. Special books, or book excerpts, can also be created to fit specific needs.

For details, write: Special Markets, Alpha Books, 375 Hudson Street, New York, NY 10014.

Publisher: *Marie Butler-Knight*
Editorial Director: *Mike Sanders*
Senior Managing Editor: *Billy Fields*
Senior Acquisitions Editor: *Paul Dinas*
Development Editor: *Nancy D. Lewis*
Senior Production Editor: *Janette Lynn*
Copy Editor: *Amy Borrelli*

Cartoonist: *Steve Barr*
Cover Designer: *Bill Thomas*
Book Designer: *Trina Wurst*
Indexer: *Celia McCoy*
Layout: *Ayanna Lacey*
Proofreader: *John Etchison*

Contents at a Glance

Contents

Appendixes

Introduction

Thrift stores are considered to be recession-proof, making this type of business one of the fastest growing in the country.

The thrift store business is exciting because it is never routine. There are always surprises to be found among the merchandise and there is always the chance that a real treasure will be discovered. An industry that was once viewed as a wasteland for the less fortunate has become a shining star in the ongoing challenge to save our planet. Reuse, recycle, and go green are now common cries, and thrift stores that have adhered to this philosophy all along are leaders in the effort to protect the Earth for future generations.

All thrift stores service the community where they are located in one way or another. They provide goods to people on limited budgets who need to find clothing and household items at reduced prices. Resale shops are also a means of support for many charitable organizations. People from all walks of life and all economic and ethnic backgrounds shop in thrift stores and donate their personal goods to be resold and reused.

There is no limit to the types of merchandise that thrift stores carry, and each store can be unique as it reflects the individual interests of its owner. Many thrift store owners have tapped into lucrative niche markets for books, collectibles, antiques, and jewelry. If you are a person who is filled with enthusiasm and anticipation every time you enter a resale shop, this may be the perfect business enterprise for you.

Thrift stores have lower start-up costs than most business ventures and have a higher success rate. A thrift store will allow you to use your talents, creativity, and ingenuity to design it, stock it, and service your community. If you have a charity or cause that needs help, a nonprofit thrift store can provide funding for it.

This book provides all the information needed to get started in the resale industry. It is presented in a simple, logical order that gives you an insight into the opportunities that exist, the challenges you will face, and the steps you must take to establish and run a successful store.

How to Use This Book

This is a guide to the many and varied aspects of the resale industry from small mom-and-pop stores to large stores with multiple locations. It will help you make important decisions about your future as a thrift store owner and explain all the complicated issues like nonprofit and tax-exempt status, the process of incorporation, and those dreaded accounting issues in straightforward, easy-to-understand language.

The book has been organized into four logical parts:

Part 1, "Planning and Research," discusses the fun and challenges of the resale business. It provides information on becoming a nonprofit entity and how to choose a charity or cause to support with your thrift store. It goes on to address the questions relating to a store organized and operated for profit. Finally, it explains the different ways of structuring a thrift store business and the process necessary to create each one.

Part 2, "Getting Down to Business," provides explanations and advice on all the decisions that must be made before your store opens for business. It includes detailed information on setting up your store and keeping all the financial records necessary to run it properly. Suggestions for advertising and promoting your new store are also included.

Now that your store is up and running, **Part 3, "Improving Your Business Operation,"** offers a wealth of information on unique ways you can improve your business operation and at the same time stand out as a business leader in your community.

Whether you want to run one store or several, **Part 4, "Expanding Your Business,"** tells you how to make the most of what you have and tap into other profitable areas of the resale business.

Throughout this book you will find notations of interesting and informative tips, suggestions, and warnings to clarify or add to the text. Take the time to read the following items as they pop up on most pages:

Added Value

Tips to help you make good choices for your business and yourself.

Helping Hands

Advice on how to help your community and your store grow and prosper.

Not for Resale

Warnings that will make you aware of potential problems that can be avoided in your day-to-day business operation.

def•i•ni•tion

Explanations of words and phrases that relate to the thrift store business.

Acknowledgments

Thanks to our agent, Verna Dreisbach, for bringing this project to us and to our editor, Paul Dinas, who helped us through the writing process.

Trademarks

All terms mentioned in this book that are known to be or are suspected of being trademarks or service marks have been appropriately capitalized. Alpha Books and Penguin Group (USA) Inc. cannot attest to the accuracy of this information. Use of a term in this book should not be regarded as affecting the validity of any trademark or service mark.

Part 1

Planning and Research

While the thrift store business is considered recession-proof, opening and running a new resale shop requires the same amount of forethought and consideration as any other type of business.

Whether the thrift store is intended to support a charitable cause or be the main source of income for the owner, it has to be structured and developed in a way that will allow it to grow and prosper.

The first five chapters of this book will guide you through the research and planning stages of opening a thrift store. Most of the information is general and applies to all resale shops. A few chapters address specific issues and concerns that face readers intending to open a nonprofit store, but these chapters also contain tips and suggestions that a store operated for profit can use.

Fun and Challenges of Thrift Stores

In This Chapter

- ◆ Making a difference in your community
- ◆ Searching for treasure
- ◆ Protecting the environment
- ◆ Investments of time and money
- ◆ Using your talents
- ◆ Meeting new people every day

Perhaps the most important question you should ask yourself before beginning any business venture is: "Will I enjoy it?"

All businesses require hard work and dedication; a thrift store is no exception, but the thrift business offers advantages that others do not. It also presents more fun and excitement than other types of businesses, because it is not the kind of undertaking where you will know exactly what you can expect day in and day out. It is the type of business that can deliver enjoyment and satisfaction with nominal *start-up costs*.

def•i•ni•tion

Start-up costs are the combined total of the actual dollars required to begin a new business venture.

Entering the world of resale is an adventure that requires advance planning and research. The challenges that we face are what make life fun and interesting, and opening a thrift store is a perfect example of how this works. In this chapter, we will examine the many facets of this growing industry and how it can impact you and your future.

Your Community Welcomes You

People used to think that thrift stores belonged in needy communities—depressed areas where the residents were forced to look for used merchandise to clothe their families and stock their households. In recent years, the resale industry has dispelled that notion. Today, thrift stores provide a seemingly unending variety of merchandise for the consumer. Although most still offer a general assortment of goods for home and personal needs, there are those that also specialize in books, furniture, appliances, and decorator items. Some believe it is the ups and downs of an unstable economy that has allowed the resale industry to flourish and expand into so many different areas. However, a look back in history shows that man has always traded what he had and didn't want for what he wanted and didn't have. Combine that practice with the fact that everyone loves a bargain, and you can see why thrift stores are thriving in cities and towns across the country.

Resale shops make a difference in any community, but the type of merchandise a shop carries often determines their place in the community. For example, a thrift shop that specializes in designer clothing and decorator items would not open up in a poor neighborhood, and a shop that carries used clothing and household goods would probably not prosper on a street like Rodeo Drive.

Regardless of its designated place in a particular city or town, thrift stores do provide the area with important choices that would not be available without their existence. While many of the benefits are economical in nature, there are also emotional benefits. Consider the feelings of an unemployed person who finds suitable clothing to wear for a job interview at a thrift store. The proper attire can bolster his or her self-confidence so that the potential employer sees the applicant in a more favorable light. There are thrift stores that solicit business attire and keep it in a section reserved for unemployed men and women who need it for job interviews or who are starting new jobs.

Another nice part of the resale business is the sweet memories that are invoked in a customer when an item from his or her past is displayed in the store. It can be an article of clothing, a painting, a book, a tool, or a certain toy treasured in childhood. People often browse through thrift shops just to revisit the past and remember the good old days.

 **Not for Resale**

In recent years, much has been publicized about toys containing lead or other elements harmful to children. Be cautious when accepting donations of toys, and make sure they are safe before displaying them for sale.

Memories for Sale

Stocking any kind of thrift store means searching for the best merchandise. This is what many owners consider their biggest challenge and, at the same time, the most enjoyable part of the business.

If your store is a nonprofit that benefits some charity or cause, you will have a built-in donation base. This base is made up of people in your community who want to help the individuals or organization your store supports. If your store is not a nonprofit entity, it doesn't mean that you won't get merchandise to stock the store given to you. It means you will have to work a little harder to get them, including purchasing your inventory. And even if you are a nonprofit business, the donations alone may not be enough to keep your inventory at the level needed to fill your store.

Before you open the doors to your thrift shop, you will have to gather donations and search out ways to obtain merchandise that can be resold at a profit. There are a multitude of ways to do this, and they will all be discussed in Chapter 15. For now, let's concentrate on the joy of the search.

If you've ever taken part in a scavenger hunt, you know the fun of the game is not the items you have to collect. It's in the search for the objects and the people you meet during the hunt who are willing to join in the game to help you win.

Searching for merchandise to resell in a thrift store is like that scavenger hunt. You will be going out into your community and other areas to make new friends and gather treasure. In the process of living and raising families, people accumulate things you may never know existed. You may think of some of these things as junk, but remember the old saying: "One man's junk is another man's treasure." That should be the motto of any thrift store or resale business.

As the owner of a thrift store, you have to keep an open mind when sorting through donations or other items that come into your hands. It's fairly easy to see the value in ordinary items like clothing, dishes, linens, and books. It's the unusual things, like a stuffed pigeon or a painted rock, that will test your imagination and prompt you to imagine its usefulness. The rock can become a doorstop, the stuffed pigeon a backyard decoration for a bird lover.

Experienced thrift store owners will tell you that people fall in love with the strangest things, and that's what makes the business so surprising. Be aware that even the most unusual items have sales potential in a thrift store.

Going Green

We have come to a point in the world when we must think twice about discarding the things that pass through our hands. Things like tin cans, glass, cardboard boxes, newspapers, plastic containers, and whatever else you can think of that were once considered garbage are now placed in recycle bins instead of trash containers. It's good for the economy and good for the environment.

Instead of filling up our land resources with garbage, recyclers are collecting these things and giving them a new life and purpose. People are becoming more and more aware of the environment and our duty to protect it for future generations.

Thrift stores are a big part of the recycling process and play an important role in saving our planet. Take a look at the benefits of recycling posted on the Environmental Protection Agency (EPA) website:

- Recycling protects and expands U.S. manufacturing jobs and increases our competitive edge in the world.

- Recycling reduces the need for landfills and incineration.

- Recycling prevents pollution caused by the manufacturing of products from virgin materials.

- Recycling saves energy.

- Recycling reduces the emissions of greenhouse gases that contribute to global climate change.

- Recycling conserves natural resources such as timber, water, and minerals.

- Recycling helps sustain the environment for future generations.

Added Value

Small appliances and electronic items that no longer work can be disassembled so the pieces can be used to build something new or used for repairs.

There has never been a better time to open a thrift store than now, when "going green" has become a national slogan. Thrift store owners are being called green-collar workers, and are proud to be in an industry that is so obviously in tune with a movement to preserve our natural resources. The "re" words are everywhere you look: reuse, reduce, recycle, and words such as repurpose, refashion and redesign are being put into practice every day by the resale industry. This is why people will donate items to your thrift store and other people will purchase those items and use them again and again.

Personal Investments

Nothing of value comes easy, but it is often the challenges and hardships that people endure in the pursuit of their goals that make attaining it so fulfilling. Becoming a part of the resale industry is going to require a lot of hard work, sacrifice, and dedication. You will have to develop managerial skills to operate a business and deal with customers, vendors, and donors every day. You will have to do this with concern, consideration, and, most of all, with a sense of humor and a good measure of pride and confidence in yourself.

You're the Boss

The other issue that has to be addressed in your planning is how much of your time this business is going to require. Be aware up front that it's going to be more than you would spend at a nine-to-five job. Once the business is up and running, the time investment could decrease, but at the beginning of the venture, countless hours will have to be dedicated to it to make it successful.

You may think that being the boss is the best part about starting a thrift store, but it isn't usually as much fun as stocking your store or as rewarding as protecting the environment.

If you've never been self-employed, you will have to learn all the rules and regulations that pertain to finances and taxes. That is information that will be explained in detail in subsequent chapters. In this chapter, we'll ease you into the role with tips on how to be an effective manager of your store.

The size of the thrift store you plan to open will determine your initial responsibilities. If you have a small store, you may only be supervising yourself. That's fine, as long as you realize that working for yourself means that everything that happens or needs to happen in your store is on your shoulders.

The benefits, of course, begin with the fact that you can make your own hours and not have to answer to the demands of anyone else.

The boss is the person with all the answers, and even if you are also the one asking the questions, providing the right answers is important to the success of your store. During this planning stage, make a list of all the duties and responsibilities a boss would have on a daily basis.

The following is a sample of what your list should include:

◆ Sort and price inventory.

◆ Operate store Monday through Saturday.

◆ Check cash drawer and verify change fund.

◆ Greet customers and offer assistance.

◆ Make periodic checks of store to keep it neat and add inventory items as needed.

◆ Search for new ways to obtain donations and maintain your inventory.

◆ Utilize advertising and promotions.

◆ Perform closing procedures at end of each business day: count money and balance cash drawer, replenish change fund, record sales, make a bank deposit.

◆ Manage the store's finances and keep it profitable.

Not for Resale

Whether you run the store yourself or have help, you should personally balance the cash and sales at the end of each day and take the deposits to the bank.

This list contains the most common tasks that need to be done each business day. Your list can be modified, depending on the size of your store and whether you have people to help you run it. If your store is large enough to have volunteers and employees, additional items such as interviewing for staff positions, preparing payroll and reports, and supervising and supporting the staff will have to be added to your list of responsibilities.

To Partner, or Not

Now that you have had a look at the amount of work a thrift store—or any business, for that matter—entails, it's time to talk about partnerships. A partner or partners would share the workload and the expenses with you. Of course, the partners would also share the income. In Chapter 6, you will learn the basics of structuring a business as a partnership. For now, just consider whether you want to do this alone or join forces with other people.

The number of hours you have to spend on your business depends somewhat on your personal situation. A man or woman with small children to tend to could be overwhelmed by the amount of time it takes to own and operate a thrift store. Yet, if you really want to do something, you will usually find a way to make it work.

If your business is well planned and organized from the start, you will enjoy being your own boss and managing the day-to-day operations of it.

Start-Up Costs

Now it's time to sit down with paper, pencil, and a calculator and estimate how much it will cost to open your thrift store. At this point, whether your final intent is to run a nonprofit store or a store that produces income just for you and your family, the costs to open it on your own will be basically the same.

Let's take a look at the items you need to include in your start-up costs:

- Rent
- Utilities: electric, gas, and water
- Telephone expenses
- License fees
- Furniture and fixtures
- Liability and fire insurance
- Promotion and advertising
- Cleaning and maintenance
- Legal and accounting fees
- Computer and software programs

The costs for the last three items can be modified, depending on how much outside help you want to use.

Cleaning and maintenance, for example, can be done by you or a member of your family instead of hiring an outside provider. Legal fees may be necessary at the beginning when you are structuring your business entity and leasing property, but will not be ongoing unless you need legal advice for other matters.

Accounting fees depend on whether you do the bookkeeping yourself or use a monthly service. Instructions and information on how to do your own bookkeeping and tax reports will be presented in Chapter 8.

Not for Resale

Accounting software programs are easy to use, but if you have no aptitude for figures and are not an organized person, you should use a bookkeeping and tax service. The cost will be offset by the money you save in penalties and interest if you make errors.

Regardless of who does your bookkeeping and tax reports, you will still need a computer. Perhaps you already own one that you can "sell" to your business. Software programs can be used for bookkeeping records and word processing for letters and other correspondence.

Once you have determined the approximate start-up costs for your business, add in what you will need to pay your personal bills for three months. Although your thrift store could make a profit from the day you open the doors, any new business usually needs time to become established and prosper.

Creative Juices

Most people who consider opening a store possess a good deal of creativity and ingenuity. Don't worry if you don't think you have these talents; they are skills you can learn and develop. You know that your thrift store is going to carry a variety of merchandise, so list the basic items such as clothing, linens, and household goods and think about how they can be displayed attractively. Planning the basic design and layout of the interior space of your potential sales area will be a good way to get your creative juices flowing.

If you are thinking about specializing in certain products, you can create a plan on paper for displaying those items. For example, if you are a book lover you will need shelves to hold the books and perhaps a small reading area where customers can sit down and browse through the titles they are thinking of purchasing.

Laying It Out

Visit other thrift stores and write down what you like and don't like about the way they are laid out. Consider the aisle space, the height of the shelves, the type of store fixtures used to display goods. There's no law against copying someone else's floor plan; it's actually a good way to get ideas that you can then modify and improve on when drawing up your own blueprint for your display area. One of your main considerations should be the ease with which customers can move through your store. Allow enough space so that people will not feel restricted or cramped.

Remember that the Americans with Disabilities Act requires that all citizens have access to goods and services.

If you can't draw a straight line with a ruler, consider finding an art or design student who can help you work out your floor plan. There's something about actually putting your plan on paper that helps you move forward to the next step—that is, the art of displaying goods in an attractive manner.

Added Value _____

Rules for accommodating the disabled can be found in the Title III Technical Assistance Manual and Supplement available at www.ada.gov.taman3. html, or by calling the Americans with Disabilities Act help line at 1-800-514-0301.

Goods Looking Good

It doesn't matter what type of goods you are selling in your store, but how they are displayed does matter. A shop that is a jumbled mess with merchandise strewn carelessly about sends a message to customers that the owner doesn't care enough to make it easier for them to shop there.

There are a number of associations with publications written for thrift stores. They are usually filled with ideas on how you can make your store more organized and attractive. Again, as you study the ideas of others, your own thoughts will surface and allow you to come up with attractive displays for your business.

Added Value _____

The National Association of Resale and Thrift Shops has a publication that is written specifically for thrift stores.

Attract Donors

Of course, the most attractive and ingenious floor plans and displays will remain empty unless the table and shelves are filled with merchandise. So you need to initiate a plan that will allow you to get donations and/or buy merchandise that can be resold in your store.

As discussed earlier, if you are a thrift store that supports a charity and has nonprofit status, you will receive donations from the other people who also support the needy group. If not, you will have to put your creativity and ingenuity to work again to solicit items for your store or search out places where merchandise can be obtained for resale.

General merchandise for your thrift store encompasses a wide array of items that can be sought and acquired. Ideas for obtaining merchandise apply to any type you are interested in reselling.

If you already have a location in mind, you can begin seeking donations in that neighborhood or general area. Here are some ways you can interest people in donating to your store.

- ◆ Contact people and offer to haul away any excess items from their home, garages, or other storage areas.

- ◆ Send out coupons giving donors a nice discount on purchases they make at your store within a set time frame.

- ◆ Plan and advertise a Donor's Day, with free refreshments and entertainment in a public area such as a park where people can drop off unwanted items.

Added Value

Visit private yard sales and offer to haul away any items not sold that day or weekend.

These ideas can be expanded to other areas of your town and city until you have enough merchandise to stock your store. In the event that you don't receive enough free donated items, budget for the possibility of purchasing stock at yard sales and swap meets where people often sell usable items at very low prices.

Other ways to obtain inventory for your thrift store will be discussed later in this book. Since we are still in the planning and research stages, the suggestions in this chapter require little or no cash outlay so that your start-up expenses can be kept to a minimum.

Making New Friends

Since you are interested in starting and running a thrift store, you are probably someone who has spent a great deal of time shopping in thrift stores. So you are already aware that it is a great place to meet interesting, friendly people.

The growth of the thrift store industry attests to the fact that people from all walks of life shop in them. Many shop on a daily basis, while others only frequent them when there is something specific they are trying to find. Still others spend their days going from store to store hoping to find an overlooked treasure. As the owner of a thrift store, you will be a resource for those people.

If a store is located in a depressed area, many of the customers will be people in need, but bargain hunters and affluent people looking for unusual or one-of-a-kind items that can't be found in retail outlets will make regular visits, too.

One of the items on the list you reviewed for the boss of the thrift store was: Greet customers and offer assistance. As the owner of the store, you will probably be the first person a potential customer sees upon entering. That means you have a chance to make a new friend every time a person comes through the door of your establishment.

Any business person will tell you that treating your customers like friends encourages them to come back again and again and recommend your store to their family and friends. Being gracious to everyone is also a good way to get more donations for your store. These are ways to ensure the profitability of your thrift store, but the real gain is invaluable to you as a person. Can anyone ever have too many friends? People tend to drift in and out of your life, so you don't have to worry about getting overloaded with friends or people you may label as acquaintances. Interacting with a variety of people from other economic and ethnic backgrounds allows you to learn and accept all the differences that make us unique human beings.

Consider the possibility that another thrift store owner enters your store, looking at your merchandise trying to find a hidden gem. Talk to him. Ask questions and l from the experiences he may share about his own business practices.

Look at the harried young mother who is trying to find decent low- her growing children. A friendly smile and a kind word can dis cause her to tell her family and friends of your kindness.

These are just a few examples of the new and interesti day. A business card can be easily discarded, but a frier handshake is something that can make a lasting impres

---

Helping Hands

At a charity book sale, a grubby, shabbily dressed man made his way through the tables and gathered a number of books. His appearance made workers wary of him until one of them noticed that he was wearing a genuine Rolex watch. He purchased a lot of books.

---

with just customers, although they should be your main consideration. Make friends with the mail person, the window washer, the pizza delivery person, and any other man, woman, or child who walks through your door. Look at the person, not at the way he or she is dressed or groomed.

Your very own thrift store will give you the opportunity to meet and greet people you might not come in contact with otherwise. It can be one of the most enjoyable things about running a thrift store. It may also be the most important way you can make a difference in your community and in your life.

So open the doors of your thrift store and welcome all the wonderful people who pass through them.

The Least You Need to Know

♦ A thrift store is a business and must be planned and organized like any other financial venture.

♦ The thrift industry is growing and prospering. Start-up costs are lower for a thrift store because inventory is often donated.

♦ All thrift stores, even those organized for profit, fulfill a need in the community. Recycling goods protects the environment.

♦ Being your own boss has its advantages, but requires managerial skills.

♦ People from all walks of life frequent thrift stores.

Chapter

2

A Store Reflecting Your Interests

In This Chapter

♦ Understanding vintage items

♦ Offering appliances and furniture

♦ Antiques and used books

♦ Decorator items and collectibles

The resale business in general caters to every social and economic group and reflects the tastes and preferences of people around the world. That is a good thing, but it also makes it impossible to provide information on all the specialty items that have found a place in this industry. For that reason, this chapter will look at the most common categories of merchandise found in thrift stores and provide ideas for those readers who have a specific vision or interest that they want to pursue and reflect in their own store.

If your store carries a variety of goods, it will attract a larger number of customers than a store that only carries specific items. However, looking at some of those stores and seeing how their owners have tapped into the lucrative markets that exist for specialty items will generate some thoughts and ideas that you can use in your store.

Added Value _____

In the United States, shopping at thrift stores has become popular enough to earn a slang term: "thrifting."

The long hours that thrift store owners must dedicate to their businesses become less strenuous and more satisfying when they are able to meld their own special interests into their business operations. So let's take a look at some of the most popular choices that exist in the thrift business and how the merchandise is handled and resold.

Never Out of Style

Since clothing comes in all shapes, sizes, and styles, it may be the largest amount of inventory in a thrift store. Over the years clothing has evolved from fig leaves, loincloths, and garments made out of animal fur into the fashion crazes that define various eras and ages. Styles change with the times but an interesting thing about clothing styles is that they never really fade away completely. This is proven by the continuing interest in vintage clothing. If you are a history buff, setting up a vintage clothing section in your store can be a source of enjoyment for you and a fascinating look at bygone days for your customers.

All Ages and Sizes

The majority of resale shops carry items for all ages and sizes. Like any clothing outlet, the items are usually separated into departments for men, women, and children and then displayed by the type of item. Shirts, dresses, pants, and accessories, such as hats, belts, and scarves, can all be displayed on separate racks or areas of the store.

Women and children would be the biggest source of donations for these stores. Women, because they often change sizes and change their minds about the style of clothing they like. Children of course change sizes as they grow, and parents often have a difficult time keeping up with costs of keeping them properly attired. For the same reasons, women are the largest group of customers for resale clothing, shopping for themselves, their young children, and their husbands. Men do purchase used clothing, too, but not as regularly; and males do not shop in as great a number as

Added Value _____

People who oppose sweatshops often purchase used clothing as an alternative to supporting manufacturers with unethical practices.

female shoppers. So if you decide to devote much of your display area to clothing, be aware that the female customers are the ones you need to please.

Youthful Clothing Styles

Teenagers are in a whole different category, but are usually so influenced by peer pressure that a resale shop that carries generic clothing would probably not appeal to them.

Some years ago a woman from Europe married a professor from the University of Arizona. At loose ends, she spent time on the campus talking to female students and took note of the fact that many of them were on strict budgets. This prompted her to open a used clothing shop that catered exclusively to the college girls.

The shop carried youthful fashions at low prices. The first shop was so successful, the woman opened other shops in other areas of town. She allowed her customers to buy clothes outright and also to receive credit for clothing they brought into the shop. The students were able to use these credits toward the purchase of new outfits—new to them, that is.

Added Value _____

Clothing from thrift stores is often purchased and modified by the teenagers who want to make their own fashion trends.

Setting up a specific area in your thrift store for youthful styles and fashions will attract the younger set, especially if you advertise the fact in publications read by students.

Baby Faces

Having a baby is a joyous experience, but babies need a lot of things. Although a newborn baby probably wouldn't know the difference between a designer crib and a cardboard box, most parents want the best for their child.

Cribs, cradles, swings, car seats, strollers, carriers, and a multitude of other things designed to keep baby safe and comfortable are on the market. Equipping a nursery can be very expensive, and many families cannot afford the retail prices charged in regular stores.

Enter the resale shops that answer this need by carrying baby clothes, equipment, and accessories at a fraction of the cost of brand-new merchandise. The nice thing about

Not for Resale

One thing to remember if you are carrying baby equipment is that everything you sell must be checked to make sure it adheres to the current safety standards for that item. This especially applies to toys and car seats.

offering items for the nursery set in your thrift store is that it's sometimes hard to tell whether an item has been used at all. Because babies grow out of clothes and certain equipment pretty quickly, the items don't suffer much wear and tear and your customers will be delighted to save so many dollars on items that look like new.

This also accounts for the fact that parents are usually willing to donate baby clothes and equipment to resale shops or turn it in for credit toward the purchase of larger clothing or equipment needed for their babies.

Large Items

When people buy new furniture of any kind, they often ask if the retail dealer will take away the old stuff that is being replaced. Hauling away the used furniture and appliances is a service you could offer in your community. These used items can then be stocked in your store if you want to bring in another type of shopper.

Some of the items donated to your shop will need work to make them saleable, but if you have an interest in woodworking, refinishing, upholstery, or carpentry, this has the potential of becoming a profitable part of your thrift store business. Sometimes a simple repair or cleaning is all that is needed to make a piece of used furniture attractive and saleable the second time around. Refinishing a piece of wood furniture gives it new life and shine.

Used furniture is always in demand, especially beds, dressers, sofas, and tables and chairs. Anyone with budget constraints—and in today's world that encompasses more people than you could imagine—looks for furniture at low prices.

Added Value

There are courses at community colleges and trade schools that will teach you the skills you need to repair and refurbish furniture and appliances.

The same thing is true for big appliances, because in a retail outlet kitchen stoves, refrigerators, washers, and dryers usually have big prices. Again, this is the kind of used item that consumers are often eager to give away to make room for their new purchases. Some of what will be donated will need repairs to get it in working order and, again, if you are interested in refurbishing and repairing things, selling used appliances may be the perfect way to get free merchandise to sell in your store.

Keep in mind that stocking large items in your shop takes up more floor space than smaller items, so plan ahead and figure out just how much you can display without making your store look crowded and cramped. As you sell the large items they can be replaced with new acquisitions you might be able to store elsewhere.

Really Old Stuff

There are thrift stores that call themselves antique shops, but most of the pieces sold are not really antiques, just old furniture, glassware, and decorator items. It is said that a real antique must be at least 100 years old, and that any piece less than 100 years old is considered a collectible. Of course, from time to time these shops do actually acquire and sell genuine antiques to their customers.

It takes a good deal of experience and training to recognize a genuine antique and determine its value. True antique dealers are experts, like the ones that examine goods and estimate their value on television's popular *Antique Road Show*. If you've ever watched the show, you know that these dealers have specific areas of interest and expertise, such as jewelry, glassware, or furniture.

If you are interested in antiques of any kind, you would be wise to study with an expert in the area in which you have the most interest before trying to add this specialty to your inventory.

Books

Used book stores provide the perfect example of a business that has tapped into a specific market niche. Each year thousands of books are published and offered to the reading public. One of the wonderful things about a book is no matter how old it is, when it is in the hands of someone who has never read it before, it becomes brand new again.

It seems that people who like to read can never have enough books on hand. If they like a particular author, they read everything the person publishes. If they have a particular interest, they buy every book they see on that subject.

If you are a person who loves to read and is interested in all kinds of books, you may want to look into the possibility of setting up a cozy area in your store where other book lovers can browse the titles you acquire without disrupting the general flow of your store's sales area.

When you are dealing in used books, there is always the possibility that you will come across a valuable *first edition.* This is especially true if your store is receiving donations of books from senior citizens or estates with extensive libraries.

def•i•ni•tion

The **first edition** of a book is one of the copies initially printed by the publisher. If it's a first edition of a book written by Ernest Hemingway or Louisa May Alcott, chances are it's very valuable. If the book is signed by the famous author, its value increases substantially.

Of course, there are millions of first editions circulating today, and most of them are no longer worth the price listed on the cover. However, these books still have resale value. The key to setting up a book area that will keep customers coming back again and again is to organize it properly. Make it easy for customers to find books they are interested in reading by stocking your fiction shelves in alphabetical order by the author's last name. Nonfiction subjects can be done the same way, or can be shelved by subject matter.

Decorator Items

Lamps, fancy tables, wall hangings, throw pillows, vases, and an assortment of knick-knacks and glassware can be displayed attractively around your shop. This is one of those categories that are large enough to satisfy many different interests.

All thrift stores must keep their shops neat and merchandise attractively displayed. The nice thing about the shop that carries decorator items is that there are usually a number of brightly colored objects in stock that can be interspersed throughout the displays to give them more eye appeal.

Added Value

White elephants are often the mainstay of decorator items. They are odds and ends that are in new or like-new condition donated to the shop because the owner no longer wants them.

If you have a flare for decorating, searching for and acquiring these unique and multihued items will be fun for you. A shop that carries lots of decorator items is also fun for the customers, and they will return to the store on a regular basis seeking and always finding something new and interesting.

Collectors Abound

Some collectibles can be considered decorator items, but in reality the vast number of collectors—and all the many and varied items they collect—dictate that these items be in a category all their own. Coins, for example, are collected, traded, bought, and sold every day. The same is true for stamps.

Through the years, doll collectors have been the source of many fads and shortages in the doll industry. Consider a time in the 1980s when the Cabbage Patch doll was so much in demand retailers couldn't keep them in stock; Cabbage Patch dolls were not just purchased, they were adopted. A few years later, Beanie Babies became the hot, most sought after items—until so many were manufactured and sent to the marketplace that they lost their elusive status. All the images of Disney characters are collected by people around the world. Stuffed teddy bears and those made of porcelain or glass continue to be sought after for children and adults. And now that Barbie has turned 50, her desirability and allure for collectors has been renewed.

Music boxes are manufactured in all shapes, sizes, and designs, with lilting tunes that enhance their appeal and salability. Trains, cars, clocks, toys, Pez candy dispensers, and the prizes found in McDonald's Happy Meals and Cracker Jack boxes are also things that people collect. The list goes on and on, and includes jewelry and other items not old enough to be antiques but old enough that they contain the power to invoke memories that make collectors want to possess them.

If you are a collector or just interested in collectibles in general, chances are you are no stranger to the thrill of finding a piece that a collector wants to add to his or her compilation. Your thrift store will enable you to widen your search for collectibles and establish a special secure area of your shop to display them.

All of the above and anything else you can think of or find can be included in a thrift store that also carries general merchandise. Because much of the inventory is made up of items that fall into the category of basic daily needs, the thrift store attracts many of the same people who shop in the specialty stores, and a lot more who don't.

Added Value

Thrift stores are popular with eBay sellers, who buy collectible items, hoping to resell them at a profit.

Dollar stores have grown in strength and popularity, but much of the merchandise carried in dollar stores is not worth that much.

In a thrift store, the customer may pay a dollar for an item that once sold for 10 or 20 times that price, and because it is still in good, useful condition it is worth much more than a dollar or whatever the thrift store is charging for it.

As a thrift store owner, if you monitor all the merchandise you offer for sale and make sure it is clean and still has some usefulness, you won't have to be concerned about the dollar stores or any other competitor.

The resale industry is wide open and filled with rewards and opportunities for all who venture inside a store or have the commitment and fortitude to become the owner of one.

The Least You Need to Know

- Your personal interests will help you determine the specialty items your store will carry.

- Thrift stores that specialize do so in the hope of tapping into a particular market niche.

- Antiques require dealers to have education and experience.

- General merchandise thrift stores attract a broad range of customers.

- Collectibles can become a lucrative part of your thrift store's inventory.

Chapter 3

Assess the Needs of Your Community

In This Chapter

◆ Helping your community

◆ Learning from established nonprofits

◆ Finding a cause to support

Whether you are planning to support a charity with your thrift store profits or yourself and your family, you need to assess the needs in your community. This will tell you where to locate your store and what kind of merchandise to stock in it. It will also be helpful to study the operations of thrift stores connected to national organizations. There may be a number of differences in the operating procedures of a nonprofit store that supports a charity and one that will support you, but those differences do not alter the fact that all thrift stores must be well managed.

You must also decide how to move forward in this planning stage. Becoming familiar with the needs you find in your community will help you decide on the path you want to follow. If your heart is touched by specific needs, you can consider ways in which your thrift store can answer their calls for help.

Helping Your Community

If you have lived in a particular area for any length of time, you may think you know everything there is to know about it. However, to really assess the specific needs of your community, you will have to dig deeper, talk to a lot of people, and gather a lot of in-depth information.

Since you are interested in the thrift store business, start visiting the ones that already exist in your area. Your visits should include all types of thrift stores, but pay particular attention to the ones that have the type of merchandise you are interested in stocking in your own store.

Introduce yourself to the owners and staff and engage them in conversation, and most importantly observe the people who shop there and, if possible, talk to them, too. Getting to know the people who shop in a particular store will help you judge the needs of the area. Are the customers poor, middle-class, or affluent? Are they simply bargain hunters, or people who need the lower-cost merchandise to survive?

> **Helping Hands**
>
> Research and join a business association in your area. Most have regular meetings that discuss the economy and overall needs of the community. You will learn a lot from the association and its members.

Look at churches and schools in your area that you are not familiar with and, if possible, attend some community meetings. The more people you see and talk to about what's going on in your community, the more you will understand its strengths and weaknesses. This will help you decide where you want to open your store and the people and organizations that may benefit from it and want to shop there.

Models to Study

You may already have a particular need or cause that you want to support with your store. However, even if you are not interested in a nonprofit venture, you can learn from the ones that operate in your area and across the country. The good works that they support with their stores are varied and worth considering for your own store. The way their stores are operated will also give you some ideas you may be able to use in managing your business.

Goodwill Enterprises

Goodwill is an international organization providing education, training, and career services to the disadvantaged in communities around the globe.

The people who come to Goodwill for these services fall into the following categories of need:

◆ People dependent on welfare

◆ Homeless individuals

◆ Uneducated and unskilled people

◆ Individuals with no employment history or work experience

◆ People who are physically, mentally, or emotionally disabled

The overall mission of Goodwill Industries is to give people a chance to transform their lives by providing opportunities to learn skills and use them to become self-sufficient. Like all nonprofit organizations, Goodwill has a *mission statement* that outlines its goals and purpose.

The mission statement of Goodwill Industries International reads as follows:

> Goodwill Industries International enhances the dignity and quality of life of individuals, families, and communities by eliminating barriers to opportunity and helping people in need reach their fullest potential through the power of work.

def•i•ni•tion

A **mission statement** is created and publicly advertised by nonprofit corporations such as Goodwill Industries. It is a necessary part of the process of being recognized as a nonprofit entity.

All or part of that mission statement can be applied to many organizations that exist to help people in need become self-sufficient. When you open any type of thrift store in your community, you can help the community in a number of ways.

Goodwill stores carry a variety of merchandise, most of it donated by people who want to support their efforts in that area. However, Goodwill also solicits donations of broken or nonworking items such as radios, televisions, computers, and small appliances. The stores then use those items to train people to repair them, a valuable skill that increases their employment potential. Then to complete the circle, those repaired items are resold in the Goodwill thrift store and the money from those sales is used to help more people in need.

While your thrift store may not help people in the same way Goodwill Industries does, the mission statement and the operation of Goodwill thrift stores may prompt and inspire you to offer simple jobs at token salaries to people in need. If you decide to do repairs on broken furniture or other items donated to your store, you can consider hiring someone who has been trained by Goodwill Enterprises. Remember that any service you provide for the community will have a favorable impact on your public image as a business owner and help you attract more donations and customers to your store. To learn more about Goodwill Industries and its work, visit its website at www.goodwill.org.

> **Helping Hands**
>
> Charitable acts performed by you or your business are a form of advertising and may do more good for your store than any other type of paid advertising campaign.

Society of St. Vincent de Paul

While Goodwill Industries is a secular organization, the Society of St. Vincent de Paul is a religious organization supported by the Roman Catholic Church. However, the work that is done through this organization is not limited to Catholics or any other religious denomination. Anyone in need may contact the St. Vincent de Paul group in their community and receive help with food, clothing, furniture, rent, utilities, and medical expenses.

The society dates back to the 1800s and was founded in France by Fredrick Ozanam, whose purpose was to do something about the poverty, sickness, and squalor found in the ghettos of Paris.

Today the society is international in scope, and in the United States is governed by a national council that oversees councils located in cities and towns that oversee the local groups called conferences. Most conferences are part of a church parish. The conferences are staffed by volunteers who take calls and make visits to those who request help. Because most parishes have a St. Vincent de Paul group attached to them, the conferences concentrate on helping people within the boundaries of their parish, but again, they do not need to be members of the parish church or any

> **Helping Hands**
>
> For more information on the St. Vincent de Paul groups in your area, contact the council office listed in the phone directory for your city.

church at all. If there is no conference in a particular area of need, those people can contact the city's council office for help.

The main difference between the St. Vincent de Paul conference and other charitable groups is that the volunteers make personal visits to the homes of those in need to deliver food if it has been requested and ascertain what other type of help can be provided, such as payments of rent and/or utilities.

Depending on the size of the city, there may be multiple St. Vincent de Paul thrift stores. Because this is a high-profile charity organization, the stores receive an abundance of donations, including clothing, furniture, appliances, linens, and other household goods.

The primary purpose of the thrift stores operated by this charity is to fill the requests of the Vincentian volunteers after the home visit has determined what is needed by the individual and his or her family.

St. Vincent de Paul conference members fill out *vouchers* for the people they visit listing their specific needs. These vouchers are turned in to the thrift stores. The clients can then go to the store and pick up furniture, clothing, or household goods.

If large items of furniture, like beds and sofas, are requested, the thrift store usually delivers the items to the home of the needy person.

def•i•ni•tion

A **voucher** is like a coupon, but it is made out to a specific person and lists the specific item or items needed. The person then takes it to the thrift store and exchanges it for his or her needs.

Any goods donated to the store that are not used to fill the needs of the people visited by the conference volunteers are sold to the public.

Again, you can look at the way St. Vincent de Paul serves the needs in its communities and borrow its voucher system for your own thrift store. Although you must be very selective about who receives vouchers for free merchandise, offering them occasionally for clothing or household goods to schools or churches in your area will give you and your thrift store a reputation for doing good works in the community. It is public relations at its finest.

If you opt to become a nonprofit thrift store that supports a particular group, school, or church, the voucher system will work well to provide for people under the charitable umbrella who need items from your store. Consider school children in a low-income neighborhood who need clothes for the winter. You can solicit donations for these items and then give the children vouchers to use to claim a jacket or coat to keep them warm.

If you have ever looked at the items requested at Christmas by poor families, you will see that they don't ask for toys or luxury items. They ask for the basic things, like shoes and jackets, that other kids take for granted.

If you are not a nonprofit store, you can still contact groups like St. Vincent de Paul conferences and offer to help them now and then. For example, there are charities that provide beds for people who don't have any, so they always need bed linens. If you find that your store has an abundance of linens at any given time, consider donating some to one of these local charities.

The Salvation Army

The Salvation Army is a Christian-based organization that reaches out to the poor and homeless and provides food, shelter, and a multitude of other services. Some of the other programs run by the Salvation Army include the following:

- ◆ Missing persons
- ◆ Disaster relief
- ◆ Prisoner rehabilitation
- ◆ Drug and alcohol rehabilitation
- ◆ Youth camps
- ◆ Elderly services

Everyone is familiar with the big red kettles that appear on street corners during the holiday season collecting funds for those in need in that community. The Salvation Army also receives funds from the thrift stores that they operate. These are called Family Stores, and like all good thrift stores they provide quality goods at reasonable prices.

One hundred percent of the proceeds from the Family Stores go directly to the operation of the Adult Rehabilitation Centers, allowing the centers to be self-sufficient. Work therapy is a major part of the Salvation Army's rehabilitation process, and some of this is done in the Family Stores. This allows the men and women in the rehabilitation programs to regain their self-esteem and learn valuable skills.

While you are probably not going to have a rehabilitation center connected to your thrift store, you could contact the Salvation Army and perhaps use its workers in your store.

You have now looked at three large, high-profile charity organizations that operate thrift stores. Learn and profit from the way their stores are run. Helping others is a smart way to help yourself.

You can also be on the lookout for charity events in your community, like raffles and auctions. Donating an item from your store for these events is still another way to make a difference in your community and promote your business.

It's all about giving back to the community where your store is located and letting everyone know that you are a person with the community's best interests at heart.

Support a Charity

If you have decided to open a nonprofit thrift shop, chances are you may already have a certain cause you want to support. If not, one effective way to help many people is to partner with a social services agency. Your store can provide coupons and vouchers that the agency can give to the needy people in their programs.

The following is a general listing of causes that always need support and additional funds:

- Medical research
- Programs for the disabled
- Veterans
- Soup kitchens

- Animal shelters
- Aid to the elderly
- Churches
- Schools

These are just general categories of people and places that need help. Under each of these are groups of people who are falling through the cracks and don't have anyone supporting them. Seek out those groups and consider answering their cry for help.

Because of the time and effort you will expend in opening and running your thrift store, choosing a charity that has a personal or emotional connection with you or your family will make everything you do for your store seem more worthwhile. People who support hospice centers are often people who have been touched by the love and care received by a friend or relative. Volunteers at soup kitchens have known hunger themselves, and people who help battered women and children may have escaped from an abusive relationship.

Take the time to really contemplate the kind of cause you want to support based on that inner voice that tells you why some needs in your community are more important to you than others.

The Least You Need to Know

- ◆ Studying the needs of your community will help you make important decisions.

- ◆ The voucher system used by larger organizations can be modified for use in your store.

- ◆ Helping people in need is public relations at its finest.

- ◆ Make a list of the needs and causes in your area that are not receiving a lot of assistance.

- ◆ Listen to your inner voice and choose a charity that has an emotional connection with you.

Nonprofit Thrift Stores

In This Chapter

- ◆ Partner with an existing nonprofit
- ◆ Organizing nonprofit corporations
- ◆ Following the articles and bylaws
- ◆ Tax-exempt status and IRS rules and regulations

If you have decided that your thrift store will be operated as a nonprofit entity that supports a charity or cause, you can move forward in the research and planning stage, concentrating on the steps necessary to achieve that end. Donning the hat of a Good Samaritan often causes people to look at you in a new light. It may also prompt them to step forward and volunteer their services. So be prepared to take names.

Although it may be several months before you are able to actually open your thrift store, having a list of people who are willing to work with you gives you an excellent start on achieving your long-term goals. At this point, you may want to enlist some of these people to be on an advisory committee for your thrift store. This will give you added support and the option of being able to discuss your ideas and problems with interested individuals.

Take Cover Under an Umbrella

A nonprofit thrift store can be newly organized or the owner can attach the store to another organization, such as an existing charity or a church. For example, if your church has an outreach program for the elderly, opening a thrift store in an available space on the church's property could benefit that program. If you have a cause that is not currently supported by the church, you could present it and your reasons for helping it to the church council for approval and receive permission to proceed under the church's nonprofit and tax-exempt umbrella.

Attaching your store to an existing nonprofit has some distinct advantages, but also has some disadvantages to consider.

The advantages are ...

♦ You automatically obtain nonprofit status.

♦ You will be covered by its tax-exempt status with the IRS.

♦ Some of your expenses will be absorbed by the parent organization.

♦ You will have a built-in donation base.

♦ You will have volunteers to help you run the business.

The disadvantages to be considered are ...

♦ Your personal income may be too limited.

♦ You will have to report to the directors of the parent organization.

♦ The vision you have for your store may have to be modified to conform to the policies of the parent organization.

♦ Any major decisions will have to be approved by the *board of directors*.

def•i•ni•tion

Most charity and church organizations are corporations that are run by a **board of directors**. This board guides the organization and oversees all of its projects and operations.

Weighing the pros and cons of attaching your store to an existing organization boils down to these two major considerations. On the plus side, you can start your store and learn the business without a large cash outlay and, once you feel confident, open your own independent store. The church or charity may have an existing space where your store can be located, and that will cut down dramatically on the time and expense of finding and leasing another location. On the negative side, you will not be your own boss because you will have to answer to the parent organization, and your income potential may be limited by its other projects and budget constraints.

Operating under the umbrella of an existing nonprofit eliminates the need to create a new entity, but this option is not available to everyone who wants to become a part of the resale industry and support a charitable cause. And even if it is an option for you, you may prefer to strike out on your own and create a business that reflects ideas and visions not compatible with the parent organization.

Open Your Own Umbrella

Establishing a new nonprofit organization requires a series of steps that must be negotiated with patience and consideration. Don't be confused by the nonprofit designation. That doesn't mean the business cannot earn profits. It simply means that the profits are used to support a charity or cause.

Although incorporation is not the only way to go, it is the most sensible and efficient path to follow because it relieves you of personal liability for the business operation and allows you to become an employee of the corporation. Being an employee of the nonprofit corporation allows you to draw a salary and receive other benefits.

Added Value _____

Employee benefits include contributions to your Social Security and Medicare taxes.

Once a nonprofit corporation is created and formed, it exists as a separate legal entity. A corporation can own property, open bank accounts, hire employees, and continue to exist and operate after you're gone. As mentioned earlier, the corporation assumes any liability that may arise in the course of its business operations, which protects you and your personal assets.

Starting any new corporation is a process that begins with the state where your thrift store will be located. While the procedure is basically the same in each state, they all have their own forms that must be completed and filed and fees that must be paid. A nonprofit corporation can also obtain tax-exempt status from the state and federal taxing authorities. Instructions on applying for tax-exempt status on behalf of your nonprofit corporation will be presented later in this chapter.

Added Value

It is prudent to obtain legal counsel and advice to assist with the process and procedures of incorporation.

The difference between a nonprofit corporation and a regular corporation is that nonprofits generally do not issue stock or have stockholders. Nonprofits do have a board of directors and the interested parties you have assembled to support your organization can become members of that board. All corporations also have a statutory agent who may or may not also be a legal advisor.

Some states have different categories of nonprofit corporations. For example, the state of California has the following designations assigned to nonprofits:

◆ A religious corporation is one organized to operate a church or otherwise structured for religious purposes.

◆ A public benefit corporation is organized primarily or exclusively for charitable purposes.

◆ A corporation organized for other than religious, charitable, civic, or social welfare purposes, whether intending to apply for tax-exempt status or not, is a mutual benefit corporation.

Helping Hands

The IRS website provides a list of all states with contact information for filing an application for a nonprofit corporation. Visit the website at www.irs.gov.

As you review the above categories, determine where the cause you intend to support with your thrift store's profits would place you in California or the state where you are locating your business. The office of the Secretary of State in your area is the place to start. This is where you will obtain information and forms that will allow you to form a nonprofit corporation in your state. An application for a public benefit corporation can be found in Appendix B of this book.

State Your Purpose

The first step in creating a nonprofit corporation is to define the purpose and intentions of the corporation in what is called a mission statement. A mission statement, such as the one issued by Goodwill Industries and included in Chapter 3, is required for incorporation in any state. Writing out the mission statement for your nonprofit corporation will help you clarify the basic goals of your nonprofit entity. It should state how and why your nonprofit is going to function and define who will benefit from the corporation's profits.

Although the mission statement can be in a wide variety of formats and lengths, it must provide specific information on why the organization is being created and who will benefit from it. The following is a list of questions that should be answered in a mission statement:

◆ What services will be provided?

◆ What individuals or groups will benefit from these services?

◆ What values will guide the operation of the organization?

◆ How do you want others to view your organization?

To help you write the mission statement for your nonprofit corporation, let's look at some of the ones created for other organizations that exist to support specific causes.

American Antigravity—The mission of the American Antigravity Corporation is to provide online scientific and educational material and support to the scientific community and general public, relating to aerospace, renewable energy, and other scientific disciplines. American Antigravity fosters learning and academic excellence by working with scientists, educators, and inventors to create a safe, fulfilling, and academically enriching environment for breakthrough science.

Second Harvest Heartland—The mission of Second Harvest Heartland is to fight hunger through community partnerships.

SAVE—SAVE's mission is to prevent suicide through public awareness and education, eliminate stigma, and serve as a resource to those touched by suicide.

Jerome Foundation—The Jerome Foundation, created by artist and philanthropist Jerome Hill (1905–1972), makes grants to support the creation and production of new artistic works by emerging artists, and contributes to the professional advancement of those artists.

PATH, Foster Care and Family Services—PATH empowers children and families to achieve lifelong successes.

Amputee Resource Foundation of America, Inc.—Its mission is to disseminate timely and useful information, to perform charitable services, and to conduct research to enhance productivity and quality of life for amputees.

PANPHA—PANPHA represents over 320 nonprofit providers of long-term care and housing services for 65,000 elderly residents across Pennsylvania. The association is committed to helping its members provide quality care efficiently and effectively for the individuals and families it serves. In an age of impersonal care, PANPHA members put people before profits.

Springboard—Their mission is simple: to offer education on the wise use of credit.

As you can see, mission statements can say a little in a lot of words, or a lot in just a few words. The main thing to remember is that the mission statement for your nonprofit corporation must accurately describe its purpose. You should be able to accomplish this in a half page or less. Don't be afraid to ask for help and guidance from your friends and advisors when preparing the mission statement for your nonprofit.

> ### Added Value
>
> Some communities have nonprofit incubators that help businesses get started. Contact the local office of the National Council of Nonprofit Associations to find one in your area.

Rules of Operation

The next step is to draft the Articles of Incorporation that must be submitted with your application to the Secretary of State. There are many books on this subject; those listed in Appendix A are recommended reading. There are also many references and samples that can be accessed via the Internet. Therefore, we will just look at the main headings required for the Articles of Incorporation to give you an idea of what this step involves. Also, these articles can vary from state to state, so make sure you provide the information in the proper order and format required by your state. The following is simply offered to make you aware of the basic information you will have to gather before trying to draft your application.

Article I

Enter the name of the corporation, the street address, and the mailing address if it is different than the street address.

Article II

State the purpose of the corporation and, in states like California where there are category designations, you must include the words Religious Corporation, Mutual Benefit Corporation, or Public Benefit Corporation to identify the type of entity you are forming.

Mission Statement

Name the statutory agent who has agreed to accept service of process in the event the corporation is sued or involved in any type of legal action. Remember that a corporation cannot act as its own agent.

Article III

List the conditions and restrictions governing the operations and activities of the corporation. This section can include anything pertaining to net profits, compensation of officers, and other legal and financial matters.

Article IV

List the directors and/or current members of the board. This list may change from year to year, and the changes are reported on the annual renewal reports required by most states.

Article V

This section states that property of the officers, members, and directors will not be jeopardized by any debts incurred by the corporation.

Article VI

This article outlines the division of the corporation's assets in the event it is dissolved.

Not for Resale

Sometimes a lending institution will require that the officers of a new corporation co-sign a loan made to the corporation, making their personal assets additional collateral on the debt.

Article VII

List the person or persons who are requesting this incorporation. Each person must sign the application and the Articles of Incorporation. Only one person is necessary, but often there are multiple incorporators.

The state where you are incorporating your nonprofit organization may also require you to submit bylaws for your entity. Regardless of whether they have to be submitted to the state, you need bylaws that specify how your board of directors will operate. The rules should be drafted by a committee chosen from the board members and then presented to the entire board for approval. Remember that bylaws can be changed and modified as needed.

Some states require other forms initially or with the annual renewal. Again, check with the Secretary of State's office in your area for specific information, forms, and requirements.

At some point in the process of incorporation, you may be required to file a fictitious name or "Doing Business As" (DBA) form with the county where your store will be

located. This is actually a public notice that usually also appears in a local newspaper. It announces, for example, that XYZ Corporation is doing business as Smart Shopper Thrift Store. The state office where you are registering your corporation (or your legal advisor) can tell you if this is necessary in your area and, if so, how to accomplish it. A sample of a fictitious name form and instructions for completing it are included in Appendix B.

When your nonprofit corporation has been filed and approved by the state where your business is located, you are ready to move on to more rules, regulations, and paperwork to ensure that the profits from your thrift store that are supporting the charity or cause of your choice are not reduced by the payment of federal and state income taxes.

No Income Taxes

Nonprofit corporations enjoy tax-exempt status with the Internal Revenue Service as long as they are properly formed and approved by the state in which they are located. Most nonprofits fall under the IRS category of 501(c)(3), a designation for public charities or private foundations like the ones whose mission statements were presented.

What does tax-exempt status mean to you as a thrift store owner? It means that you will not have to pay income taxes on the profits earned by your store. If your store is located in a state that also taxes income, and most states do, you can also be exempt from those taxes. States usually honor IRS rulings, but you may have to make a separate application to extend your tax exemption to the state taxing authorities.

Being tax exempt means that the charity or cause you support with your thrift store will not have its proceeds reduced by tax liabilities. This tax-exempt status only applies to the net profits of your store. It does not alter or reduce your personal tax liability for the salary or other earnings you receive for operating and managing the thrift store.

Study the Rules

The IRS rules prohibit certain activities for tax-exempt corporations. The following is a list of those activities that could cause a nonprofit to lose its tax-exempt status:

♦ Participating in the political campaigns of candidates for local, state, or federal office.

♦ Lobbying activities that are not restricted to an insubstantial part of its total activities.

♦ Not ensuring that earnings do not benefit any private shareholder or individual.

♦ Operating for the benefit of private interests such as those of its founder, the founder's family, its shareholders, or persons controlled by such interest.

♦ Operating for the primary purpose of conducting a trade or business that is not related to its exempt purpose, such as a school operating a factory.

♦ Having purposes or activities that are illegal or violate fundamental public policy.

Those are all the things a nonprofit corporation seeking tax-exempt status may not do. The IRS goes on to list the exempt purposes, one or more of which must be stated in its *organizing documents*.

Exempt purposes can be charitable, educational, religious, scientific, literary, fostering national or international sports competi-

def•i•ni•tion

Organizing documents include the mission statement and the Articles of Incorporation that are part of your state's nonprofit corporation application.

tions, preventing cruelty to children or animals, and testing for public safety. For a more detailed list of exempt purposes, visit the IRS website at www.irs.gov and access the various publications that are available for nonprofit corporations seeking tax-exempt status. Publication 557 is one of the most informative and should be downloaded and thoroughly studied.

When applying for tax-exempt status for your newly formed corporation, there is specific language the IRS recommends you use. The following is an example of the type of language required by the IRS to qualify the corporation as a tax-exempt entity.

The corporation is organized exclusively for charitable, religious, educational, and scientific purposes, including for such purposes, the making of distributions to organizations that qualify as exempt organizations under Section 501(c)(3) of the Internal Revenue Code or the corresponding section of any future tax code.

As you may suspect, being granted tax-exempt status requires that the corporation complete a number of forms that will be reviewed before final approval is received from the IRS. However, the corporation is allowed to function as tax exempt while waiting for this approval. Its contributors may also assume that any donations made to the organization while the application is pending will be tax deductible.

Even if the corporation has no employees, it should have already obtained an Employer Identification Number (EIN), as that is used on all forms and correspondence you need to complete and file with the IRS in order to be approved as a tax-exempt organization. Obtaining an EIN can be done instantly online at the website www.irs.gov, or by calling the IRS at 1-800-829-4933 Monday through Friday.

Now let's look at the forms your nonprofit corporation may have to complete before receiving tax-exempt status.

Form 1023: Application for Recognition of Exemption Under Section 501(c)(3) of the Internal Revenue Code. The required user fee stated on the form must be mailed with the form to the address indicated on the 1023 before the IRS will process it.

Form 2848: Power of Attorney and Declaration of Representative must be attached to Form 1023 only if someone other than the principle director represents the corporation on matters concerning the 1023 application.

Form 8821: Tax Information Authorization needs to be attached if you want the IRS to provide information about your application to an employee other than the principle director of the corporation.

There is a deadline for filing Form 1023. Most corporations must file the application by the end of the fifteenth month after the corporation was created, but there is an additional 12-month extension that can be granted.

As with most things relating to Internal Revenue codes, the secret is to complete the forms fully and in a timely manner so the IRS does not have to come back to you for more information.

Once all the paperwork is done, the corporation will receive what is called a determination letter from IRS recognizing the organization's exempt status and providing it public charity classification. This is an important legal document and should be kept in a safe and secure place.

Smaller nonprofit corporations must register their information each year. Larger organizations may have to file a tax report, but no taxes will be paid on profits of the business. Check with your financial advisor at the end of each year to see what is required of your nonprofit corporation. More information on those tax and information returns will be presented in a later chapter.

Don't Miss a Step

This chapter has presented a lot of information for starting a nonprofit entity, and structuring it as a corporation is strongly suggested. Yes, as mentioned earlier, there are other ways a nonprofit business can be organized, but a corporation gives you the best tax advantages and the ability to operate your thrift store efficiently and also draw the income you need to support yourself and your family.

The following checklist is a review of all the steps necessary for organizing the nonprofit corporation that can run your thrift store. Listing the tasks in the order that they should be considered and performed will help you negotiate the steps quickly and accurately.

1. Contact the office of the Secretary of State in your area and get information and forms needed to file for incorporation.

2. Draft a mission statement that clearly states the purpose of your nonprofit and who will benefit from its operations.

3. Invite people you know and trust to be on the board of directors of your nonprofit corporation.

4. If needed, seek legal advice to help you with the state forms and Articles of Incorporation.

5. Draft the Articles of Incorporation with the help and approval of your board.

6. Draft the corporation's bylaws with the help and approval of your board.

7. File the incorporation forms with your state.

8. Apply for an EIN for your corporation.

9. Find a bank with good customer service people and open a bank account for the corporation.

10. Set up a bookkeeping system following the procedures in Chapter 8 of this book.

11. Find an insurance agent to help you with liability insurance and other policies your nonprofit may need.

12. Apply for tax-exempt status with the IRS.

13. Apply for tax-exempt status with your state.

14. Find out what other tax exemptions are available, such as property taxes, and file for them, too.

15. Apply for any state or city licenses that are needed to operate your business or solicit donations.

Not for Resale

Avoid what is called "founders syndrome" that occurs when a corporation is operated according to the personality of its founder or someone else on the board.

Remember that when in doubt about any of the steps listed above, you need to seek competent legal and/or financial advice. You can also find organizations, websites, and other means of help on the Internet. Last but not least, remember that this book has a resource section (Appendix A) that lists several books you can read to help you structure and manage your nonprofit entity.

The Least You Need to Know

♦ Attaching your thrift store to an existing nonprofit has both advantages and disadvantages.

♦ Incorporating your nonprofit business is the best way to structure it.

♦ Mission statements define your goals and the benefits to your charitable cause.

♦ Recruiting good members for your corporation's board is imperative.

♦ Drafting Articles of Incorporation and bylaws is necessary for the application process in many states.

♦ To attain tax-exempt status for your corporation, study the publications and necessary forms provided by the IRS.

Chapter 5

For-Profit Thrift Stores

In This Chapter

- ◆ Buy in or start your own
- ◆ Understanding business organization and structure
- ◆ All your state and city licenses
- ◆ Business insurance and financing
- ◆ Where to find resources and help

There is a lot to be done before the doors to your thrift store will actually open and customers walk in. In this chapter, you will look at the first crucial steps that need to be negotiated by you and/or your partners in your business venture.

Up to now, you have considered the basic reasons for opening your own store, and you should have decided whether you want to open a nonprofit store and support a particular charity, or you want your store to simply produce income for yourself and your family.

If you have decided to become a nonprofit entity, all the information you need to get started was presented in the last chapter. Much of that information could also be applied to a profit-making corporation. However, stores

def•i•ni•tion

Legally organized basically refers to the way the Internal Revenue Service and the state where you reside recognize and treat your business entity.

run for profit have a number of other choices other than incorporation, and this chapter will present other options for *legally organizing* your business. It will also include basic information and offer advice and suggestions on business details and proven methods that can help you run a smooth, more successful business.

Yours or Ours

Although a business operated for profit cannot attach itself to an existing church or charity, it can buy into a business that is already up and running. Thrift stores are considered to be recession-proof. While retail stores often lose sales and customers during an economic slump, second-hand stores prosper because people are forced to look for lower-cost merchandise.

This is probably why you don't often see a resale shop for sale. However, that doesn't mean opportunities don't exist for someone who wants to invest in the business. Look at the want ads in your daily paper. Talk to people in the business. Are any of them near retirement age? Are any of them having health problems?

Once again, there are pros and cons of walking into an existing business, and here are some things you need to look at before signing a contract:

- Study the books and financial statements.

- Set up a trial period to see how the store is operated.

- If the owner is going to be your partner, determine if you are compatible with each other.

- Make sure the contract covers all your needs and concerns.

- If the owner is leaving the business, include a clause in the contract that prohibits the owner from opening another thrift store within a certain radius and time frame.

- Review the list of regular donors to the store.

- Review the customer mailing list.

- Check out the existing lease for terms, rates, and maintenance fees.

- Check out the area. Make sure the city isn't going to widen the road or dig up the parking lot.

A regular corporation issues stock and is owned by its shareholders, who may or may not be officers of the corporation.

The percentage of ownership is determined by the number of shares each shareholder has purchased. You may have heard the term "controlling interest." That refers to the stockholder of a corporation who owns the majority of the stock issued by the company. Often the person who has founded the corporation also owns a controlling interest in it.

A corporation is established in the state where the business is located and is formed according to the rules and regulations of that state. The application process for a regular corporation is much like the process followed by a nonprofit entity. It has a mission statement, articles of incorporation, and bylaws. Like the nonprofit business owner, if you plan on forming a corporation for your thrift store business, check with the Secretary of State in your area and get all the information and forms needed to register it.

A corporation assumes all the liabilities generated by the business as well as responsibility for operating the business and the resulting profits or losses.

A corporation is assigned an EIN by the IRS and must file a tax return every year. Any taxable income is subject to the corporate tax rate schedule, and the federal income taxes, payroll taxes, and state taxes are all paid by the corporation.

 **Added Value**

Corporations protect the personal assets of their founders and board members.

The Secretary of State oversees corporations, and some states have a separate office called the Corporation Commission, where Articles of Incorporation must be filed and approved before the corporation is officially established. See the instructions and checklist in the previous chapter for organizing a nonprofit corporation, as the process is the basically the same for a corporation that will be operated for profit.

One difference between the nonprofit corporation and a regular corporation is in the issuance of stock. Forming a regular corporation requires that you provide information such as the number of stock shares that will be issued and whether it is common stock or preferred stock. However, since you are probably not going to become a public corporation that sells stock to other people, the shares of stock can be minimal and owned by you. Check with your legal advisor as to how this should be handled on your application for incorporation.

A corporation that is operating for profit must also state its purpose in a mission statement. You reviewed a number of mission statements for nonprofit entities in the last chapter, so we will just provide one example for a profit-making corporation in this chapter. The following is a one-line statement from the retail giant Wal-Mart: To give ordinary folk the chance to buy the same thing as rich people.

The important thing to remember when drafting your mission or vision statement and bylaws is to make both clear and to the point. Consider including some of the following information:

♦ The moral and/or ethical views of the company

♦ The key strategies the business will follow

♦ A description of the products and services

♦ The expected customer base

♦ Expectations for growth

Depending on the state statutes, there may be other steps that must be taken before the corporation is approved. Of course, there are also fees to be paid. The quickest and most efficient way to go through the process is with a competent legal advisor who is familiar with the procedures and the fees charged. The advisor will also charge a fee for his or her services, but will take care of all the details and make the entire process smoother for you.

All corporations are subject to review and renewal each year and must file a report with the state office that governs them.

S corporations are smaller versions of regular corporations and relieve the business owner of the liabilities that could result from the actions and debts of the business operation. S corporations are assigned an EIN by the Internal Revenue Service and file a tax report each year. However, like the partnership entity, the profit or loss of the business is filtered back to the owner or owners for reporting on their personal tax returns.

All types of corporations can have employees. Even if you are the sole person running your thrift store, you can be an employee of the thrift store. The corporation will then pay you a salary and be responsible for reports and payroll taxes. Corporations can also purchase vehicles and other equipment needed to run the business.

State and City Licenses

Once your business entity is structured, start investigating the cost and requirements to obtain your licenses to operate a business in your city and state.

These licenses all have fees attached to them. The fees vary from city to city and state to state. Usually, a nonprofit organization is also exempt from sales tax on the items it sells. However, that may not be true in all cities and states, so check it out thoroughly to make sure you know exactly what will be required of you as a business owner.

The licenses probably won't be issued until you have a location for your store, but you should check out the costs and rules and regulations before you start looking for a location. Some areas may have restrictions about the type of business that can be opened there.

Business Insurance Needs

Even though you're opening a thrift store with low-cost merchandise, the accumulated value of your inventory may be more than you expect. You will also have furniture and fixtures and equipment like a computer and cash register that need to be covered for fire and theft.

You will also need liability insurance in the event a customer sustains an injury in your store. Auto insurance must be purchased on any vehicles you will use for your business.

Business interruption insurance is also a smart thing to have. In the event that your store and its contents are lost in a fire, it will take you time to repair the premises and replace the inventory. Business interruption insurance pays you a set fee for the income lost while you are getting your store up and running again.

You may also consider additional life insurance or disability insurance on yourself if you are the primary person running the store. If you have an accident or become disabled, it will help you and your family until you recover or find someone else to run the business for you.

 **Added Value**

Contact a reputable commercial insurance agent to research the cost of all your business insurance needs.

Some insurance coverage is totally necessary, but carefully consider the costs of any extra coverage an agent tries to sell you.

Start-up Capital

In the event that you need help financing your business, the planning and research you have completed while reading this book will show a lender that you have given considerable thought to the business venture and understand what will be required of you as the owner. When negotiating a business loan, make sure the payments and terms of the loan are ones you can handle.

Helping Hands
If you need a bank loan, it is better to take a longer term with lower payments to get your business started. With less being paid out, your cash flow will be better, and the loan can always be paid off early to save the interest expense.

Banks and investors are often unwilling to lend money to a new business, even one that is incorporated. Here are some options you may consider if you need to raise capital to start your thrift store:

♦ Use the equity in your home to secure a second mortgage.

♦ Seek investments from private parties.

♦ Co-sign a loan for your corporation using your personal assets as collateral.

♦ Find a silent partner who will supply funds in exchange for a percentage of ownership in your store.

Be aware that any of the above suggestions have risks. Do not enter into any financial arrangement without a thorough investigation and advice from a competent lawyer and/or accountant.

Ask for Help

There are a number of places that will help you organize your business regardless of the structure you decide to use. Review the following list of places that will answer questions and give you advice:

♦ Small Business Answer Desk and/or SCORE (Service Corps of Retired Executives): 1-800-827-5722

♦ Small Business Development Center: 402-595-2387

- ◆ American Home Business Association: 1-800-664-2422

- ◆ National Association for the Self-Employed: 1-800-232-6273

- ◆ Department of Commerce Business Assistance Service: 202-483-3176

- ◆ National Business Association: 1-800-465-0440

- ◆ Your local Chamber of Commerce

You should now have sufficient information and a basic plan for your thrift store. Once you decide how you want to structure the business organization and have the necessary capital, you can move forward to actually finding a location, and getting your store stocked and ready for customers.

When all the paperwork is behind you, you can concentrate on the more creative aspects of the resale industry. Stay focused on your initial reasons for opening a thrift store. If you are a nonprofit, start organizing the volunteers. If you're not, call on family and friends to help you scout locations, gather merchandise, and a hundred other details that will have to be attended to before your store opens.

The Least You Need to Know

- ◆ Sole proprietors put their personal assets at risk for the actions and debts of the business. Limited liability companies (LLCs) provide some protection for the owner's personal assets.

- ◆ Partners should be compatible, each possessing skills that benefit the business operation. Partnerships file tax returns each year that then assign the income to the partners based on the percentage of ownership each partner retains.

- ◆ Creating a corporation allows you to become an employee of the business as well as the owner/manager. Regular corporations file a tax return each year and net earnings are taxed at the corporate rate.

- ◆ An S corporation is a smaller version of a regular corporation with income filtering down to the officers much like the partnership tax returns.

- ◆ There are organizations that you can contact for help. Seek them out if you need assistance.

Part 2

Getting Down to Business

Now that you have learned how to structure your business to fulfill your needs and the needs of your charity and community, it's time to make more decisions that will affect your future success.

In Part 2, you will learn about all the decisions that must be made prior to opening the doors of your thrift store. Some of the tasks that have to be done include finding the best location, establishing operating procedures, and becoming familiar with new laws that apply to thrift stores.

These chapters are full of information that will make your store's opening really grand. Some chapters deal with setting up a good bookkeeping system. While that may not be your idea of fun, learning how the money your store generates should be handled and recorded will ensure that the fun of making the money continues.

Chapter **6**

Preliminary Business Decisions

In This Chapter

- ◆ Finding store locations
- ◆ Determining your type of merchandise
- ◆ Negotiating a lease with the landlord
- ◆ Choosing a good name
- ◆ Staffing the store with volunteers and employees

As have you already learned, opening a new business requires a series of steps, lots of thought, and many decisions. The purpose of this chapter is to give you information and suggestions that can be used to open the thrift store that reflects your vision and suits your plans for the future. The first person a new business has to please is the owner. If you are happy with the way the store takes shape, you will not mind the hard work and sacrifices necessary to open the doors for business.

If you have a partner or partners who are going to be involved in the venture, no firm decisions can be made until all the partners are consulted and agree on how to proceed. Again, all these business decisions should be thought through and provide a measure of satisfaction and a sense that you are on the way to obtaining your goal.

Find a Space

Choosing the right location for your thrift store is probably one of the most important business decisions you will make. It is not something that can be rushed and not something you should do on your own. You need to arrange for the services of a licensed commercial property real estate agent or broker. A commercial property real estate professional only handles sales and rentals of business property such as stores, shopping centers, warehouses, and other income-producing buildings.

Added Value

Take a cue from real estate agents who say the three most important things about a piece of property are location, location, and location.

An agent who is experienced in commercial property will be able to give you the guidance and advice you need to make a good choice. Before you start looking at available commercial space, sit down with your agent and discuss your needs. That includes the monthly rent you expect to pay and the neighborhoods in your city that may be best suited for a thrift store.

If the agent is managing shopping centers or malls, he or she may try to rent you an empty space in one of those locations. Be aware that shopping centers and malls offer some good advantages, but they also have disadvantages you have to take into consideration.

Some of the advantages of a shopping center or mall are ...

- Other businesses to attract customers.

- Large paved parking lots.

- General advertising for the center.

- Security.

- General maintenance of public areas.

All of these advantages come with a price tag to the businesses located in the mall. In addition to the monthly rental fee for a store in a shopping center, fees are added on for maintenance, security, and advertising. Being in a shopping center is always more costly, but the costs could be offset by the number of customers the mall attracts.

However, commercial shopping centers often restrict the type of activities a store can promote. They also set the business hours for the stores, which means your store has to be open when the mall is open and closed when the mall is closed.

While there are some thrift stores located in large shopping malls, most rent space in smaller centers known as strip malls, or rent stand-alone commercial space.

Research the Neighborhood

Perhaps you already know the general area or neighborhood where you want to rent store space. The first thing you may want to look at in that area is your competitors. How many other resale shops are located there? Having other thrift stores in the same area is not necessarily a disadvantage. It can actually be an advantage, especially if your store is going to carry merchandise that is different from the other shops. That's because shoppers like to have a choice of stores in one area, which explains the popularity of shopping malls.

If you are not very familiar with the area, do some research before your agent begins showing you rental spaces. Contact your local law enforcement agency and request the crime statistics for the area. If that information is acceptable, spend some time visiting other stores in the neighborhood. Talk to the owners and tell them that you want to open a thrift store. Monitor their reactions and get their opinions on the area and the needs of the people who live there.

If you are considering a new strip center, find out if there were any protests from neighborhood associations about its construction. The people who live near your store are your first potential customers and if they didn't want the shopping center in their neighborhood, they may boycott all the businesses that rent space in it. Of course, people come and go from a particular area, but a changeover or a change of heart can take a long time.

Once you and your agent have settled on a particular area, it's time to start inspecting available properties.

Room to Grow

Your agent should know the approximate population of the area. If you are not sure how much space you need, you can estimate the right size with a simple formula. You will probably need 1,000 square feet of floor space for every 1,000 people within a 5-mile radius of your store's location.

You may also want to look at stores that have the potential for expansion, because if you run your store properly you will probably need more space in a few years.

Rent

Once you have determined the amount of space you need, the next question is how much will it cost. Commercial rents are usually based on a set amount per square foot. If the storefront is in a strip center, find out what the fees are for maintenance and other services the owner of the center provides.

While a strip center does not have the high fees charged by large malls, there are always some additional fees to be paid by the tenants.

You also need to find out if the landlord is willing to make repairs or remodel the premises to suit your needs. While some will not, others will, and still others are willing to split the cost of modifications with you. This may depend on the type of lease you are willing to sign. A longer lease usually makes a landlord more generous.

Not for Resale

When you are estimating the amount of space you will need for your store, don't overlook your need for storage space and customer service areas.

It's okay to pay more than you originally budgeted. Perhaps you can save money by reducing something else in your cost estimates. However, don't rent any space that you know you can't initially afford. It is better to start small and outgrow the space than to rent a store that will have you sweating the payments each month.

Storage Space

Although you need a certain amount of storage space, remember that storage areas are not income producing. Don't turn down a good store location because it lacks the storage space you think you need. There are ways to make the most of the storage space you have with shelving units and good organizational skills.

If you outgrow your storage space, you can always rent space in one of the many storage facilities that exist in every city. Or you can add a storage building to the yard area of your home.

Remember that unless you are saving specific types of items for a special sale, you want your merchandise on the sales floor where customers can buy it.

Customer Parking

The ideal location for your thrift store will have good, adequate parking. People actually avoid shopping in stores where finding a parking space is a problem.

Also consider any special events your shop is going to sponsor to attract customers, and estimate how many parking spaces will be required for those events. You must also consider parking for yourself and any employees or volunteers that staff your store. In addition, parking areas must be paved and well lit, especially if your store is going to be open in the evenings.

A store that does not have good parking facilities has two strikes against it from day one, so make sure any location you are considering satisfies that criteria.

Added Value

Providing customers with easy access to your business will help it to become profitable.

Types of Merchandise

Women who walk into an empty house they are thinking of buying always look around and think about where they are going to put their furniture. They also contemplate the need to add or eliminate pieces. When you walk into a rental space, you must think about the type of merchandise you are going to display in the store, and where and how it can be placed in this space.

Because you are going to sell general merchandise, think about how the space can be divided for the different categories you will carry. Where will you place racks for displaying clothing? Where will you put shelves to store used books? Where will you place tables for household items like towels and bed linens?

Remember back to Chapter 1 when you drafted a floor plan and designed a display area for your shop. You should be carrying those plans and rough drafts with you when you look at stores. They will tell you whether the space you are looking at will work for you or if it can be modified to suit your needs

Working with the Landlord

It may take some time, but eventually you will find the perfect location for your thrift shop. Once you find the right location, step back and let your real estate agent negotiate the initial lease terms for you.

One reason to let the agent do it is to avoid any disagreements with the landlord or leasing agent. If you are going to occupy the property, you will have to work with this person for a number of years and you don't want to start out on the wrong foot.

This doesn't mean that you blindly accept the lease terms your agent has worked out with the landlord. A lease is a legal document and must be carefully reviewed and considered before you sign on the dotted line. It's worth the legal fees you will pay an attorney to advise you on a lease that often has complicated clauses that need clarification. This is especially important if your real estate agent is also the leasing agent for the center or mall where the store you want is located.

> **Not for Resale**
>
> No matter how much you like the rental space, be willing to walk away from the property if any of the lease terms will make running your store difficult.

Once the lease has been signed, you will be anxious to get into the empty space and start turning it into your thrift store.

Furniture and Fixtures

Shopping for furniture and fixtures for your business will not take much time. Since you have already planned out the basic layout of your shop, buying the fixtures will be easy. Used furniture and fixtures are appropriate for a thrift store.

There are a number of outlets where store fixtures are displayed and sold, and many of them carry used merchandise. You can also look for stores that are going out of business and see about buying some of their fixtures. Don't forget to get shelving or tables you will need for your storage area, too.

A good cash register and service counter are necessary items. Today, electronic registers make ringing up sales and balancing the receipts at the end of the business day simple and smooth. If you decide to purchase a new computerized register, make sure there is a good instruction manual for it or a training class is provided on how to use it.

> **Not for Resale**
>
> Don't attempt to run an accounting software program without first learning the basics of accounting.

A home computer with enough memory is usually fine for running accounting and bookkeeping software programs. Again, when purchasing a software program make sure it comes with a good operating manual and technical support service. Much of what you need to know for running accounting software will be found in Chapters 8 and 9 and in the books listed in Appendix A.

What's in a Name?

Most authors will tell you choosing a title for a book is extremely important. People are warned not to judge a book by its cover, which may be true of many things, but when it comes to literature the cover and the title displayed on it are usually what attract a reader to the book. The name you choose for your thrift store should attract customers to your store.

Perhaps from the moment you considered opening a thrift store, a particular name jumped into your conscious mind. Hopefully, it is a name so clever and witty that it will stick in the minds of thrift store shoppers as resolutely as it stuck in yours. Throughout this book the name Smart Shopper Thrift Store is used to discuss examples and other information. It's an adequate name, but does it have the sing and zing you want for your store?

Take into account the fact that the name of your store will not just be painted on a sign attached to the front of the building. It will be used every time you place an ad or do any type of promotion for the store. A catchy name is always easier for people to remember, and they often enjoy a name with a pun or a sound-alike phrase, such as a book store called Buy the Book. Trade names are usually protected to keep others from using them. If you think of a great name and want to keep it exclusive, you can register it.

Added Value _____

Visit www.smallbusinessnotes. com for tips, resources, and information on choosing a good business name.

A nonprofit thrift store that supports a charity or cause may want to work that into the name of the store. For example, a thrift store in southern Arizona that supports a home that cares for distressed infants and toddlers is called Casa de los Ninos, a Spanish term that means "home of the children." The thrift store carries the same name, letting everyone know that the proceeds from this shop go directly to the children's home. This works well in that part of the country, because with its close proximity to Mexico, Spanish names and phrases are commonly used.

If your mind is a blank when it comes to naming your thrift store, enlist the aid of your family, friends, and advisors. Sometimes a good brainstorming session produces an array of wonderful names for consideration. You can also look through the telephone directory and see what names are already being used in your area. You don't want to choose a name that is too similar to another store's name; you want a name that is exclusive to your store and the image you want to project to the public.

You can also go on the Internet and do a search for thrift stores and see what names owners in other parts of the country are using. You can use a similar name as long as the name isn't copyrighted and isn't in the same state as your store. Or you can take one of the names you like and modify it to suit your store. There are also companies that will design a name for your store based on the information you supply on your personal vision for the business.

Remember that the subconscious mind often has fabulous ideas if you'll just let them surface. Concentrating too hard on a subject, like a name for your store, can stifle the subconscious, so relax and be open to suggestion. You'll be amazed at the good ideas that suddenly make their way into your conscious mind. Keep a pad and pencil handy to write down these spontaneous thoughts as they come along.

Another method that works is writing down names for your shop that include words that convey the image you have of it. Then, look up some of those words in the dictionary and/or thesaurus to get a fresh perspective on them. This may allow you to change a word or two and come up with something new with a clever twist to it.

The name you settle on for your store will become a permanent part of your business. Therefore, take your time and come up with a name you will be happy to use for a long, long time.

Help Wanted

Store owners are usually the primary people who staff a store. This is especially true in new business ventures before the profits start rolling in to pay additional help.

Hopefully, a good deal of what you are going to sell in your store has already been acquired, but you will still need to sort and display the goods.

After your store actually opens for business, you will probably still need to purchase merchandise and accept donations. That means you will need help because no matter how talented you are, you will not be able to be in two places at one time.

Volunteers

If you are opening a nonprofit store, you will be able to use volunteers. These people are drawn from the supporters of your particular charity. These people will work in your shop and not expect any payment or benefits.

Volunteers will, however, expect to be treated fairly and with respect. One of the ways you can keep volunteers happy is to be organized and to work side by side with them.

Setting up work schedules for the volunteers is essential so you know that all the tasks will be covered. Before you make up a schedule, you must interview your volunteers to find out what jobs they would like to do and then determine the days and hours they will be available to do those jobs.

> **Helping Hands**
>
> Always try to keep a list of alternate volunteers. These alternates will fill in when someone is ill or quits working unexpectedly.

The main thing to consider when staffing a store when you are responsible for its operations is this: If you don't have enough volunteers to service customers, sort donations, stock the shelves, clean the store, and do paperwork, then you will have to do it yourself.

As a nonprofit store grows and prospers, more and more volunteers will be needed to help you run it. So talk to the supporters of your charity. Get them lined up to step in and do some work.

Some staff people are going to be better workers and more efficient than others, but don't play favorites or cut out anyone who wants to volunteer. If someone isn't capable of doing their share, assign someone else to help them get the job done. Since they are not earning salaries, you can use as many people as you can get.

Employees

A store that is operated for profit also needs to be staffed. If you have partners or family members that are going to help you, you probably won't need to hire employees immediately. However, if your store is structured as a corporation, nonprofit or not, employees can be hired by the corporation, and this includes you, your partners, and family members.

You will be learning all about payroll and taxes a little later in this book. For now, let's concentrate on the actual hiring of employees in the event you don't have partners or family members to help you run your thrift store.

Interviewing potential employees is crucial. Look for people who have had experience working with the public, ideally in some type of resale or retail store. You always check the references of the people you are considering for employment. Many past employers won't say anything really derogatory about a former worker, but be wary if they are not willing to give the person an enthusiastic endorsement.

When looking at the work history or resumes of potential employees, watch for these signs that may mean they will not be good additions to your store staff:

- Prior jobs of short duration

- Vague reasons for leaving prior jobs

- No experience with sales or public contact

Employees are an expense to your business, and having to go through the hiring process often adds to that expense. So give your full attention to interviewing and getting a personal feeling about applicants. One of the biggest mistakes employers make is passing over an applicant whom they feel is overqualified for the job. Don't you want the best person you can find to work in your store? An overqualified person is a much better choice than an underqualified person. Employers often think that overqualified individuals will leave their employ as soon as something better comes along. That may be true, but while they are working for you they will do a good job and probably help you increase your business income.

Added Value

Small courtesies go a long way in keeping your employees happy and satisfied.

Employees, just like volunteers, expect to be treated fairly and be appreciated for the work they do. These things can be more important to some people than the wages they earn. As your store grows and prospers and a need arises for additional staff, always promote from within, giving current employees a chance to take on more responsibilities and earn a higher salary.

If employees like you and like the job, there is a greater chance that they will become long-term employees that you can depend on to help you make your store successful.

The Least You Need to Know

- Choose a store location that suits your immediate needs and has the potential for future expansion.

- A lease is a legal document with terms that have to be carefully considered.

- The type of merchandise you carry will determine the kind of furniture and fixtures you need for your store.

◆ Nonprofit stores can use supporters of the charity to fill staffing needs.

◆ Interviewing potential employees thoroughly and checking references is crucial to the success of your store.

◆ Don't pass over a potential employee who is overqualified.

Chapter 7

Establish Basic Business Practices

In This Chapter

- ◆ Determining your store hours
- ◆ Organizing your sales procedures
- ◆ Establishing inventory control
- ◆ Training your store personnel

It is up to you to set up a basic plan for the day-to-day operation of your store. Don't worry—this plan can be changed any time you feel it is not working for you. These are simply guidelines that you will use to open and close your store each day, handle sales, and a number of other things related to managing a thrift store.

Some of these procedures will have to be set before you start staffing your store with volunteers or employees. That's because people want to know what time they need to report to work and what time they can leave work. You will also need these initial guidelines for training personnel on how to handle customers and inventory.

Open and Close Times

Setting the hours for your store is a more complex decision than you might have thought it would be. There are several factors that need to be considered before you print up a sign for your front door listing the hours of operation. The sign listing your business hours must be prominently displayed on your front door. The front door is the first place customers will look for it. Also, whenever you advertise your shop, include the hours of operation in the ad.

The location of your store has a direct bearing on the hours of operation. If you are in a shopping mall or large shopping center, the hours your store is open for business will be dictated by the hours that the shopping mall is open.

If you are in a smaller strip center or a location where you have similar businesses for neighbors, you should probably talk to them so that your hours can be coordinated with the other stores. If they are open later in the day, you should try to stay open later as well. Customers who visit their shops may very well decide to visit yours, too, as long as they are in the vicinity.

The neighborhood where your store is located will also help you decide the days and hours your business should be open to the public. If the neighborhood residents are mainly working-class people, they need to shop on the weekends. That means your shop should be open Saturdays and perhaps Sundays also, even if you make the Sunday hours shorter than the weekday hours.

Again depending on the area, you can close your shop at 5 or 6 P.M. or keep it open later one or two evenings a week. Keep in mind that when you are not at your store, you may be busy collecting donations or obtaining merchandise for your store from other sources.

Added Value

Start with the longest hours you can manage until you get a feel for the times when the most customers are in your store.

So unless you're in a shopping mall where you must set your store hours to their hours, consider how much time you personally will have to be at the store. If you have staff to help you, longer hours will work. If you are doing it alone, you may want shorter hours or at least have the store closed one day a week to give yourself a break.

Making Sales

Hopefully, once your store opens there will be a steady stream of customers purchasing your merchandise every hour that you are open. These sales will be the main source of income for your business. So you must set up some guidelines to handle them properly.

Using the newer electronic cash registers will cut down immensely on your daily paperwork. They are actually computers programmed to total sales, add sales tax if applicable to your store, and print out a receipt for the customer, while posting the sales figures into a program that will print out a report at the end of the business day.

Do yourself a favor and get a good computerized cash register. You can probably find a used one that will do the job at a much lower cost than a brand-new one. It will pay for itself in the time it will save you and the errors that will be avoided.

In the case of cash sales, the clerk only has to input the amount of cash received from the customer and the register will display the amount of change the customer needs to get.

Today most people shop with debit cards and credit cards. Debit cards can be used for any size purchase, but because of the merchant fees connected to credit card purchases, you may want to limit the use of credit cards to sales of $10 or more. Posting a sign notifying customers of that limitation on credit card sales would be necessary.

The computerized cash registers are set up to work with processing machines that your bank will provide to handle debit and credit card sales. The information from the processing machine is transmitted electronically to the cash register to record these payments on sales. When a customer uses a debit card to pay for a purchase, that amount is instantly and automatically transferred from the customer's bank account to your business account—a quick, simple, and safe transaction.

Some people still prefer to write out checks, and that is fine. The computerized register will validate the check for you. Don't hassle customers about using checks, but a look at an identification card such as a driver's license should be done just to verify that it matches the information on the check, especially the mailing address. You will need that information in the event the check does

Not for Resale

The electronic equipment for processing credit and debit cards has to be in place before the store opens for business.

not clear your bank, to contact the customer and ask them to make good on the check. Always do that in writing and keep a copy of the correspondence. Making a photocopy of checks before they are deposited into your bank account is a good idea.

Some training is required to run electronic cash registers, but learning to operate one is not difficult. You will also have to train your staff on other sales procedures, such as handling and wrapping merchandise and answering any questions the customer may have about the various items you are selling in your store.

If for some reason you are unable to install a computerized cash register, sales slips will have to be handled manually, creating a much greater margin for error. It's best to use sales slip books that make duplicate copies. You keep the original and the customer gets the copy. At the end of the day all the sales slips will have to be totaled and balanced against the money collected in your cash drawer.

Setting sales guidelines for you and your staff will help you run your store more efficiently.

Inventory Control

Because retail stores purchase all their merchandise from *vendors*, keeping track of inventory often requires a separate bookkeeping department.

There are clerks, warehouse workers, and computer software programs all dedicated to controlling inventory in the retail sales business. This helps them determine the profit margin on the products they sell, and also tells them what is selling and what is not. Most of the time, this is not necessary for members of the resale industry. In fact, merchandise in thrift stores often comes and goes so quickly there's no time to record it or count it. In addition, much of the inventory that comes into your store will be donated, especially if you are a nonprofit corporation.

def•i•ni•tion

A **vendor** is a supplier that sells products or services to other businesses.

Handling consignment items does require some paperwork, but like donations, there is really no purchase price on the merchandise. Some items may be purchased for your store and could be recorded in an inventory account, but that is up to you as the owner. If you want to do that you will find more information on inventory control in the chapters dealing with accounting and bookkeeping. You will also learn how to handle any outright purchases you may make for your store.

For a resale shop, controlling inventory simply means sorting and stocking and making sure all the items you sell are in reasonably good condition and provide a good value for your customers.

Inventory control in a thrift store also means that you and your staff know where specific items are; that way you will be able to fill requests for certain things and answer any questions about your current merchandise that your customers may have.

Added Value

If you keep your shop and storage areas clean and neat, you will be able to tell at a glance what is selling and what is not and make adjustments to your inventory.

You're a Trainer

Whether your staff is made up of volunteers or employees, it is up to the owner or manager to train them in the basic business practices that are going to be used to operate the thrift store.

How your staff responds to the training will tell you what jobs they can handle in your store. Some people are better suited to deal with customers day in and day out. Others may be more suited to working behind the scenes and can be trained to sort and price merchandise and keep the shelves and racks properly filled.

To Work with Customers

People with patience who do not get easily rattled are ideal for customer service of all kinds. These are the volunteers or employees you want out front helping customers and ringing up sales. These attributes must also be present in you, the person who is managing the store.

Train your salespeople to use the cash register properly and make sure they fully understand it. You should stay alongside all new people for the first few hours to answer questions and help them deal with any unusual problems that arise. Most customers are easy to service, but there will always be a few that complain and demand special

Added Value

The age of the customer should be taken into consideration when handling a complaint. Older people often need special assistance.

treatment. Train your staff to ask you for assistance with difficult people. It is your store, and the decision to honor complaints or special requests is up to you.

Remember that the customer is right most of the time, but not always. Also be aware that some people will not be satisfied not matter what you do for them.

To Accept Donations

The best procedure for taking donations is to accept them gratefully. There may be items you won't be able to resell, but you can dispose of those later after the donor has left your store.

Always get the donor's name and address and ask if they would like a receipt. Your procedure for receipts should be to give the customer one at the time of drop-off. This saves you the task of mailing them at a later time, which could become quite a big job as your donating customer base grows.

> **Not for Resale**
>
> If there is an odor attached to any donated goods, they should be moved outside immediately so the odor will not offend customers.

Always keep some boxes handy in the event the donations are not carried into your store in a container. Your staff should not handle the items when they are brought in that way. The boxes should be carried to the storage area or another area of the store for sorting. Only staff that has been trained in the safe handling of donated items should be allowed to sort through the boxes. The safe handling of donated goods is covered in detail in Chapter 12 of this book.

It's a good idea to make up a list of acceptable donations for your staff members to refer to when you are not on the premises. With strict adherence to those guidelines, any member of your staff can be trained to accept donations.

To Handle Stock and Inventory

As you have already learned, some staff people are more useful to your store by working behind the scenes. These people can fill in occasionally to help with customer service, but should not be assigned to that job on a regular basis.

Keeping your store stocked with new items all the time is what will keep customers stopping in regularly to see what has been added to the racks and shelves. So having people who can keep the store properly stocked is essential.

You or your staff will have to walk the display areas every day to see what type of items need to be added or deleted. After a while you will know what goods sell best and which items are slow movers.

You also want to train people to rearrange the items in the shop regularly, especially if you don't have an abundance of new goods to put on display. If customers see the same old merchandise in the same old place every time they come in the store, they will quickly get bored and go elsewhere.

Train your staff people to clean all the areas of the store, including the storage areas. All the displays and racks must also be kept neat and attractive.

Customers have a habit of picking up clothing or other items and then dropping them somewhere else in the shop if they decide not to purchase them. Again, your staff should be vigilant about looking for those discarded items and returning them to their proper place.

As you manage your thrift store, you will come up with many different jobs and tasks that have to be handled. Training your staff in these areas is important because it frees you up for all the many tasks owners and managers must train themselves to do.

Remember, any procedure can be changed in the event that you think of a better, simpler way to handle things.

The Least You Need to Know

- Store hours should be convenient for customers.
- Schedule at least one day off from the store for yourself.
- A good computerized cash register is essential.
- Credit cards fees reduce your profits, so set limitations on the use of them.
- Set up very simple procedures to manage your inventory.
- Staff must receive good training and support.

Chapter 8

Setting Up a Bookkeeping System

In This Chapter

◆ Opening bank accounts

◆ Computerizing your accounting procedures

◆ Debits and credits and opening entries

◆ Posting your daily business transactions

Whether you plan on doing your own bookkeeping or not, you need to understand the process and learn how to read financial statements. Financial statements should be issued at the end of every month and are the best way to monitor the success of your thrift store.

All the income and expenses are totaled and reported on the financial statements and will tell you if your store is operating at a profit or loss. These reports will also show you where adjustments can be made to improve your cash flow and financial condition.

This chapter will provide a crash course on the basics of accounting and bookkeeping so that you will be able to do your own books—or at the very least understand the procedures and reports issued by anyone you hire to do the books for you. The information that will be presented in this book assumes that you are opening and running a small thrift store with either no staff or only a small staff to assist you. Larger businesses would need more complex accounting procedures and a computerized system that prints out checks for bills and payroll. However, whether your first store is large or small, owners without a background in accounting are advised to seek professional help to set up the books and daily bookkeeping procedures for their business.

Not for Resale

Get recommendations for accounting professionals in your area and meet with them to discuss your needs before turning your financial records over to them.

There are, of course, a number of books you can read that will give you more detailed instructions for handling your own bookkeeping. A few good ones are listed in Appendix A of this book.

Find a Bank

If you do not already have a separate checking account for your business, one should be established as soon as you have settled on a location for your store.

It is important that you choose a bank that suits your needs. Don't be swayed by a bank that gives out free gifts when you open an account. Look beyond the free gifts and make sure the bank has all the conveniences and services your business will require now and in the future.

Here are some of the things you should look for in the bank where you will do business:

◆ Convenient location

◆ Convenient banking hours

◆ A minimum of fees and service charges

◆ Credit card processing

◆ Debit card processing

◆ Electronic equipment you can purchase or lease for processing credit cards and debit cards

◆ Good customer service people to help you set up your accounts and handle your banking needs

Because most thrift stores sell merchandise at such a reduced price, many do not accept credit cards in payment of the goods they sell. However, it is a proven fact that when a customer is using a credit card to pay for purchases, they spend more.

If you decide to accept credit cards, keep in mind that there are processing fees associated with them. That means that the bank or credit card processor will take a percentage of every credit card sale in addition to a standard monthly service charge on your bank account. As mentioned in a prior chapter, some stores establish a sales policy that limits the use of credit card sales on purchases of less than $10. Your bank should explain all the fees and monthly service charges and provide you with the equipment needed to process credit card sales.

Make sure that the bank will issue statements on your account that cover the first of the month through the last day of the month. This is for your benefit because you want your bank records to correspond with your bookkeeping records. This makes it easier to reconcile the cash balance that will be kept in your bookkeeping system with the balance the bank shows for your account.

Thrift store owners should always keep control of the bank accounts, especially the checking account. Even if you have someone else doing your books, you need to know how much money is going into the account and how much is being paid out of the account on a daily basis.

Joint accounts with your spouse or partners as additional signers on your account are fine, as long as you monitor the account activity. Other than your spouse or business partners, no one else should be able to sign your business checks.

Update your checking account balance every time a deposit is made and every time a check is written. The balance in your checking account will tell you instantly whether your business is doing well or heading toward a financial crisis.

Your checking account is a mini–financial statement that you can review every day to keep your thrift store running smoothly and profitably.

Added Value

Initially you can use your checking account to record income and expenses, and transfer the information into a software program once you have learned how to use one.

Purchase a Program

If you are going to keep your own books, you should invest in a computerized accounting program. There are many good ones on the market. All of the programs claim to be easy to use and understand, but some are more complex than others. Again, talk to businesspeople or accounting professionals and find out what programs they use and like.

As mentioned earlier, before trying to enter financial information into an accounting software program, you need to learn some basic accounting procedures. The best software program in the world won't do you any good if you don't enter the information correctly.

> **Helping Hands**
>
> It is better to get a software program that includes everything, even if you don't need it initially. It will save you the expense of adding to the program or having to purchase another program if your needs change.

Accounting software programs include an array of features and reports that you may not need. For example, most of these programs have built-in functions for keeping track of employees, payroll checks, and payroll taxes. If you have no employees, you can just ignore those areas of the program. However, you can easily activate and access those functions in the event you expand and hire employees.

Set Up Your Accounts

The first step in setting up a bookkeeping system is deciding what accounts are needed to record the financial information related to your thrift store. You will be creating what is called the *chart of accounts*, and it should be structured to suit your specific business activities. It can be easily expanded or modified at any time.

def•i•ni•tion

> A **chart of accounts** is a listing of accounts in your bookkeeping system that is used to record financial information in an organized, categorized manner.

Most computerized software programs allow the user to select a Chart of Accounts from a list categorized by different types of businesses. While you may not find one specifically for thrift stores, you can select one for a nonprofit business or a retail business that can be used for your store.

The Chart of Accounts is broken down into two main sections: Balance Sheet Accounts and Profit and

Loss Accounts. The charts built into your software program will probably have more accounts listed than you will need, but as mentioned, you can modify the accounts to suit your bookkeeping needs.

All the accounts in a computerized accounting program have a number assigned to them. These numbers are used to distribute the financial information entered into the system to the correct accounts. Each section of the Chart of Accounts assigns numbers within a particular range. More information on the account numbers will be discussed a little later in this chapter.

Assets and Liabilities

The Balance Sheet is a report that is part of the financial statements that lists assets, everything of value owned by the business, and any *liabilities* associated with those assets and the thrift store and its operations.

The assets portion of the Balance Sheet is broken down into specific categories. The following list is a sampling of some of the accounts you might need to list your thrift store's assets, and a brief explanation of why and how each account would be used.

◆ Cash in Checking—The balance in your store's operating account is reflected here.

◆ Cash in Savings—If your business has a savings account, this where the balance in that account is shown.

◆ Cash on Hand—This is the account that holds the amount of the change fund you keep in your cash register.

◆ Building—This would only be needed if you purchased the building that houses your store. The purchase price of the building would be shown as the value of this asset.

◆ Land—The value of the land you purchased where your thrift store building is located is posted in this account.

def•i•ni•tion

Liabilities are loans or other debts that have been incurred by a business.

Added Value

The values of a building and the land it occupies are listed as separate assets because the cost of a building can be written off over time, but land cannot be.

def•i•ni•tion

Depreciation is a tax deduction businesses can claim to write off the costs of tangible assets such as equipment, vehicles, buildings, and the improvements to them.

♦ Leasehold Improvements—Often a leased store has to be renovated or remodeled to suit the needs of a particular business, and the costs associated with that are included in this account and can be *depreciated*.

♦ Deposits—This account is used to record any prepaid amounts that are not expected to be returned in the near future. This would include security deposits on rental property and the deposits often required by utility companies.

♦ Prepaid Expenses—Not to be confused with deposits, this asset account holds the amount paid in advance for things like insurance premiums and equipment rentals that will then be written off on a monthly basis.

♦ Vehicles—This account holds the purchase price of any car or truck owned by your thrift store.

♦ Furniture and Fixtures—Shelving, clothing racks, tables, and purchases of other items used to display merchandise or service customers can be listed under this category.

♦ Equipment—This account is created to hold the total value of things like computers and cash registers.

♦ Other Assets—This is a catch-all account that would be used to list the value of items that do not fit into the other categories in the asset section of the Balance Sheet. An account called Accumulated Depreciation would be listed after each tangible asset or grouping of tangible assets that can be written off as a tax deduction, based on the rules established by the IRS. Often these accounts are only posted to once a year when the federal tax return is prepared by the owner or tax accountant.

♦ Inventory—The value of merchandise purchased for your store can be posted to this account, but most thrift stores, especially nonprofits, would not use this account.

Every computerized system has an account called Accounts Receivable programmed into it. This account would not be used by a thrift store that operates on a cash-and-carry basis. While most programs will not allow the user to delete Accounts Receivable, if it is not being used it will have no balance and therefore will not be listed on any of the financial reports. This is true of any account in your bookkeeping system that is not in use.

The second section of the Balance Sheet accounts is where all the liabilities of the thrift store are listed, with the outstanding balance on each loan or other debt. It is rare that a business, especially a new one, can be established without incurring some liabilities that have to be paid each month.

The very first account in this section is Accounts Payable. This is a general heading for the total of all the bills that have to be paid out for one particular month. Instructions on how bills are posted to this account and paid each month will be given in a later chapter of this book. For now, just make a mental note that this account is a part of the liability section of every Chart of Accounts and every bookkeeping system. Like Accounts Receivable, if you decide not to use this account it will not appear on your financial reports.

All debts can be classified into two types: secured liabilities or unsecured liabilities. A secured debt is one that is guaranteed by the value of an asset that exceeds or is equal to the amount of the original loan. A mortgage is a secured liability because the property financed by the mortgage loan guarantees it. An auto loan is a secured debt because the vehicle is used for collateral on the loan.

Not for Resale _____

If the loan is not repaid, the lender can take possession of the asset used as collateral to satisfy the balance on the loan.

In the liability section of your Chart of Accounts you would list any loans or debts connected to the assets you have listed.

For example, if your thrift store has purchased a delivery truck financed by a bank, it would become part of your Chart of Accounts and could be labeled as follows:

- ◆ Loan Payable ABC Bank: Delivery Truck—Accounts in this section would also have to be created for unsecured debts. Credit card debt is an unsecured liability. If you are making payments on a credit card balance, it should be listed on your Balance Sheet liabilities like the following sample:

- ◆ Visa Payable Merchant Bank—If you pay a credit card in full each month, it is not necessary to list that account as a liability on the Balance Sheet. An example of how the payment would be handled in your bookkeeping system will be presented in the posting instructions in this chapter.

If you use more than one credit card for business expenses and do not pay each one in full each month, you would have an individual account listing for each of them and the balances they carry.

The number of accounts listed in the liability section of the Chart of Accounts depends on your thrift store and how you have financed its assets. If you have employees, liability accounts for payroll and payroll taxes would also be included. More information on those accounts will be provided in a later chapter.

> **Not for Resale** _____
>
> Even though debts are unsecured, the lenders can still take legal action against you or your corporation to satisfy the debt if you don't make your payments.

The last two accounts in the Balance Sheet liability section are the Owner's Capital account and the Retained Earnings account. The Owner's Capital account is used to record the amount of money or the value of any tangible assets the owner invested in the store. Retained Earnings is used to report the accumulated profit or loss generated by the store's business operations.

Retained Earnings should not be confused with the term "net worth," which has nothing to do with the profit or loss of your store's operations. Net worth is the difference between the value of the assets your store has and the total debts or liabilities it is responsible for paying. Keep in mind that your store has a net worth only if the value of its assets is greater than the total of its liabilities.

Income and Expenses

Moving on to part two of the Chart of Accounts, let's look at the group of accounts that are needed to compile the Profit and Loss Statement. This report, along with the Balance Sheet, makes up the financial statements that should be issued for your business at the end of every month.

> **Helping Hands**
>
> St. Vincent de Paul thrift stores have a lot of different sales accounts to report income. This allows them to issue detailed reports to their local and national offices. Smaller resale shops should not need this type of detail.

Income accounts are listed first in this section of the Chart of Accounts. Your store can report sales in a number of different categories, but it is best to keep it simple, unless you are a nonprofit corporation that needs the detail for other reports.

If your thrift store carries specialty items, such as books or collectibles, you may want to have a sales category for each of those along with a general sales category for all the other merchandise. The accounts could be labeled as follows:

- Income—General Sales

- Income—Books

- Income—Collectibles

Other categories may be added as needed, but these accounts are created for your personal use and information. If you are only interested in the gross sales of your shop, you only need to establish one sales account where anything and everything you sell can be totaled and recorded.

If you do choose to have different sales accounts, you may want to list the amounts in each category separately when you record the day's deposits into the checkbook. This will make posting the sales into your book-keeping system faster and easier.

The next accounts in this section are called Cost of Sales accounts. These accounts immediately follow the income accounts and reduce the total sales reported in them. Cost of Sales accounts reflect the amount, if any, for the purchases of any merchandise sold in your store. If you are a nonprofit thrift store that only sells donated items, you won't need the Cost of Sales accounts.

Not for Resale

Don't confuse the expense accounts with the liability accounts. Liabilities are debts that are related to business assets, while expenses are a variety of bills connected to the business operation.

Every business has regular monthly expenses to pay, and the next accounts in this section are created to record the amounts paid out of your checking account for regular and not-so-regular bills incurred by your business.

The following list is a sampling of the most common accounts needed in the Expense section of the Chart of Accounts:

- Advertising Expense
- Auto Expense
- Bank Fees
- Depreciation Expense
- Insurance Expense

- Interest Expense
- Meetings/Seminars
- Miscellaneous Expenses
- Office Expense
- Rent Expense

- ◆ Repairs and Maintenance
- ◆ Supplies
- ◆ Telephone Expense
- ◆ Utilities

The titles of these accounts indicate the type of expense that should be reflected in each of them. Again, if you have employees or buy merchandise from outside sources, you will have to set up accounts where those liabilities and expenses can be recorded. However, the Chart of Accounts built into your accounting software program includes many expense accounts that you probably will not need.

There is a function in the Chart of Accounts section of the program that allows you to modify or delete accounts. You can always add a new account, but some programs will not allow the user to modify or delete certain accounts. The accounts mentioned earlier—Accounts Receivable and Accounts Payable—are what are known as control accounts in the software programs and therefore cannot be deleted. Again, if you do not post amounts to those unnecessary accounts, they will not be printed on the financial reports, so you can just ignore their existence in the Chart of Accounts. Appendix B has a sample Chart of Accounts for your review.

The General Ledger

All the accounts you will use for keeping track of the financial data for your thrift store are listed in the Chart of Accounts. Once the Chart of Accounts is created, it becomes what is called the General Ledger.

The General Ledger is where the accounts that have balances in them are stored. Eventually, all the accounts that have dollar amounts posted to them become a part of the financial statements. They are printed out of the General Ledger in a specific order according to the account number assigned to them by the software program and its user.

The accounts numbered 1000 to 3999 will appear on the Balance Sheet report.

Added Value

Accounts 1000 to 1999 are printed in the Asset section of the Balance Sheet. Accounts 2000 to 3999 will be used to print out the Liability section of the Balance Sheet.

The information for the Income Statement or Profit and Loss Statement of the financial reports is gleaned from the accounts numbered 4000 to 9999. Day-to-day expenses are usually in the 6000 to 6999 accounts. The other numbered accounts are for more complex financial reports than the ones presented to you in this simple crash course that is designed to acquaint you with a simple bookkeeping system for your thrift store.

Now that your Chart of Accounts has become the General Ledger, the next step is to get financial data into the General Ledger accounts. This is where posting debits and credits comes in.

Posting Transactions

The first and most important rule to remember about posting debits and credits is this: every transaction posted to the General Ledger will have both debits and credits, and those debits and credits must zero each other out.

In other words, if you are posting a debit of $50.00 to one account, you must also post a credit of $50.00 to another account so the transaction is in balance.

The good news is that accounting software programs will not let you enter a transaction that does not balance. Debits must always equal credits or the computer will not let you complete the posting. This doesn't mean you can't make a posting error, such as posting an amount to the wrong account. It just means your entry has to be in balance or the computer won't accept it.

Before you try to post transactions into the General Ledger, you need to become familiar with which accounts generally are considered to be debit accounts and which accounts are generally considered to be credit accounts.

Added Value

Often a credit amount in an entry will be shown in parantheses as (50.00).

Take a look at this list of account groupings and note whether the balance in the account is expected to be a debit or a credit balance:

◆ Asset Accounts—debit balances

◆ *Accumulated Depreciation Accounts*—credit balances

◆ Liability Accounts—credit balances

◆ Capital—credit balance

◆ Retained Earnings—credit balance

◆ Income Accounts—credit balances

◆ Cost of Sales Accounts—debit balances

◆ Expense Accounts—debit balances

def•i•ni•tion

Accumulated Depreciation Accounts reflect the amounts that can be used as tax deductions; these accounts reduce the value of the asset as it is written off for tax purposes.

Added Value

The amounts in the Cost of Sales Accounts and the Expense Accounts reduce the amount of income generated by sales.

Not for Resale

Never allow your bank account to become overdrawn. In addition to the amount your account is short, you will incur a number of other fees that will make matters worse.

The Cash in Checking account is an asset and is always expected to have a debit balance, but this is the account that is used most often to offset an entry. A debit balance in this account reflects the fact that there is money in the account. A credit balance in this account means that the bank account is overdrawn.

Here's another important rule to remember: never write a check from your account unless there are sufficient funds to cover that check. In today's world, electronic banking means that checks reach your account with lightning speed, and if you don't have sufficient funds to cover a check it will bounce just as fast. Besides the fact that it is illegal to write a bad check, it also damages your credit rating and the bank fees could end up being more than the check amount.

So the bottom line is that you always want to keep a debit balance in your checking account, but when you are posting any transaction that involves cash, a deposit for sales income, or a check to pay a bill, the entry in the General Ledger has to be balanced with a debit or credit to Cash in Checking.

Money going into the bank account is always a debit to Cash in Checking and a plus in the check register. Money taken out of the bank account is always a credit to Cash in Checking and is a subtraction in the check register.

Post This First

Now that you have created the Chart of Accounts and it has become the General Ledger, and you know which accounts are supposed to have debit balances and which ones have credit balances, you are ready to begin entering your financial information into the accounting system. The General Ledger is ready and waiting for what is called the opening entry.

Like every other entry you post to the General Ledger, the opening entry has debits and credits and must be in balance. As a matter of fact, once the opening entry is posted, you will be able to print out a Balance Sheet.

Let's assume a new thrift store is about to open and the owner has made the following financial transactions in order to get the store set up and ready for business:

◆ Bank loan obtained in the amount of $10,000.

◆ Personal funds in the amount of $5,000 invested in the business.

◆ Electronic cash register purchased for $1,500.

◆ Used store fixtures purchased for $2,000.

◆ Supplemental merchandise purchased from various sources for $1,800 cash.

◆ Truck purchased for $23,000. Owner gave the dealership a down payment of $2,300 and financed the balance through Toyota Financial Services.

◆ Security deposit and last month's rent on store in the amount of $1,000.

◆ Insurance policies for auto and general business liability coverage paid for six months at a total cost of $900.

Let's start at the top and post each transaction separately. This will give you the best understanding of how each one is entered into the General Ledger. It will also demonstrate how each posting contains debits and credits that zero each other out, resulting in an entry that is acceptable to your accounting software program because it is in perfect balance. All of the postings are called Journal Entries and are usually numbered.

Account#	Account Title	Debit	Credit
1000	Cash in Checking	$10,000.00	
2010	Loan—ABC Bank		$10,000.00
To record bank deposit and liability payable to ABC Bank			
1000	Cash in Checking	5,000.00	
3050	Owners Capital		5,000.00
To record owner's investment			
1110	Equipment	1,500.00	
1000	Cash in Checking		1,500.00

continues

continued

Account#	Account Title	Debit	Credit
To record purchase of cash register			
1130	Furniture & Fixtures	2,000.00	
1000	Cash in Checking		2,000.00
To record purchase of store displays			
1140	Inventory	1,800.00	
1000	Cash in Checking		1,800.00
To record purchase of used furniture and household goods			
1150	Toyota Truck	23,000.00	
2050	Loan Payable—Toyota		20,700.00
1000	Cash in Checking		2,300.00
		23,000.00	23,000.00
To record purchase of truck			
1101	Deposits	1,000.00	
1000	Cash in Checking		1.000.00
To record payment of security deposit on store			
1105	Prepaid Expenses	900.00	
1000	Cash in Checking		900.00
To record payment of 6 mos. insurance premiums			

Added Value

The loan amount posted as a liability is usually only the principal on the debt. The interest charged by the lender will be included in the payments and written off as an expense as each payment is made.

If you were to actually put these entries into a computer software program, it would post each item to the proper account and then balance each account. Since every entry required a posting to Cash in Checking, let's take a look at how this account would look in the General Ledger after the opening entry was posted.

The software program will always let you review an individual account in the General Ledger. If you were to access the Cash in Checking account after posting all of the above entries, it would appear as follows:

1000	Cash in Checking	Debit	Credit
JE#1	Loan	$10,000.00	
JE#2	Capital	5,000.00	
JE#3	Equipment		1,500.00
JE#4	Furniture and Fixtures		2,000.00
JE#5	Inventory		1,800.00
JE#6	Down Payment Truck		2,300.00
JE#7	Security Deposit		1,000.00
JE#8	Insurance Premiums		900.00
	Totals	15,000.00	10,000.00
	Balance	5,000.00	

Note that on JE#6 only the amount of the down payment is posted to the cash account, because it is the amount of the check that was written from the account.

With the opening entry posted in the bookkeeping system, the owner would be able to print out the first financial report, the Balance Sheet. The Balance Sheet would look like the following sample:

Smart Shopper Thrift Shop
Balance Sheet
June 30, 2010

Assets:

Cash in Checking	$5,000.00
Deposits	1,000.00
Prepaid Expenses	900.00
Equipment	1,500.00
Furniture and Fixtures	2,500.00

continues

continued

Smart Shopper Thrift Shop	
Balance Sheet	
June 30, 2010	
Inventory	1,800.00
Vehicles	23,000.00
Total Assets	35,700.00
Liabilities and Equity:	
Loan Payable—ABC Bank	10,000.00
Loan Payable—Toyota	20,700.00
Owner's Capital	5,000.00
Total Liabilities and Equity	35,700.00

Added Value

When a software program prints out a financial report, it is always dated for the last day of the month the report covers.

The entries and the Balance Sheet for a nonprofit thrift store would be exactly the same, except it probably would not have an Inventory account because its merchandise usually comes totally from donations from the supporters of the charitable organization it benefits.

Daily Transactions

The opening entry you just reviewed is an excellent example of how to post financial information into your bookkeeping software program. Posting the daily income and expenses of a thrift store works the same way, except that instead of just working with the accounts in the Balance Sheet, you will be entering financial data into the Income Statement accounts, too.

The majority of your daily transactions will involve cash and the checkbook, and if you have a good electronic register to ring up sales, your bookkeeping chores will be simplified. At the end of each business day, your cash register will give you the following information:

- ◆ Total amount of sales
- ◆ Cash collected
- ◆ Checks tendered
- ◆ Debit or credit cards processed

Once you have this information, all you have to do is verify it against what is in your cash drawer. The most efficient way to do that is to make up a worksheet. The following is an example of the type of worksheet you should create and use for your thrift store:

Sales/Cash Verification	
Date: June 24, 2010	
Cash in Register	$842.00
Checks Tendered	136.00
Debit Cards	50.00
Total in Register	1,028.00
Less Change Fund	-100.00
Total Sales	928.00
Less Debit/Credit Cards	-50.00
Bank Deposit	878.00

Remember that the processor automatically deposits the debit and credit cards into your bank account. So your bank deposit will only consist of the cash and checks collected for that business day. You may be thinking that if you have one of those magical electronic registers, you don't need to take the time to do a daily verification sheet. Think again. If the total sales, cash, checks, and credit cards processed balances with what is in your cash drawer, you know that every sale was rung up accurately and all customers received the correct change. A good bookkeeping system is built on the checks and balances that verify its accuracy.

When you enter the daily sales into your checkbook, do a separate entry for debit cards, credit cards, and the deposit you had to carry into the bank. That will make it much easier to reconcile your checkbook to the monthly statement you will receive from your bank. The reconciliation process will be explained in detail in the next chapter, as that is a procedure that is done at the end of the month.

Keeping the debit and credit card amounts separate is not necessary when you post the daily sales into the General Ledger. The entry to post the sales from the above example is as follows.

Account#	Account Name	Debit	Credit
4000	Income—Sales		$928.00
1000	Cash in Checking	$928.00	
To record sales receipts for 6-24-10			

Of course, many of the financial transactions your thrift store has will involve money going out of the bank account to pay monthly bills or other incidental expenses.

The following example explains the posting procedure for checks written out of your checking account for a regular expense.

Account#	Account Name	Debit	Credit
6000	Advertising	$92.00	
1000	Cash in Checking		$92.00
Check # 2356 payment of newspaper ad			

The next sample entry shows you how a check written for a payment on a liability that has been set up in the liability section of your Balance Sheet should be posted.

Account#	Account Name	Debit	Credit
1000	Cash in Checking		$500.00
2050	Loan Payable—Ford	$450.00	
6200	Interest Expense	50.00	
Check# 2357 Truck Payment			

Note that the interest on the truck loan is being expensed monthly as each payment is made. This breakdown of principal and interest will be on the loan documents provided by the lender at the time the loan is funded so you will know how much of the payment to expense each month. Only the interest included in this payment will reduce the profit on your books, because interest is an expense. The rest of the payment simply reduces the principal amount of the loan that you set up as a liability on the Balance Sheet.

Earlier, you learned that a credit card bill that is paid in full each month does not have to be set up in the liability section of the Balance Sheet. Let's assume you used your credit card to purchase the following items that are listed on your bill:

Gasoline for Delivery Truck	$72.00
Plastic Hangers	25.00
Paper for Printer	30.00
Gasoline for Delivery Truck	80.00

At the end of the month, the balance to be paid on this credit card account is $207.00. After you write the check to the credit card company, the transaction would be posted as follows:

Account#	Account Name	Debit	Credit
1000	Cash in Checking		207.00
6010	Auto Expense	152.00	
6350	Supplies	25.00	
6300	Office Expense	30.00	
		207.00	207.00

Note that the two purchases of gasoline were added together for the posting. All the purchases made with the credit card were posted to the proper expense accounts as debits offset by the credit posted to Cash in Checking for the amount of the check that was written from the bank account.

Entries into the General Ledger can be made daily, weekly, or monthly, depending on the volume of business your thrift store generates. As mentioned previously, no matter how often you post entries into the General Ledger accounts, your checkbook must be updated on a daily basis.

Added Value _____

To help you post entries correctly, print out a copy of the Chart of Accounts you create for your thrift store and make a notation next to each account to remind yourself if the account balance is supposed to be a debit or credit.

Keep in mind that a debit posted to an account that normally carries a debit balance increases the balance in the account. A credit posted to the same account reduces the balance in the account.

Computer software programs have prompted many business owners to do their own books. That is a good thing because it keeps owners aware of the overall financial status of their stores' operation. It also saves the expense of hiring an outside accountant to issue financial reports. If you decide to keep your own books using a computerized software program, remember to back up the accounting records stored on the computer on a CD or memory stick. Like anything else kept on a computer, a power failure or other computer problem can cause you to lose all the information entered into the program. Most programs will prompt you to back up the accounting information each time you exit the program. Do it.

Even though you are doing your own books, a professional accountant should always be consulted if your business encounters questions and problems. Also unless you are an experienced tax preparer, your books should be taken to a professional to have the tax return for your thrift store completed and filed.

The Least You Need to Know

- Learning to use the information on financial reports is important to the success of your store.

- Creating a Chart of Accounts is the first step to setting up a bookkeeping system.

- Computerized programs require that you learn the basics of accounting before using them.

- The checkbook for your store must be updated every day. The check register is a mini–financial statement.

- When posting entries into your accounting system, debits must always equal credits.

- The information stored in your accounting program should be backed up on a regular basis.

End-of-Month/Year Accounting Procedures

In This Chapter

◆ Recapping your income and expenses

◆ Reconciling your bank accounts and making adjustments

◆ Organizing your filing system

◆ Creating monthly financial statements

◆ Preparing year-end closing procedures and tax returns

In this chapter, you will learn about end-of-the-month and end-of-the-year bookkeeping procedures. A shortcut to posting transactions that is an easy alternative for a small business will also be presented. Tips on balancing your checkbook with the bank's monthly statement will help you catch any errors before they cause problems in the cash flow of your thrift store. Cash flow is the amount of money that comes in and goes out of your bank account.

Again, keep in mind that the instructions presented here are very basic. They are intended to help you manage a very simple bookkeeping system.

Even if you have no intention of doing your own bookkeeping, you can benefit from the information in this chapter. At the very least, it will prepare you to discuss your financial condition with your accountant, ask questions, and get answers that will make your day-to-day business operations run smoother.

Posting Shortcut

Posting to the General Ledger every day is a good way to become familiar with your bookkeeping system and the software program you use for it. However, if you are diligent about keeping your checkbook updated, you will know the most important thing you need to know, and that's how much money you have to work with.

Many businesses take their checkbooks to an accountant at the end of every month to have the checks and deposits posted and financial reports issued. If you are doing your own bookkeeping, you can wait until the end of the month, too, and post all the deposits and checks individually all at one time. Another option is to recap the income and expenses and do one entry to post all of the activity for the month.

Either method is fine, but recapping the activity and doing one entry is a little faster and more efficient. Here are step-by-step instructions for recapping and posting all your business transactions at the end of the month.

1. Make up a worksheet with columns for each category you have set up for sales. If you only have one sales category, you only need one column. Then, add a column for all the expenses you have paid out of the checkbook that month. Leave extra blank columns for expense accounts you may have to add as you fill in the worksheet.

2. Start with the deposits and list every deposit that is recorded in the check register, separating it if necessary into the various sales accounts.

3. Total the sales accounts.

4. Go back to the beginning of the month and list all the checks you have written, entering them in the expense columns you have set up on your worksheet.

5. Total all the expense columns.

Added Value _____

Anytime you are adding up a column of figures, even using a calculator, always do it twice to verify its accuracy.

6. Go to your Chart of Accounts and enter the account number for each income and expense column on the worksheet. You need the account numbers in order to post the amounts into the General Ledger.

7. Post all the income and expenses from your worksheet into the General Ledger as one Journal Entry. Remember that income amounts are posted as credits; expense amounts are posted as debits. When all the figures have been posted, the accounting program will tell you the amount that must be posted to Cash in Checking in order for your Journal Entry to balance.

8. Post the amount needed to balance the entry to Cash in Checking. The entry will now be in balance and the program will allow you to save the entry.

Added Value

When you "save" any entry in a computerized program, it automatically posts all the figures you have entered to the accounts in the General Ledger that you have designated.

Recapping income and expenses is not recommended for a thrift store that does a high volume of business. Those stores need to post activity into the bookkeeping system daily or weekly.

Review Account Balances

After all the financial transactions have been posted for the month, you need to verify that the ending balance in your checkbook agrees with the ending balance in the General Ledger. There are two reports that you can access in your software program that will give you this information.

As you learned earlier, you can check the current balance in the Cash in Checking account in the General Ledger at any time. This will tell you if the General Ledger balance is the same as the balance in your check register. However, at the end of the month you should always print out what is called the Trial Balance.

The Trial Balance is a report that shows the current year-to-date balance for every account in the General Ledger. The accounts in this report are printed according to the account number assigned to each. So it begins with the Balance Sheet accounts and ends with the Profit and Loss accounts. Therefore, the first account listed on the Trial Balance report is Cash in Checking, and you can verify the balance in your check register with the one shown on the Trial Balance. In addition, this report gives the bookkeeper an overview of all accounts that have had financial activity posted to them during the year and provides the bookkeeper with the opportunity to correct any posting errors and make other adjustments before the actual financial statements are issued.

Be aware that verifying the checkbook balance with the Cash in Checking balance in the General Ledger does not ensure that there are no posting errors. If the cash account balance does not agree with the checkbook balance, the following procedures will help you find the discrepancies so they can be corrected:

◆ Review the postings and see if you entered a debit as a credit, or vice versa

◆ Start with the last verified checkbook balance and double-check all the additions and subtractions

◆ Double-check your worksheet figures against the deposits and checks taken from the checkbook

◆ Double-check the totals of all accounts on the worksheet

◆ If the difference between the General Ledger and the checkbook is a figure that can be divided by nine, look for a *transposition error.*

def•i•ni•tion

A **transposition error** is a reversal of two figures in a posted amount—e.g., 149.00 is posted as 194.00.

If the discrepancy is due to an error in the checkbook, correct the checkbook. If the discrepancy is a posting error, you will have to make a correcting entry into the General Ledger. Let's assume you transposed the figure you posted to the Office Expense account. Instead of the actual amount of $149.00, you posted $194.00. Here is how the correcting entry would be done:

Account#	Account Name	Debit	Credit
6300	Office Expense		$45.00
1000	Cash in Checking	$45.00	

The transposition error meant that $45.00 too much was posted to the Office Expense account (a debit), which resulted in the same amount being deducted from Cash in Checking (a credit). The above correction reverses the posting with a credit to Office Expense and a debit to Cash in Checking, correcting the error and bringing the cash account in balance with the checkbook.

Once the cash is verified, go through the Trial Balance and see if you can spot any discrepancies in other accounts. The following guidelines will help you find other errors:

- A credit balance in an account that is expected to have a debit balance
- A debit balance in an account that is expected to have a credit balance
- A loan payable balance that is the same as it was the month before

The last item is an easy error to make, especially if you are posting principal and interest on the loan. Sometimes the entire payment amount gets posted to Interest Expense and sometimes the principal amount on an auto loan is erroneously posted to Auto Expense. Just keep in mind that if you are making your loan payments every month, the balance on each one will be reduced each month by the amount of the payment made on the principal.

Any time you make a posting error, you can make a correcting entry like the one you have just seen, or you can go back to the original entry and void it. The computer will then erase the entry and all the figures posted within it from all the accounts. After you have voided the original entry, you will have to post the entire entry again, making sure you correct the figures that were wrong.

Computerized accounting programs allow you to go back and forth between months because all entries are sorted and posted by the dates you designate for them. That means you can post all the January activity through the end of the month and then move forward and start posting February activity. The program will keep the two months separate as long as you have used the correct posting dates.

So even though you have not completed January, the computerized program allows you to begin posting February data and will keep it separate from January's data. However, at the end of the year to avoid confusion, it is wise to post everything for one year and then close it out before starting to input the next year's transactions.

Not for Resale

Financial data for a particular month must have a posting date within that month.

The Bank Statement

Keeping the financial data correctly by months is important because there are tasks to be performed before the financial statements are issued for that month. One of the most important tasks is reconciling the bank accounts. That should always be done before the financial statements are issued, but the bank statements end on the last day of the month and are usually not mailed before the first week of the following month.

If you get your bank statements online, you will obviously have them quicker, but keep in mind that some banks do not separate the online banking data by months and that makes it more difficult to reconcile. Also, having a hard copy of your monthly bank statement gives you more organized access and ensures that you have the proper backup information for tax authorities—such as the IRS.

Even if you are one of those people who never balances his or her personal checking account, you will have to change your ways when it comes to your business account. Just as it is vital that you keep your check register updated at all times, you must sit down and balance it with the bank's records every month. When your checking account is verified by the bank's monthly statement, it tells you that your books are in order. Keeping your books and your bookkeeping system orderly and accurate is the only way to keep control of your finances and avoid problems.

There are a number of different ways you can reconcile your bank account with the bank records, but since this is still a crash course, we'll look at the easiest method. You will find this method printed on the back of your bank statement, and though the instructions may vary from bank to bank, the basic procedures are the same. The following is a sample worksheet from a bank statement.

Balancing Your Checkbook

1. The ending balance shown on this statement: $_____

2. List and total all deposits & additions not shown on this statement:

Date   Amount   Date   Amount   Date   Amount

____   _____   ____   _____   ____   _____

____   _____   ____   _____   ____   _____   Total: +_____

3. Add Step 1 and Step 2 totals   Total: _____

4. List and total all checks, ATM withdrawals, debit card purchases, and other withdrawals not shown on this statement:

Balancing Your Checkbook

Check # or Date of Electronic Posting

_____

_____

_____

_____

_____

_____

Step 4 total   Total: –_____

Subtract Step 4 total from Step 3 total

                                                      Total: _____*

*This should match your checkbook.

If this does not match your checkbook, review this statement for any adjustments or bank fees not recorded in your checkbook.

If there are fees or other adjustments on the bank statement that are not recorded in your checkbook that you don't agree with or don't understand, call your bank and get an explanation. Any adjustments you make in the checkbook must be posted to Cash in Checking and the Bank Fees accounts in your General Ledger. Any checks you have written that have not yet cleared your account are called Outstanding Checks.

A savings account is a lot easier to balance, unless you've made a lot of deposits and withdrawals during the month. Usually you will just have to update the savings account in the General Ledger by posting the interest earned that month as a debit to the account you set up for the Savings Account in the Asset section of the Balance Sheet, and a credit to the Interest on Savings account you set up in the Income Section of the Profit and Loss Accounts. If you're fortunate enough to have a Certificate of Deposit, you would have a separate account for that included with the Assets Section, but you could use the same Income account for the interest earned on the CD.

Cash or Accrual?

Up to now, the bookkeeping systems presented have all been what are categorized as the cash method of accounting. The cash method is one where only the income that actually came into the store for that particular month is recognized and only the payments that were actually paid out of the business that month are claimed.

Thrift stores would not have customers who purchase merchandise on credit, so there is no need for Accounts Receivable, which is part of every computerized accounting program. Remember that if you are not using an account in the General Ledger, it will have no balance in it and therefore will not be printed on the financial statements.

Thrift stores may have bills that are incurred in one month, but not paid out until the first of the next month. It is up to the owner/bookkeeper to decide if those payments should be claimed as expenses in the month when they were incurred. Claiming these expenses before they are actually paid out of the business will reduce the store's net profit, but the accrual method is used more than the cash method because it provides a more accurate financial picture.

If you want to use the accrual bookkeeping method, you must use it all year long and declare that you are using it on your annual tax return. You may recall that Accounts Payable was set up in the sample Chart of Accounts, and that is the account you would use to record bills incurred in the current month that will not be paid until the next month.

Assume that you have a bill for a filing cabinet you acquired and used in your store in May, but the payment on your account with the vendor was not due until June 1. Here is how that data would be entered into the General Ledger.

Account#	Account Name	Debit	Credit
6300	Office Expense	$157.00	
2000	Accounts Payable		$157.00
To record purchase of file cabinet			

This entry would be posted in May and the expense would then be included on the May financial statement. In June when the bill is actually paid, the check would be posted as follows:

Account#	Account Name	Debit	Credit
2000	Accounts Payable	$157.00	
1000	Cash in Checking		$157.00
Check# 5203 to Acme Office Supplies			

This entry zeroes out Accounts Payable and deducts the check amount from the Cash in Checking account. Note that the Office Expense account is not used because the expense was already recorded in that account when it was set up for payment in Accounts Payable. The expense was also already included in the financial statement for the month of May.

Most new thrift stores may want to use the cash method of accounting. The information on the accrual method is presented here to make you aware that you have the option of choosing that method for your bookkeeping system.

Adjusting Entries

At the end of each month, before the financial statements are issued, a few other adjustments may have to be made. In our sample Chart of Accounts and Balance Sheet in Chapter 8, an account was created for Prepaid Expenses. This account was set up to hold the insurance premiums that were paid in advance for six months.

The original amount in this account in the Asset section of the Balance Sheet was $900. If you divide this amount by six months, you see that the cost of insurance is $150 per month. That is the amount that needs to be expensed each month into the Insurance Expense account. The entry to do that at the end of every month is as follows.

Account#	Account Name	Debit	Credit
1105	Prepaid Expenses		$150.00
6205	Insurance Expense	$150.00	
To expense one month's insurance premium			

Perhaps you are wondering why the total amount of $900 was not expensed at the time the check was written. It's because it would have reduced the profit for that month by $900 when the actual cost of insurance for one month is only $150. Of course, the other option would be to use an insurance company that would accept installment payments, and there are many that do. Again, this particular scenario is only to make you aware of another strategy used by professional accountants to ensure that your financial statements reflect the most accurate information.

Another adjustment that can be made monthly is depreciation expense. Keep in mind that this is primarily a tax deduction that the IRS allows businesses to use to reduce their tax liability.

If you own the building that houses your thrift store, you can write off the cost of it year after year, but in reality, a building that is properly maintained will increase in value.

That is usually not true with other tangible assets such as vehicles and equipment. These items do lose their value year after year and may even need to be replaced before they are fully depreciated.

Not for Resale

The rules for depreciating assets change from year to year, so be sure to obtain and use the most current information.

You're already aware that a computerized accounting program does much of the work for you and will enable you to print out monthly financial reports. However, at the end of the tax year, depreciation of major purchases and other tax credits your business can use to reduce its income tax liability will have to be calculated and entered into your bookkeeping system.

Contact your accounting professional to have these calculations and entries done correctly, so that your tax return is accurately prepared. Unless you are a tax expert, you need a professional to prepare your business return correctly and make sure you get all the tax credits and deductions your business is allowed to claim. The money you save in tax liabilities will more than make up for the fees the accounting professional charges.

Hard Copies

Although your financial records are in the accounting program on the computer, you will still need to set up a filing system to keep copies of some of the paperwork. The filing system can be a cardboard box or a drawer in your desk, as long as you set up folders to hold the various papers and label the folders properly.

Use the headings on the following list to set up folders and keep the hard copies you need in their respective files:

♦ Loan information and legal papers for each liability your store has acquired

♦ Bills to be paid

♦ Paid bills marked with the date and check number used to pay them

♦ Paperwork on any guarantees or warranties for vehicles or equipment purchased

♦ Bank statements

- Check register stubs
- Payroll files (if applicable)
- Financial Statements
- Tax Returns

It is necessary to maintain a neat, orderly filing system for all of the above financial records and any other financial data applicable to your business. The few minutes it takes to file paperwork properly will save you hours of time in the event there is a dispute about a bill being paid or you are audited by the IRS.

If a vendor claims you didn't pay an invoice, looking in the paid bill file will give you the date and check number for the bill, and you can then go to the bank statement for that month and see if the check cleared your account. If you have a lot of vendors, it is best to keep a separate file for each.

In the event that any deductions you have claimed on your tax return are questioned or your return is audited, the IRS will want to see hard copies of the paperwork that supports your tax deductions. This is another reason you must set up and maintain a proper filing system. The books on accounting and bookkeeping listed in Appendix A of this book will provide you with detailed instructions and suggestions for setting up a good filing system.

Viewing the *Bottom Line*

Once the bank statement has been reconciled and all the monthly adjustments have been entered into the General Ledger, it is time to issue the monthly financial statements.

Most computerized accounting programs have an area where all the financial reports are listed and can be chosen for printing. Usually, the Balance Sheet is considered one report and the Profit and Loss Statement is another. The statements can also be previewed on the computer screen so that you can have an advance look at the reports before printing them out.

def•i•ni•tion

The **bottom line** is an accounting term for the Net Profit or Loss of a company, used because it is the last amount displayed on the financial statements.

It is recommended that your financial statements be printed and reviewed carefully. The information on them will help you pinpoint any financial areas that need your attention. Don't be unduly upset if your first few months in business result in a loss. It often takes time for a new business to become profitable. That's why there are a number of other chapters in this book that discuss ways you can promote your thrift store and raise your visibility in the community.

Also, remember that being a nonprofit thrift store doesn't mean you don't run a profitable enterprise. It only means that the profits support a specific charitable cause or organization.

Taxing Decisions

The end-of-the-year financial statements are the ones that are used to prepare the annual tax returns. If you are doing your own bookkeeping, take extra time to review the financial data for the year. If you are using an accounting firm to do your books, meet with the staff member who will be preparing your tax return to make sure that person has all the information needed.

As stated a number of times in this book, unless you are knowledgeable in tax matters, have a tax professional prepare the annual tax return and reports for your thrift store. However, be sure that your bookkeeping information is in order and as accurate as possible before bringing it to the tax accountant.

The type of tax return that your business files each year depends on how your thrift store was structured. Let's review the different types of business entities and look at the tax return or report that is required for that particular business structure.

A thrift store run by an individual as a sole proprietor must include the profit or loss of the store on his or her personal tax return.

Added Value

On Form 4562 under the Section 179 area, a business owner is allowed to write off the entire cost of business equipment up to a certain limit rather than depreciate it over time.

The following tax forms are required:

- Form 1040 Individual Tax Return

- Schedule C (Form 1040) Profit or Loss from Business

- Form 4562 Depreciation Schedule

- Schedule SE Self-Employment Tax

To give you an idea of the financial information a sole proprietor needs in order to file his or her tax return, the sample forms in Appendix B include review copies of Schedule 1040-C, Schedule SE, and Schedule 4562 that may need to be filed with the business owner's individual tax return.

Properly formed partnerships that run a business must file a partnership return with a schedule that divides the profit or loss between the partners. The partners must then carry the profit or loss over to their individual tax returns.

The following tax forms are required:

- Form 1065 Partnership Return
- Schedule K-1
- Form 1040 Individual Tax Return

A small corporation called an S Corporation works much the same as a partnership. The corporation must file a tax return and the officers of the corporation must then carry the profit or loss over to their personal returns. The principles are usually also employees of the S Corporation and receive a W-2 for the wages earned which, of course, must be included on their 1040 filing.

Required tax forms are the following:

- 1120S S Corporation Return
- 1040 Individual Tax Return

A regular corporation running a business for profit files a corporation tax return. The principles are employees of the corporation and receive a W-2 for their wages. The profits of a regular corporation are not carried over to the principles' tax returns, but are taxed at the corporate rate and paid by the corporation.

There's only one required tax form:

- 1120 Corporation Return

A nonprofit corporation that has tax-exempt status with the Internal Revenue Service and has earnings of more than $35,000 a year is required to file a report with the IRS but does not pay taxes.

One tax form is required:

◆ Form 990

A nonprofit corporation that has tax-exempt status and earns less than the minimum amount above has to register with the IRS each year, but is not required to file a Form 990.

For more information on these tax forms, visit www.irs.gov, where all the forms can be viewed and instructions for completing all of them are available.

All the information in this chapter and the previous one is presented to help you understand how to set up and run a simple bookkeeping system. While the computerized program does much of the work for you, it still requires the basic knowledge you have reviewed in order to provide your thrift store with the financial information needed to grow and prosper.

The Least You Need to Know

◆ There are shortcuts you can use to help you update your bookkeeping system more efficiently.

◆ Balance your checkbook with the bank statement every month to avoid costly errors.

◆ End-of-the-month adjustments must be reviewed and posted before issuing financial statements.

◆ Accurate tax return information is the result of managing your bookkeeping system properly.

◆ Study the tax forms that must be filed for your store to make sure you have all the necessary data.

Advertising and Promotion

In This Chapter

- Creating signs, window displays, and posters
- Using flyers and direct mailings
- Creating an Internet presence
- Benefiting from word of mouth
- Staging a grand opening charity event
- Setting up interviews and public service announcements

Getting a good start for your thrift store will take a good deal of time and energy. When a new store opens, it automatically attracts people in the neighborhood because they are interested in seeing how the newly opened business will fit in and benefit the area. So even if you don't do any advertising or promotion, you will have some customers just because you have located your store in their neighborhood.

The challenge is twofold. One is to impress the neighborhood shoppers so that they continue to come into your shop. Two is to reach out beyond the boundaries of your area and attract customers from all over the city. This chapter is all about doing both.

Make It Big and Bright

The sign affixed to your store is a permanent means of advertising your business. Assuming that you have taken the advice from a prior chapter and chosen a name that people will remember, the task at hand is to put that name front and center so anyone driving and walking by will see it.

Most stores have an area above the front door and display windows where a sign can be attached to the building. There are a number of different ways this can be done. The sign can be made up of individual letters that spell out the store's name and are affixed one at a time in the proper order, or the name can be painted on a metal sheet that is then anchored in place. The advantage to this method is that if you decide to move to a different location, the one-piece sign is easier to move.

Like all the other items that are important to the success of your thrift store, you must do some research before choosing a sign, and a professional to make it and hang it for you. First of all, most cities have ordinances that dictate the size and type of sign that can be displayed in a given area. Check out the sign stipulations and restrictions for your area. Find out if you need a permit to hang a sign for your store and what fees, if any, are required.

Don't just pick a sign maker out of the phone book. First look around at signs in your area and other parts of the city. Decide what you want and then get recommendations and references for businesses that create, construct, and install signs. See samples of a company's work and get an estimate of the cost before hiring them to do your sign.

Getting the sign up on your store is one of the first things that should be done after signing the lease. It needs to be up there advertising your thrift store as soon as possible. It will help build interest and anticipation in everyone who sees it before you open for business.

> **Not for Resale**
>
> Be present when your store's sign is installed to make sure it is done properly.

> **Added Value**
>
> Have a temporary sign made to hang under the permanent sign or in the window to advertise the day your store will open for business.

Window Shoppers

Some stores hang paper or drapes across their display windows to hide the disarray that exists when the shop is being set up and organized. If you are worried about people seeing the clutter in the store during the preopening process, hang drapes behind the display windows to hide it, but set up an attractive, eye-catching display in the window area to give potential customers a preview of what your shop is going to offer them.

If your window display is good, passersby will be so busy looking at it, they probably won't notice or care about any untidiness that may exist in the store itself. Remember the old adage, "Put your best foot forward," when exhibiting items in your store's front window or windows. Select the best of what you are going to sell to the public in the window as a way to tempt shoppers before and after it opens.

You might also consider hiring a window artist to decorate your front windows with colorful cartoons or scenes to hide whatever organizational efforts are going on behind them. Large posters and signs are another option you may want to utilize. These could also include information about your shop and the type of merchandise you will be offering to the public. In the case of a nonprofit shop, you can let people know what charity or cause your store is going to support.

The main thing to remember is that you are not just trying to cover the preopening activity in your store. You are advertising and promoting your store. This is especially important if you are located in a shopping center or other area that has a lot of foot traffic. Promoting your business is something that should go on 24 hours a day. Consider the shopping centers around the country, where people come in early before the stores open to exercise. As they walk through the mall, they look at the window displays and if they see something they like, they will probably come back when the store is open to buy it.

Attractive window displays, posters, and any kind of cute or pretty paintings on your store's glass front will attract attention, and all of these are low-cost, effective ways to bring people into your store.

Information Sheets

Another effective, inexpensive way to advertise your store is by distributing flyers. There are lots of computer programs that will enable you to design and print out decorative and colorful sheets to introduce your thrift store to buyers. If you don't have the computer skills to design your own flyers, find a friend who can do it for you or visit your local office supply or copy shop and have them do it for you. All you have to do then is supply the pertinent information needed for the flyer.

Look around the area where your store is located and you will find that most grocery stores and other retail outlets have bulletin boards where flyers can be posted. Libraries, churches, and other public places also have areas where stacks of flyers can be put out for people to take. If your thrift store is nonprofit, you will be able to use volunteers to help you distribute flyers. If your charity is affiliated with a church, consider stuffing the flyers in the church bulletins before Sunday services.

Not for Resale

Some cities have ordinances that prohibit placing flyers on the windshields of parked cars, so check before distributing them that way.

Computerized programs will guide you through the process of making flyers and have built-in art clips that can be used to make them fun and colorful. One advantage to designing your own flyer on a computer to advertise your store's opening is that the sheet can be easily changed for future promotions, such as sales and fund-raising events.

Mail Them Out!

Once you have a clever, colorful flyer to inform potential customers of the existence of your thrift store, they can be mailed directly to their homes or businesses. Direct mail is a tried and proven method of getting promotional material into the hands of consumers. This is something you can do yourself with a phone book and postage, but it is time consuming and may actually be more expensive to do it yourself.

There are many businesses that offer direct mail service. You can bring them the flyer you designed, or they will design a flyer or a postcard for you. These companies have mailing lists containing the names and addresses of thousands of consumers. They also have permits to send bulk mail, and that results in big savings over first-class postage.

Specific areas of your city can be targeted to receive your mailings, or you can send information out to everyone in town.

With some direct mail businesses, the cost goes down with the volume of mail you want sent out, so blanketing the entire city with information about your new thrift store may be the best way to go. Again, don't just pick a random company from the phone book listings of direct mail companies. Ask around and find one that is established and reputable.

One good way to know how effective your direct mail campaign was is to add a coupon or other incentive to come into your store to the flyer. For example, you can say that anyone who brings the flyer into the shop during a specified time period will receive a 10 percent discount on all purchases. Collect and keep the flyers when the customer comes into your shop to redeem it and you will have a pretty good idea of what areas of the city to target next time you do a direct mailing. You will also know if the money you spent on the mailing was worth it.

Added Value

If you include a discount coupon on your direct mailing flyer, be sure to specify an expiration date on the coupon.

Some advertising professionals believe that direct mail is the best and most cost-effective way to advertise a business. Seeing the same business advertised on television or hearing about it in a radio ad does not provide that tangible item to hold on to that will remind them of the store's existence.

Electronic Ads

The electronic age of computers and the Internet has gotten us accustomed to instant information. Granted, there are still some people who don't own a computer, but for most of us, when we want to know about a person, place, or thing, we go straight to our computers and do an Internet search. For this reason, you should think about creating an Internet presence for your thrift store that includes a website.

Building a website may not be something you feel qualified to do, but over the years creating one has become easier. However, this is not going to be a lesson in website design; it is just a suggestion that if you are technically challenged there are several alternatives to consider. There are people who do websites for a fee, you can take a class and learn how to do it yourself, or you can find a friend who knows how to do it and enlist his or her participation in the endeavor.

Websites are wonderful venues for promoting just about anything, but they do have to be maintained and updated in order to keep them fresh and interesting. Keep in mind that if you learn how to create your own website, you'll also be able to update it with new information any time you choose. Otherwise, you may have to pay someone to do it for you, or talk your friend into updating it.

If you do an Internet search for thrift stores, millions of matches will be presented to you. Obviously, if you tried to access each one of them, you would be on the computer for years and not have time to do anything else—including run your thrift store. However, any search on the Internet can be modified to just include the thrift stores in your city or state. For example, you can search for Kansas City thrift stores or Bar Harbor thrift stores, and the first matches that come up will be for stores in Kansas City, Kansas, or Bar Harbor, Maine.

So go on the Internet and do a search for thrift stores in your area and take a look at their websites. This will give you some good ideas and information on how to structure a website for your thrift store.

Since there are millions of people interested in thrift shops and the bargains they offer, your website should give visitors the option of signing up for a newsletter or just quick e-mail updates on special sales or merchandise.

When the Internet was new, it was like the Wild West with no rules or restrictions, but now it has been regulated to a certain degree and unsolicited e-mails about products or services are frowned upon and labeled as "spam." Most Internet providers either don't deliver e-mail deemed to be unsolicited sales pitches or relegate it to a special junk folder. That's why people who visit your website would have to sign up for your newsletter or e-mail alerts—so they would become solicited rather than spam.

def•i•ni•tion

A **blog** is a contraction of the word "weblog" and is maintained by an individual, with regular entries of commentary, event descriptions, or other material.

If you don't want to do a newsletter or e-mail alerts, you can establish a *blog* to direct people to your website to learn about your store. You can also use blogging to tell them about special sales and other events. A typical blog contains text and links to other blogs or websites related to its topics. Blogs are interactive in that people who read them can post comments about the subject.

There are specific sites on the Internet that you can join and blog every day about your store and the merchandise you sell there. Again, we're not going to give blogging directions. It's something you learn by joining a site and doing it.

If you want to know more about this unique method of promotion on the Internet, visit www.blogger.com, where you can establish a presence and blog away for free.

eBay is another way to market and sell goods and would be especially useful when your thrift store uncovers one of those hidden treasures everyone in the business finds from time to time. eBay has an auction option that can be used by owners who want to sell a particular item. For more information, visit the eBay site.

The Internet is a powerful tool, and if used wisely can be quite effective for marketing your thrift store. If you are a nonprofit entity, the Internet can also help you attract more attention to the charity your store supports and even enable people to donate money or merchandise to the charity.

People Will Talk

The main purpose of any type of advertising or promotion is to get people talking about your business. While it might seem like your advertising dollars are not working, remember that everyone who sees your sign, receives a flyer in the mail or at the grocery store, visits your website, or reads your blog is a potential customer.

Even if those people never set foot in your store themselves, chances are they will mention your store to a friend, neighbor, or co-worker. That's what is known as word of mouth, and it is one of the best sources of advertising. However, if you don't erect a sign, send out flyers, and establish a presence on the Internet, word of mouth cannot get started.

It's getting word of mouth started that requires all that initial cost and effort, but once you get it going it will keep on spreading and bringing new people into your store. Once a customer comes into your store, the ball is in your court and it is up to you to keep them coming back and talking positively about their shopping experience there. Also be aware that any vendors you deal with talk to people, too. Always treat them with respect.

Have a Grand Opening

Nonprofit thrift shops usually have a committee of volunteers to assist with special events, and when they open a thrift store they can count on the people that are dedicated to their cause to shop there on a regular basis. However, the nonprofit thrift shops also realize that in order to become really successful, they must reach out into the community and let everyone know about their store and the charity it supports. For this reason, the nonprofit store often hosts special newsworthy events, and a thrift store that operates for profit can do the same.

Added Value

A grand opening can actually take place anytime. You can wait and plan an event for weeks or months after your store has opened for business.

In an earlier chapter, you learned about assessing the needs in your community. Even if your store is not going to donate its profits to a charity on a regular basis, you can certainly find one to help make your store opening a newsworthy event. Choose from smaller charities or schools that don't get the attention and support that the national charities get. The extra benefit to doing this is that the volunteers and supporters of the group you sponsor will help you plan and run it.

def•i•ni•tion

A **silent auction** requires that bidders write down the amount they are willing to pay for an item instead of shouting it out.

Here are some activities that may draw extra attention to your thrift store for the days or week of your grand opening:

- A diaper drive
- A *silent auction*
- A car wash
- A food drive

Your flyer, postcard, or website can include the information for any of the above suggestions. Let's look at them individually to give you an idea of how they can help you attract more people to your place of business.

A diaper drive could, of course, benefit any number of organizations that work with infants and toddlers. This works well if your store is situated near a grocery store, and you may even be able to get the store to hold a sale on a particular brand of diapers for that day or week.

For the silent auction, you would need to set aside a number of nice pieces of merchandise. Find a charity to donate the proceeds of the auction to and the group may even provide you with some additional auction items. You will need at least one person to man the auction table and oversee the bids. Present the auction items a few at a time so you can spread it out over a period of several hours.

If your store's parking lot has adequate space and a way to access water, a car wash is a good way to bring people into the area. You can work with local high school kids who want to earn money for a trip or athletic equipment. They will wash the cars and keep the proceeds. Their parents, teachers, and friends will come into your store because you have gone out of your way to help the kids.

You can also adopt your local food bank, a shelter, or a soup kitchen that feeds the poor by collecting donations of canned goods or other nonperishable food products.

Any organization that services the poor would be grateful for your help and will in turn help you spread the word.

There is no limit to the type of special event you can sponsor, and you will find that there are plenty of small organizations that will be happy to benefit from your efforts.

Free Publicity

Once you have settled on an event and a cause that will benefit from the event, you can begin contacting the media and trying to get publicity for it. Newspapers, radio stations, and television stations are all part of your community, and they are always looking for news bites. All media in your city should be sent a press release describing your event. Keep it short and to the point, but remember to follow the rule of the five W's that all journalists and reporters are supposed to include in a story. The five W's are who, what, where, why, and when.

Depending on your event, the news media may be interested in interviewing you. Getting an interview in the newspaper or on radio or television is a combination of luck and timing. Sometimes interviews are done and bumped off the air or the page when a big news story comes along that requires special coverage. It's the chance you take, but it is definitely worth the effort; if your piece does receive publication or airtime, you will reach thousands of people with your story.

Most newspapers, radio stations, and television stations have community calendars that are generally posted on their websites. Make sure to submit your information according to the instructions that are included on the website. Some newspapers, especially small weeklies, include a page with upcoming community events.

Radio and television stations all broadcast public service announcements (PSAs), and if your grand opening is centered around an event that helps the people in your community, you qualify for a public service announcement (PSA). The Federal Communications Commission requires that all stations donate a certain amount of airtime to service the public and the community.

Added Value

A public service announcement is usually no longer than 30 seconds, so when you write one up keep it to that time limit.

There are no definite rules for writing a PSA to submit to your local stations, but the following guidelines will give you the basic format. Using this format to write up your PSA should be acceptable to any media outlet that receives it.

If you have letterhead for your store, use that to write up the PSA. At the middle of the page, center the title: PUBLIC SERVICE ANNOUNCEMENT. This immediately identifies the purpose of the correspondence to the recipient, and if this person does not handle PSAs, he or she can forward it to the proper department.

Go down a few spaces and enter the date you would like your announcement to air. Follow that with the name, address, phone numbers, fax numbers, and e-mail address of the person the station can contact about the announcement.

Skip a few more spaces and provide a title for your event, such as, DIAPER DRIVE FOR CASA BABIES. The event title should be in bold type and capital letters. Skip a line and write a short, concise explanation of what you want announced on air. Keep in mind that most PSAs are only about 30 seconds long. At the end, write the word "end" or ###.

Your submission should be sent to the media outlets at least three weeks in advance of the grand opening event. Depending on the number of stations you are submitting to in your area, it's a good idea to call the stations and get the name of the person who handles the PSAs. If that's not possible, address your request to the public service director.

If you are not sure how to word your PSA, listen to the ones your local stations are airing and learn from them. You can also do an Internet search for public service announcements and find samples to study.

If you are fortunate enough to know some media people, contact them directly and ask for their assistance and advice on getting your announcement aired.

Getting publicity for your thrift store requires a lot of time and effort. Try to enlist the help of family and friends for all the preopening work. If you are working alone, make a list of all the tasks that have to be accomplished in the order of importance. Do the most difficult jobs first and then move on to the smaller, easier items. Remember that problems are going to arise that may throw you off the schedule you have set for yourself. For that reason, set up a time frame that allows for the setbacks that are bound to occur. Never leave important items until the last minute. That's a sure way to court a nervous breakdown. Every time you complete an item on the list, cross it off and pat yourself on the back for being so centered and efficient.

The Least You Need to Know

- Have your store's sign installed as soon as possible. It's a great source of advertising.

- Set up attractive window displays before the store opens to build anticipation and interest in passersby.

- Direct mailings of flyers or postcards should be done by companies who can provide bulk mailing postage rates.

- Some type of Internet presence is vital in today's fast-paced electronic world.

- Be friendly and respectful to any vendors you deal with to get them talking positively about you and your store.

- You don't have to be a nonprofit to connect a charity to your grand opening. Take advantage of free publicity, such as public service announcements.

Daily Business Operations

In This Chapter

- Establishing rules for accepting merchandise
- Determining how to price merchandise
- Knowing how to display merchandise
- Servicing your customers
- Maintaining your store

The many challenges of opening your store have been met successfully. All you have to do now is tackle the new challenges that will present themselves to you on a daily basis. While there is no way to predict exactly what you will encounter as a thrift store owner, you can prepare yourself to meet whatever comes along by remembering that your ultimate goal is customer satisfaction.

Every decision you make and every procedure you establish affects the customer in the end. The quality of merchandise, the way it is displayed and priced, and the way customers are treated while they are in your store determines whether they will be satisfied or not. Obviously, a satisfied customer will return again and again, and will spread that positive word of mouth discussed in the last chapter to family and friends.

Granted, there will be some customers you won't be able to satisfy no matter how hard you try, but even difficult people can be won over with sincerity and good intentions.

Accept It or Reject It

All thrift stores must acquire merchandise. Nonprofit stores get most of what they sell through donations. Thrift stores that operate for profit must go out into the community and obtain it from other sources. No matter how your store stocks its shelves, you must establish guidelines for the type of merchandise you want to display and sell in your store.

Even if you are getting free merchandise through donations, you can't automatically accept everything that is offered to you. What you accept and what you refuse to put in your store is where thinking about customer satisfaction begins.

> **Added Value**
>
> IRS rules state that to be deductible, clothing or household items donated to charities must be in good used condition or better.

Let's face it: people donate items that they no longer need or want, and the value and usefulness of some donations is a big fat zero. If you are not in the company of someone who donated an item that makes you cringe, you can simply recycle it or drop it into the trash container. If the donor personally gives you the item and wants a receipt, you have a problem to solve.

Although it is said that honesty is the best policy, that's not always the best way to deal with a donor who may also be a customer of your thrift shop. Here are some suggestions for diplomatic ways of handling this situation:

- Thank the donor and write out a receipt for the merchandise. It is up to the donor to claim a value for what is donated.

- Tell the donor you have many similar items that you have been unable to sell in your store and cannot accept another one.

- Tell the donor that the item does not meet the standards you have to adhere to for your merchandise, but for their convenience, you will be happy to recycle or dispose of the item for them.

Refusing to display junk in your store is the first step in achieving customer satisfaction, but dealing tactfully with a donor is also important, especially to a nonprofit shop that depends on their generosity.

Receipt Rules

If you are running a nonprofit thrift store, you and your staff need to be aware of the rules regarding tax-deductible donations. Keep in mind that donations are reported as an itemized deduction on an individual's tax return. That means that taxpayers who take the standard deduction on their tax return instead of filling out Schedule A for itemized deductions cannot claim a deduction for donations of tangible items that they made to charitable organizations during the year. If the donor does itemize deductions on his or her annual return, then the value of the goods is deductible in the year that they were donated to a qualified charity.

There are other rules governing monetary donations, but for the most part, cash donations would go directly to the charity and the thrift store would only be receiving items for resale.

For all donations of clothing and household items, the IRS prefers that the donor get a receipt from the charity that includes a description of the donated property and an estimated value for it. However, taxpayers are allowed to keep their own records for items left at an unattended drop site for charitable donations and deduct the value of those items on their tax returns. A sample of a donor's receipt can be found in Appendix B.

> ### Helping Hands
>
> IRS publication 78 lists the types of charitable organizations that qualify to receive tax-deductible donations. Visit www.irs.gov to access the list.

Although clothing and household items must be in good condition to qualify for a deduction, a taxpayer may claim a deduction of more than $500 for a single item regardless of its condition. In this case, the taxpayer must include a copy of a qualified appraisal of the item with the tax return. For deduction purposes, the IRS considers furniture, furnishings, electronics, appliances, and linens to be categorized as household items.

Keep the Best, Dump the Rest

Some thrift stores have a relationship with storage facilities and buy the contents of unclaimed lockers and units. Usually the thrift store can obtain the contents of a storage unit by paying the rent that has accumulated and then taking the time and trouble to clean it out properly.

If your shop specializes in certain items, you will be quick to separate those items from boxes and containers filled with potential merchandise for your store. Because of the hazards that can be found in donated items and other potential resale stock, a later chapter in this book deals with safe handling.

For now, we are concentrating on the constant challenge of keeping your store stocked with merchandise that your customers will regard as being good enough and useful enough to bring into their own homes.

The more you sort through the boxes, crates, and storage facilities looking for that type of merchandise, the more practiced you will become at snatching up the good items and discarding the bad. You will also learn that although some items look bad because they are covered with dust and grime, a thorough cleaning can make them shiny and saleable. When sorting, you may want to have three places to put things categorized as yes, no, and maybe.

A foul odor permeating any item dictates that it go directly into the trash barrel. Nothing will chase customers away faster than bad odors in your shop. Clothing, linens, and some furniture items absorb odors that are often very difficult to eradicate. You must also be on the lookout for clothing with moth holes or any other sign of insects. Be cautious about acquiring items from the following places:

- Any room or storage facility that has water damage

- A smoker's home or place of business

- Bug-infested rooms or storage areas

- Any place that smells of mothballs

- Any place that has an unpleasant odor that you can't discern

Customers will purchase clothing that shows signs of wear and may be missing a button or two, but most will not want anything with unsightly stains. Don't waste your time stocking clothing that will probably make a customer walk out of your store.

Not for Resale

Research cleaning products that eliminate odors but calculate the time and effort it will take to make something odor-free.

Keep in mind that stained clothing or those with an odor are not always a complete waste of time to inspect. If the clothes have usable buttons, they can be removed and you can set up a button bin in your shop. Customers who sew or do other crafts are always looking for odd buttons to have on hand.

When your first sorting is done, look through your "no" items to see what needs to go directly to the dumpster and what items can be recycled. There are companies that pay for certain items such as used ink cartridges, cell phones, and other small electronic devices. Do some research and make some extra cash for yourself or your store.

Added Value

A good way to sell odd buttons is to have small plastic bags on hand and allow customers to fill up a bag for $1 or $2.

White Elephants

The term "white elephant" originated from the Burmese belief that albino elephants are sacred. Unlike the more common gray elephants, the white elephant could not be used for work and required the owner to provide the finest, most lavish care for the animal. Legend has it that the King of Siam would bestow the white elephant as a gift to a disagreeable courtier, believing that the care of the animal would lead to financial ruin for the courtier.

Through the years the white elephant has been defined as a possession unwanted by its owner but difficult to dispose of, or a possession that's value is much less than the cost of maintaining it. Today, the white elephant is equated with unusual objects that an owner no longer wants. Often these items are cumbersome or bizarre and some seem to have no usefulness at all. However, it is their questionable design and purpose that make them attractive to people. Consider the popularity of white elephant sales and gift exchanges, and you can see that these unique items scorned by the original owners can be treasures to someone else.

As a thrift store owner you will undoubtedly come across white elephants on a regular basis. You may even want to set up a special display of white elephants in your store or in your front window. The common items you sell— like clothing, linens, and other household goods—may be the mainstay of your business, but it is the surprisingly outlandish pieces that can draw in new customers and have them telling their friends about your flare for the unusual.

So as you are sorting, recycling, and disposing of the goods donated to your shop or picked up in lots from garage sales and storage facilities, keep an open mind and remember the old adage, "Beauty is in the eye of the beholder."

Price Tags

Whether you are a nonprofit store that gets most of its merchandise free of charge or a thrift store run for profit, pricing things right is an ongoing test of your business sense.

You must always be aware that the customers who come into your shop expect to get something they want or need for less than they can get it in a retail outlet.

> **Added Value**
>
> The Internet is a good place to do research on any merchandise you are pricing. Besides all the online catalogs, you can also check out the prices on eBay.

Thrift store patrons are often very knowledgeable about the items they are searching for in your store. This is especially true of people looking for antiques, collectibles, and old jewelry. This means that you must also become well educated in the retail value of the merchandise you sell.

Before you start pricing merchandise, sit down and figure out the cost of your overhead. That is the amount of money it takes each month to operate your store. Your operating costs include rent, utilities, and maintenance. If you have employees, you have to figure in the costs of payroll, too. For example, if the monthly cost of running your store is $1,000, you will have to sell a thousand items at a profit of $1 each or 500 items at a profit of $2 each, every month, to meet your expenses. It may sound silly, but once you have that information firmly planted in your mind, establishing a price structure becomes easier.

Pricing may not be as much of a problem for a nonprofit entity as it is for a shop operated for profit. That's because shoppers in a nonprofit store realize that the money they spend in the store is going for a worthy cause. On the other hand, nonprofit stores may have better prices overall because they are not paying for the merchandise they sell. However, if you are running a nonprofit store, you must also take your overhead expenses into consideration. Your prices cannot be so low you end up operating at a loss, or your shop will soon be out of business.

There are different approaches to the pricing dilemma. You can simply price everything at 50 or 60 percent below retail. This assumes that the merchandise is in good condition. For any goods that show visible signs of wear and tear, the discount will have to be more. If you have purchased the goods in your shop, like any retailer, you will have to estimate the cost of the stock and take that into consideration when putting a price tag on it. Remember that if stock doesn't sell, you can always have a sale, but also keep in mind that your prices have to be fair or customers will not come back again.

Send Them on a Search

If you've ever run a yard sale or garage sale, you know that people show up just to ask if the owner has any books, jewelry, or china for sale. That is all they are interested in buying, and if they get a negative response from the person running the sale, the potential buyer doesn't waste time looking at any of the goods that are available there. A good answer to the question these selective shoppers ask when they come through the door of your shop is, "There may be some pieces like that displayed around the store." Some shoppers may not fall for that noncommittal answer, but most will take the time to walk around your shop looking for the treasures that they seek.

It is a well-known fact that grocery outlets usually have bread at one end of the store and milk at the other end. That's because bread and milk are two of most common staples of life, and the two items that are most often purchased at the same time. By separating them by the length of the store, shoppers are forced to walk through the store, and in the course of their journey from the bread aisle to the dairy cases generally find other grocery items they end up buying.

Even large items like furniture can be spread around your thrift store and can even be used as display racks. A baby crib, for example, can be used to display baby blankets, sheets, stuffed animals, and other toys. A dresser can be used to display collectibles, hand mirrors, or small items of clothing like socks and scarves.

Of course, you will still have certain areas where clothing and household goods are bunched together, but there's no reason those areas cannot also contain a different type of item, like one of those amusing white elephants that don't fit a specific category.

Added Value

Hang pictures on the walls, but be creative based on the theme of the picture—a painting of a bowl of fruit can be displayed with the kitchen utensils, an outdoor scene with the camping equipment.

Make shopping in your store an adventure. Make it a place where customers will walk around every time they come in to see what new surprises you have in your store for them.

Make Friends

The importance of being friendly to everyone who comes into your thrift store has been mentioned several times in this book, but it is so vital to the success of your business, it bears repeating again. The following suggestions are reminders of the ways that you can make your customers feel wanted and welcome:

- Try to personally greet everyone who comes into your shop and ask them how you can help them.

- Keep candy or balloons on hand for the kids who come in with their parents, but always check with the parent before offering a treat to a child.

- Have baskets available for the shoppers to use as they walk through your shop.

- Have a full-length mirror and, if possible, a dressing room area that customers can use to try on clothing.

- If you can manage it, offer to carry large purchases to the customer's vehicle.

If your thrift shop carries toys, set up a play area for the kids. Chances are, any toys the kids play with there will be purchased for them. Just be sure the play area only contains safe items.

Not for Resale

Be sure that the play area is located where parents and you can keep a watchful eye on the children as they play, or assign a staff member to supervise the area.

Although the low prices in thrift stores make layaways unnecessary, be willing to hold an item for a customer if requested. If and when you provide this service, make it clear that you will only keep the item off the sales floor for a limited amount of time, no longer than a day or two. If the customer does not return to claim it in that amount of time, you can return it to the display area without having lost too many other opportunities to sell it.

As you get to know the clientele that your store attracts, you can adapt to their needs. A play area if young families frequent your store or some chairs in various places where an older person can rest for a few minutes will be welcome additions to your store. Use your own common sense and ingenuity to make sure that your customers find a visit to your store is always a pleasant experience.

Keep It Neat

How many times have you been in a grocery store and found a perishable item sitting on a shelf with snack items? How many times have you been in a retail store and found nonsale items on the sale racks? Shoppers are not always neat and they are not always considerate. It is up to the store manager and the staff to check for misplaced items, spills, and damaged goods. As a thrift store owner, you will be faced with these problems and more.

Periodic checks of your store during business hours are the best way to find small problems before they escalate into bigger problems. However, that may not be possible unless you have volunteers or employees helping you. If you work alone, make sure you inspect the store before you leave every day. Earlier, we discussed not stocking any merchandise that had an odor. Now consider the fact that someone might leave a half-eaten lunch or a soiled diaper in an obscure corner of your store. If left overnight, you could have a big odor to deal with the next morning.

The following is a checklist of tasks that should be done frequently to keep your store neat and attractive inside and out:

- Floors should be swept, mopped, or vacuumed.

- Merchandise should be returned to its proper place in the store.

- Look for items discarded or left behind by customers.

- Dust displays and display items if needed.

- Check entryways for debris.

- Check dressing rooms for abandoned items.

- Clean mirrors, glass doors, and windows.

- Sweep sidewalks and walkways.

- Check parking areas for hazards and messes.

Even if you are not responsible for the parking lot convenient to your place of business, you should check that on a regular basis as well. Potholes, burned-out lights, standing water, and other safety or health concerns should be reported to your landlord for immediate attention.

You should also set up a lost and found box for items you find in your store. If a customer comes back and is able to retrieve the lost item, he or she will be grateful for your consideration.

Post a sign on your front door prohibiting food and drink in your store to cut down on accidental spills. Be courteous about reminding customers who do not heed the sign and make exceptions for small children with spill-proof cups.

Don't let your storage areas get too overrun with junk, as that tends to spread out into your sales area. Also, keeping the storage area neat and in order makes it possible for you to quickly restock your store when needed and find an item not on display that is requested by a customer.

After running your store for a period of time, you will establish your own routine and list of chores necessary to keep your store in good condition inside and out. Although there are some people who love to rummage through a tangled, jumbled mess to find bargains, most people prefer shopping in a shop that is neat, attractive, and organized.

The Least You Need to Know

- ◆ Customer satisfaction should be your foremost concern in choosing merchandise.
- ◆ The IRS guidelines for tax-deductible donations should be followed when issuing receipts.
- ◆ Your merchandise should be priced fairly, but not so low your store operates at a loss.
- ◆ Display merchandise in a way that encourages shoppers to walk through your whole store.
- ◆ Be willing to offer extra assistance to your customers.
- ◆ Keep your store clean and neat both inside and outside.

Chapter 12

Safe Handling and Disposal of Merchandise

In This Chapter

◆ Taking standard precautions

◆ Managing the obvious hazards

◆ Handling glass, furniture, and clothing

◆ Stocking small appliances, toys, and cribs

◆ Working with computers and other electronics

Every item that comes into your possession has to be handled in some way or another. Whether you are a nonprofit that receives all of its merchandise from donors or you are a store that must go out into the community and get merchandise from other sources, you will have to develop safe handling practices for yourself, your staff, and ultimately your customers.

Safety issues connected to products have always existed, but today those issues become public knowledge instantly. New merchandise reported to be hazardous is quickly pulled from the shelves of retail stores, but anything purchased before the alarm was sounded can make its way into your hands.

This means you have to be twice as vigilant and cautious in choosing the items that will be sold in your store.

In this chapter, you will learn how to avoid problems with the multitude of products you handle. You will find out where you can go to get answers and information when you have questions and concerns about a particular item or class of items. Safe disposal of hazardous products is also a big part of your responsibility as a thrift store owner.

Be Prepared

Often people will bring in boxes full of donated items that have to be handled. If you are running a for-profit business, you will also receive boxes and sealed containers from storage facilities and other sources where you obtain merchandise. Before touching anything packed in those boxes, you and anyone else you have working with you should don your safe-sorting equipment. This may include the following items:

- ◆ Safety glasses

- ◆ Surgical mask

- ◆ Heavy-duty gloves

- ◆ Long-sleeved shirt or coveralls

- ◆ Long pants

- ◆ Sturdy rubber-soled closed-toe footwear

If you're thinking this list is over the top as far as caution is concerned, you are right. That's because when you start sorting and moving things, you never know what lies underneath and what type of item you may uncover. Even a harmless-looking piece of clothing can have a dangerous needle or other sharp object hidden in a pocket or fold.

Reaching into a pocket or fold without heavy-duty gloves on your hands can result in injury.

While you are always hoping to uncover a hidden treasure, you could also uncover an aerosol can or other container with hazardous contents ready to break open or explode. Without a mask, safety glasses, and the protection of the right clothing and shoes, you can suffer burns or breathe in toxic fumes.

Not for Resale

Set up a place in your storage area or outside of your store for sorting through any boxes or containers that could contain hazards to protect your sales area and customers.

This is especially likely with boxes in a storage locker that have been abandoned, because the lockers generally do not have heating or cooling. This means everything stored in the locker may have been damaged by extreme heat or cold.

These warnings and suggestions for safe sorting are definitely needed for sorting boxes and containers that have been packed by someone unknown to you. While you still have to be careful with large objects such as furniture, appliances, or electronics, you can see usually see what you are getting, so the risk in handling them is greatly diminished.

Don't let all these warnings and precautions keep you from acquiring boxes and containers from unknown donors, storage facilities, and other places. Thrift store owners often find first-class used merchandise in the boxes and containers from these sources. Just be aware that hazards may exist, and be prepared to handle the boxes with the proper safety precautions in place.

Look but Don't Touch

Obviously, you would not knowingly allow chemicals or other dangerous materials to pass over the threshold of your thrift store business. Unfortunately, many common household products contain dangerous chemicals and will sometimes appear in the most unlikely places. The following is a list of common products you may run across that are deemed to be hazardous:

- ◆ Automotive products: motor oil, brake and transmission fluid, antifreeze, car batteries, and car wax with solvent

- ◆ Household products: drain cleaners, oven cleaners, toilet cleaners, spot removers, silver polishes, furniture polish, liquid and powdered cleansers, bleach, and dyes

- ◆ Paints and solvents including latex, oil-based, auto, and model paints; varnish; wood preservers; mineral spirits; and glues

- ◆ Fertilizers and pesticides

- ◆ Aerosol products; dry-cell, disc, or button batteries; mothballs and flakes; shoe polish; photographic chemicals; smoke detectors; air fresheners; and deodorizers

 **Not for Resale**

Look for the not-so-obvious hazards like car wax, which contains petroleum and is associated with skin and lung cancer.

What makes a product hazardous? Here's another list that answers that question:

- Ignitable: can burn or cause a fire

- Corrosive: can eat away at materials and destroy living tissue with contact

- Explosive or reactive: can explode or release poisonous fumes when exposed to air, water, or other chemicals

- Toxic: immediately poisonous or poisonous over a long period of chronic use

- Radioactive: can damage and destroy cells and chromosomal material

Compare the list of products with the list of what makes them hazardous and use proper caution when any of these products are included in donor boxes and found in boxes and containers that you obtain from other sources. While most donors would not put these hazardous products in a box donated to your store, you never know what will be deposited in a donation bin located in a public place, which is why it is important to be familiar with these product lists and the dangers associated with the products. A good rule to follow is when any such product is found in an open container or a container that is damaged in any way, it should be disposed of immediately.

Before purchasing any of these products, such as furniture polish or silver polish to use on items you will offer for sale in your store, read the labels on them. The Federal Hazardous Substances Act of 1960 requires that manufacturers place warning labels on all products containing hazardous substances. The labels you will find will be in the following categories of cautions:

- **Danger:** substances that are extremely flammable, corrosive, or highly toxic

- Poison: substances that are highly toxic

- Warning or Caution: substances that are moderately or slightly toxic

Added Value

Visit the Environmental Protection Agency website at www.epa.gov for questions about hazardous products and waste disposal.

Does all this mean that you cannot purchase or use any of these products in connection with your thrift store business? No. It simply means you should use and store the products as directed on the labels to avoid problems. You can still sell these products if you purchase them from a bankrupt stock sale, but be sure to display them safely, out of the reach of children.

The EPA has district offices across the country that will provide information on disposal of hazardous materials. In addition, many colleges and universities around the country will also help you dispose of hazardous materials and give you instructions for safely handling and storing the materials prior to disposal.

Remember to keep yourself informed of potential hazards and safeguard yourself, your staff, and your customers by handling potential merchandise safely and intelligently.

Breakables

Fragile items need special care to be transported and displayed safely. It's a good idea to keep a supply of wrapping paper, sturdy boxes, and other items needed for packing glassware or other breakable items in your store and in any vehicles used for picking up donations or visiting locations where you might find merchandise for your store.

When displaying these items in your store, try to place them on shelves or tables that are out of the reach of little hands. Also, do not display any items that are cracked or damaged. A small chip or two might not matter, but visible cracks may make the item unsafe for customers to handle and undesirable to purchase. Again, wear gloves when unpacking boxes containing any type of glassware to avoid cuts in the event that items have broken during transport to your store. Recycle any glass items that are no longer useable.

Glass and ceramic items may not be the only fragile products that you will stock in your store. Things made of wicker and certain types of wood can be fragile as well. These items must be inspected for sharp edges or damaged areas where wood splinters could get embedded in someone's hand or fingers when the item is examined. Often customers will still want to purchase something that is damaged—at a reduced price, of course. Like the manufacturers of products containing potentially hazardous materials, attach a label or prominent tag on the item to advise people that it has chips, cracks, or splinters to be wary of.

Any used furniture must be carefully inspected for defects in the wood, loose nails, or dried-out joints. If the furniture has fabric, examine it for holes or obvious signs of wear and tear. Also, as you learned in a prior chapter, if any fabric in a piece of furniture has an odor attached to it, such as cigarette smoke, don't accept it as potential merchandise for your shop. Sometimes, a donor will have you pick up such a piece and you may want to haul it away for them in the name of good will and customer service, but haul it away from their living quarters straight to the dump unless you can salvage some part of it.

Never put a chair, bench, or stool on the display floor until it has been thoroughly examined and declared safe and sturdy enough for someone to sit on. Consider the consequences of a customer sitting down on a chair with a wobbly leg and having it collapse. Or think about someone sitting down on a bench with damaged wood edges and picking up a splinter. These are problems you don't want to have, and these are problems you can avoid by employing safe handling procedures.

There have been some safety issues reported on various types of lawn furniture. Lists of these defects that have caused injuries to consumers are posted on the U.S. Consumer Product Safety Commission (CPSC) website (www.cpsc.gov) and should be reviewed before placing outdoor furniture on display in your store.

Clothing has already been discussed in detail in other chapters, noting potential problems with insects, odors, and wear and tear. Now we must address the issues of safety that mostly exist in the area of clothing for children. Some years ago, laws were passed that required manufacturers to make sleepwear for children only with flame-retardant fabrics. In recent years, the CPSC has uncovered potential hazards in children's clothing that has led to a number of recalls.

Added Value _____

Dyed or undyed children's clothing made out of natural, untreated fibers such as cotton, silk, or wool is generally okay to be resold.

Added Value _____

Go to www.cpsc.gov and sign up for e-mail alerts on recalls and other safety news for all products.

Because kids grow out of their duds so quickly, thrift stores receive donations of children's clothes on a regular basis. That's why it's doubly important for owners to be aware of recent problems and recalls. For example, children's outerwear with drawstrings at the neck or waist have been cited as a safety hazard because these drawstrings can catch on things like playground equipment, bus doors, and cribs, leading to injury or death. Guidelines were issued by CPSC to consumers and manufacturers to help prevent children from strangling or getting entangled in the drawstrings of garments like jackets and sweatshirts. Since your store will be acquiring used kids clothing, it is up to you to discard any outerwear with drawstrings that comes into your hands.

While it is not likely that you or your staff would be injured in the handling of children's outerwear with drawstrings, it is your responsibility to ensure that all items displayed in your store are safe and have not been recalled by CPSC. When in doubt, visit their website for updated information. CPSC also maintains a toll-free telephone hotline seven days a week from 8:30 A.M. to 5 P.M. Eastern Standard Time. Call 1-800-638-2772 to obtain product safety information.

Electrical Concerns

Clocks, radios, hair dryers, lamps, and other small appliances will cease to work if dropped or banged around too much. In general, check out the cords and plugs on all electrical appliances to make sure there are no frays, splits, or bent metal. If the electrical cords and plugs are in good condition, test the items to be sure they are in working order, and then check with CPSC to see if any of them have been reported for safety issues.

It has been determined that older hair dryers do not have protection against electrocution. In 1990, the manufacturing industry adopted a voluntary standard that affords extra protection by adding a large rectangular-shaped safety plug at the end of the cord. If hair dryers come into your store without this safety feature, it is best to discard them.

Added Value

If an electrical appliance with a frayed cord or damaged plug is in good condition otherwise, the plug and/or cord can be replaced to make the item saleable.

Older halogen floor lamps pose a fire hazard. In 1997, 40 million of these lamps were recalled because of fires that resulted from unintended contact between the lamp and combustible materials. Like hair dryers, newer models have an added safety feature of a wire guard over the bulb, making it harder for flammable materials to come in contact with it.

Again, be aware of the dangers of older models of these lamps, and any other electrical appliance that you are considering for sale in your shop.

Not Safe for Kids

Products for children—such as cribs and toys—seem to receive the most scrutiny for safety issues. That's because the little ones have yet to learn what is safe and what is not. Infants and toddlers generally put everything they can pick up into their mouths and often stick their little heads into any available space. Older kids often have no fear. They climb and jump and take their toys apart.

Cribs, playpens, car seats, infant swings, toys, and even books have been reported to cause injury and death. With so much anxiety and concern over items for kids, many thrift store

Helping Hands

Vintage children's books and toys can be sold as collector's items. Their value and age make it unlikely that they would be given to a young child.

owners have opted not to carry these products or accept donations of them. This is a personal decision that you must make, but before you turn your back on what could be a fairly lucrative market, take some time to learn the facts and be aware of the information that is available to guide you.

Once again, the Consumer Product Safety Commission has a wealth of information on children's products and lists that can be accessed on recalled items that should not be stocked in your store. When any of these items come into your possession, simply put them aside and do some research before automatically rejecting them for resale. Everyone is aware that lead poisoning is one of the most frequently reported dangers and lead is found in many toys, especially those manufactured in foreign countries. Be aware that if your shop receives suspect merchandise with good resale value, it can be tested to determine if it does indeed pose a threat to child safety. Check local telephone and business directories to find a qualified, trained person in your area who can quickly screen items with a handheld device called an x-ray fluorescence (XRF) machine. Depending on the resale value of the item, this may be a good way to determine if the product can be safely stocked and sold in your store. You can also contact the manufacturers of any products you have questions about for answers and additional information.

Added Value

CPSC has a checklist written specifically for thrift store owners that can be accessed at its website (www.cpsc. gov).

Another huge area of concern for toys is the possibility that they might contain phthalates, which are plasticizing and softening chemicals. CPSC cautions thrift stores to be wary of any plastic toy that is soft enough to allow a baby or small child to grasp it easily.

Studies have shown phthalates cause a number of reproductive problems in males and have also been linked to liver and kidney damage. In recent years, toy manufacturers like Early Start, Little Tykes, Lego, Prime Time Playthings, Sassy, and Tiny Love have stopped using phthalates in their products.

If you decide to take the extra precautions necessary to handle toys and other children's products, display them with a notice to customers that the products have been inspected and tested and have been deemed safe for resale. This is another one of those things that will spread positive words of praise for your store.

Any item that is not safe should be properly disposed of to prevent its reuse.

Beginning in February 2010, selling a recalled item will be punishable by law. For more information about the laws and the products covered by them, read the information taken from the Guide to the Consumer Product Safety Act that is included in Appendix A of this book.

The Electronic Age

Computers, cell phones, iPods, and a vast array of other related electronic products are sold every day. Because the manufacturers are constantly coming out with new, improved models of all these products, they are constantly being donated or sold to thrift stores. If you have decided to specialize in used electronics, this is a good thing for you. However, handling these products requires that you know enough about them to be able to sell them to your customers. You must also know how to test the items as they come into your store to make sure they are in resalable condition. You must also communicate with donors or anyone you obtain a computer from to make sure they have cleared the computer's hard drive of all their personal information.

On the other side of the coin is the fact that many of these electronic devices donated to your shop will not be worth the time and trouble and floor space to display them. So, for you as a thrift store owner and the public in general, many, many, many electronic products have to be disposed of or recycled.

As mentioned in another chapter, there are actually recycling programs that pay for electronic items (*e-cycling*). Nonprofit organizations can sign up with programs through companies like Safeway Foods and receive extra cash for turning in cell phones and other specified products and accessories.

def•i•ni•tion

Recycling electronics has become such a huge undertaking that it has become its own program, called **e-cycling**.

The following list of programs that may exist in your local area is provided by the Environmental Protection Agency:

- Earth 911 (earth911.com), a comprehensive communication network for the environment, has hotlines, websites, and other informational sources. The Earth 911 network will put you in touch with programs in your community for e-cycling and much more.

- My Green Electronics (www.mygreenelectronics.org), sponsored by the Consumer Electronics Association, is a resource for opportunities to recycle or donate used electronics.

- Electronic Industries Alliance's Consumer Education Initiative E-Cycling Central website (www.eiae.org) helps you find reuse, recycling, and donation programs for electronic products in your state.

- TechSoup (www.techsoup.org) provides information to promote computer recycling and reuse.

- Rechargeable Battery Recycling Corporation (www.rbrc.org) helps you recycle portable rechargeable batteries commonly found in cordless power tools, cellular and cordless phones, laptop computers, camcorders, digital cameras, and remote control toys. You can search for collection sites by zip code.

According to the EPA, manufacturers and retailers offer different approaches to give you several options to recycle electronics. Some programs developed in connection with the EPA's Plug-In To eCycling partners are national, while others are regional. Here are some of the options these programs offer, including some that may help you earn extra income for your e-cycling efforts:

- Take-back, mail-in, or trade-in programs

- Programs supporting local organizations that collect equipment

- Programs that host collection events at retail locations and other stores within a city or state.

Some of the manufacturers and retailers that offer a variety of the e-cycling options listed above are Dell, Best Buy, Intel, and Sony. A complete list with specific information for each company can be found in Appendix A of this book.

Added Value

Hosting an e-cycling event at your thrift store with the help of one of these companies is a good way to publicize your store.

Last but not least, remember that safe handling and proper disposal procedures begin the moment the products come into your possession. As a thrift store owner, it is your responsibility to take precautions and do anything else necessary to ensure that the items that eventually end up on your sales floor pose no danger to you, your staff, or the customers who purchase them.

The Least You Need to Know

- Donning protective gear before handling boxes of unknown contents or origin is essential.

- Educate yourself on the hazards of chemicals and other potential dangers.

- Careful inspection of glass, wood, and clothing before it goes on sale will prevent problems.

- Hair dryers and some lamps have been recalled because of reports of injuries, deaths, and fires.

- Children's equipment and toys can pose the biggest safety problems for resale shops.

- Electronics can be recycled and provide extra income for thrift store owners.

Chapter 13

People and Paperwork

In this Chapter

- ◆ Establishing hiring procedures
- ◆ Processing payroll
- ◆ Employer/employee taxes and reports

Whenever you bring staff members into your store—whether they are volunteers or employees—you increase your own responsibilities. As the owner or manager of the store, having volunteers on your staff means you must deal with issues like scheduling and training. Employees also require scheduling and training, as well as extra paperwork and a whole new area of bookkeeping procedures and tax liabilities. The good news is that if you need staff members, it means your store is doing so well, you cannot manage the workload yourself. The extra people and paperwork are therefore worth the added responsibilities and costs because your store is becoming more and more profitable.

The paperwork necessary to employ people is based on the rules and regulations imposed by the state where you are located and by the federal government. If your business is structured as a corporation, you may already be an employee of that corporation. That means all the information in this chapter regarding taxes and reports applies to you as well as any other people you add to your payroll.

Finding Good Help

In Chapter 6 you reviewed some basic considerations and thoughts regarding staffing your nonprofit store with volunteers. You know that supporting a cause or charity generally ensures that you will have help running your store. While volunteers are not paid to work for you, they still need to be chosen carefully. The same type of review process you would use to hire paid staff members can be modified to make sure volunteers are placed in the right positions in the store.

Make up a simple form for the volunteers to complete before you schedule them to work in the store. The following information should be requested on the volunteer form:

- ◆ Name, mailing address, telephone number (home and cell)
- ◆ Number of days or hours per week volunteer can give to the store
- ◆ Days or specific hours volunteer wants to work
- ◆ Area of the business volunteer prefers to work in
- ◆ Prior experience in the preferred area

As you can see, having your volunteers complete a form that provides the above information will give you necessary contact information. It will also help you assign the volunteers to the right jobs in the store. Scheduling the volunteers will also be easier if you have their preferences down on paper.

Hiring employees requires a lot more paperwork. An application form to collect all the information you need for employment consideration should be filled out by anyone who answers your help wanted ad. One of the most important parts of the application form is a section where previous employment and experience can be listed. Suggestions for interviewing and checking references and hiring were presented in Chapter 6, so let's skip ahead to the hiring process.

Added Value

For easy access, place all the volunteer information sheets in alphabetical order in a folder in your filing system.

In the United States, potential employees must provide you with a valid Social Security number. Since the employer is required to verify that the employee is a citizen, legally entitled to work in the United States, he or she must also provide a driver's license, a certified copy of a birth certificate, or citizenship papers. Form *I-9* must be completed and kept in a file along with photocopies of the documents the employee provided.

def•i•ni•tion

I-9 is a form required by the federal Immigration and Naturalization Service (INS) verifying United States citizenship.

The employee must also complete IRS form W-4 that indicates marital status and the number of deductions the employee is claiming. This form must also be kept on file and used to determine the amount of withholding taxes deducted from the employee's paycheck. Copies of forms I-9 and W-4 can be viewed or downloaded by visiting www.irs.gov. You will also find several publications the IRS provides with all the rules and regulations employers must follow.

The frequency of payroll checks can be weekly, biweekly, twice a month, or even monthly. Obviously, a weekly pay schedule requires a little extra time as the wages have to be computed and the checks written every week. Regardless of how often you issue paychecks, the tax reports are filed either quarterly or annually.

Not for Resale

Even if your corporation operates on a fiscal year, all payroll reports and taxes must coincide with the calendar year.

Payroll records are very important and should be updated every payday. Your computerized accounting program will have a payroll section, and once you have entered the basic information into it, it should calculate gross wages, taxes, and benefits such as insurance premiums and print out a net payroll check. You will initially have to enter each employee separately and input their personal data, gross salary or hourly rate of pay, and the information from the completed W-4 form. If the employee works for an hourly rate, you only have to input the hours worked in the payroll period and the computer will calculate the gross wages and the tax deductions based on that amount.

If you have set up your bookkeeping system to print checks from your software program, you can print out the paychecks. If you are not using the computer to print checks, simply print out the payroll ledger and write the checks out manually from your checkbook. Either way is fine as long as you remember to save the information in the computer so that it posts the paychecks to the employee's ledger sheet and the tax information into the liability accounts that are included in the Balance Sheet section of the General Ledger. However, if you only have one or two employees, you may want to calculate the paychecks yourself, write them out, and then enter the data into the bookkeeping system for posting.

Tax Liabilities

The payroll liability accounts that are already included in a computerized accounting program are as follows:

- ◆ Federal Withholding Tax Payable

- ◆ Social Security Tax Payable

- ◆ Medicare Tax Payable

- ◆ State Withholding Tax Payable

- ◆ *SUTA* Payable

- ◆ *FUTA* Payable

def•i•ni•tion

SUTA is the abbreviation for State Unemployment Taxes. **FUTA** is the abbreviation for Federal Unemployment Taxes.

Some cities impose income tax on the wages of its working residents. If you are located in such a city, you will have another liability account for Local Withholding Tax Payable.

In the Income and Expense section of the General Ledger, there will always be an account for Gross Wages to record the amount you are paying the employees and Payroll Tax Expense where the employer's portion of Social Security and Medicare taxes and unemployment taxes are recorded.

These are all taxes associated with employee wages. The employer is responsible for collecting all the taxes and remitting them to the proper taxing authorities. Let's take a look at the taxes individually and see whether the tax is paid by the employee through a payroll deduction, is an expense employers pay as a benefit to their employees, or if the tax is shared equally by the employer and the employee.

Federal withholding tax is deducted from an employee's gross wages and is based on his or her marital status and the number of dependents listed on the W-4 in the employee's file. The IRS provides tax rate schedules that the employer uses to determine the correct amount of the withholding tax.

At the beginning of each tax year, the IRS issues Circular E Employer's Tax Guide with the new tax rate schedules for withholding taxes and the current tax rate needed to calculate Social Security and Medicare taxes. Circular E is generally mailed to employers, but can also be accessed online at the IRS website. Employers who do not receive a copy of Circular E in the mail can order one by calling the IRS at 1-800-829-3676. Since these taxes are subject to change each year, the owner or bookkeeper needs to update the payroll information to reflect the new rates.

Social Security tax is the government's retirement plan, and participation in the plan is mandatory for all wage earners.

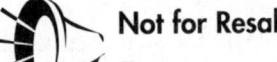

Not for Resale

Tax-exempt status for nonprofit corporations only applies to income tax on the net profit of the business. Employment taxes must be reported and paid by every employer.

Medicare tax provides health insurance benefits for retired and disabled workers and is also a mandatory program. These two taxes are covered under the Federal Insurance Contributions Act (FICA), and payments into the plans are shared equally by employees and employers.

Tax rates on FICA taxes are subject to change from year to year. There is also a wage limit on Social Security tax that is set at the beginning of each calendar year. Once an employee reaches the wage limit set for the current year, Social Security tax is no longer deducted from his or her paycheck, and the employer no longer has to pay into the fund for the employee either. There is no wage limit on the Medicare tax. Again, all this information can be found in the annual Circular E booklet or online at the IRS website.

Most states also require employers to collect and remit income tax on employee wages. Check with your state revenue office for information and tax rates as well as reporting and remittance requirements. The states may also have their own version of a W-4 form for employees to fill out and indicate how much state tax they want withheld from their wages. For example, the state of Arizona's form allows employees to choose a percentage of the federal withholding tax for their state deduction. An employee can choose 10, 15, or 20 percent of the amount withheld for the federal taxes to be withheld for state income taxes. State revenue departments usually assign employers an account number, but also use the federal Employer Identification Number as an additional reference.

FICA taxes and withholding taxes should be calculated and posted into the General Ledger accounts each time paychecks are issued. This will keep your liability accounts updated for the Federal Tax Deposits (FTDs) that most employers have to make on a monthly basis. Keep in mind that the frequency of federal tax deposits depends on the dollar amount of gross wages paid out each week and the tax liabilities related to those wages. Generally, payroll taxes accrued in one month must be deposited by the fifteenth of the following month.

If the taxes and procedures associated with payroll seem like a lot of extra work for you as the owner of a thrift store, be aware that there are a number of payroll services that will do it all for you for a fee. These services calculate and issue paychecks, figure your tax liabilities, and then give you a detailed printout of what you need to post into the General Ledger of your bookkeeping system each payday. Some services will even make your Federal Tax Deposits for you—for an extra fee, of course. However, like any other accounting function that involves taxes, the owner is ultimately responsible for the accuracy of the tax calculations and paying the taxes in a timely manner. So even if you use a payroll service, you still need to understand how it all works. Therefore, we will continue this portion of the crash course on accounting with an example of a typical payroll and how it should be posted into your store's General Ledger.

The following is an example of how a weekly payroll worksheet would look.

Added Value

"The ABCs of FTDs Quick Reference Guide for Understanding Federal Tax Deposits" can be accessed online at the IRS website: www.irs.gov.

Added Value

Many banks offer payroll services, and that may be a convenient way for you to avoid the time and effort of doing it yourself.

Smart Shopper Thrift Store Payroll for Week Ending 3-15-10

Name	Gross Wages	SS	Med	FWH	SWH	Net Check
		6.2%	1.45%		20%	
J. Smith	$600.00	37.20	8.70	60.00	12.00	482.10
B. Brown	400.00	24.80	5.80	40.00	8.00	321.40
Totals	1,000.00	62.00	14.50	100.00	20.00	803.50

Not for Resale

The tax rates and percentages in this book are for demonstration purposes only. Be sure to obtain current rate information before calculating payroll for your store.

Now study the following example to see how the weekly payroll in the previous table would be posted to the General Ledger. Keep in mind that the employer portion of the Social Security and Medicare taxes must be calculated and posted to keep the liability accounts properly updated.

Account#	Account Name	Debit	Credit
6000	Gross Wages	$1,000.00	
2050	FWH Payable		100.00
2051	SS Payable		62.00
2052	Med. Payable		14.50
2053	SWH Payable		20.00
1000	Cash in Checking		803.50
2051	SS Payable		62.00
2052	Med. Payable		14.50
6308	Payroll Tax Expense	76.50	
		1,076.50	1,076.50

The tax liability accounts hold the amount of payroll taxes that have to be remitted to the federal and state revenue departments. When the payments are made, the checks are posted as debits to these accounts and credits to the Cash in Checking.

Unemployment taxes are paid to the state where your business is located and to the federal government. These funds are used to pay benefits to people who are laid off or fired from their jobs. Unemployment taxes are an expense to the employer. Some states base the tax rate for unemployment on how many unemployment claims the business has filed against them in a specific time period. The good news is that the federal government allows employers who pay into the state funds a reduced rate on the federal unemployment tax.

As an employer, it is your responsibility to contact your state unemployment revenue department to obtain information and tax rates. This department will assign an account number to your business and send you all the necessary information and forms.

Unfortunately, in some states a new business with no experience record for claims is generally charged the maximum rate for the first year. If no unemployment claims are filed against the business, the rate is reduced the next year. State unemployment tax rates are usually no more than 3 percent, and in most states only have to be paid on the first $7,000 of the gross wages of each employee. After an employee's earnings reach the set limit in that state, the remainder of earnings for that year become exempt from unemployment taxes. If a company is paying state unemployment taxes, the federal tax rate is reduced to .008 of the first $7,000 in wages paid to each employee.

> **Not for Resale**
>
> Unemployment tax rates and rules vary from state to state. The rates in this book are estimated averages, and the rules are general, not specific to any particular state.

Using the previous payroll example and assuming a state unemployment tax rate of 2 percent and a federal rate of .008, the unemployment taxes would be posted in the General Ledger as follows.

Account#	Account Name	Debit	Credit
2054	SUTA Payable		20.00
2055	FUTA Payable		8.00
6308	Payroll Tax Expense	28.00	
Totals		28.00	28.00

State unemployment taxes are usually reported and paid quarterly. Federal unemployment taxes are reported annually, but depending on the tax liability may have to be paid quarterly.

In Chapter 9 you learned the difference between a cash basis accounting system and an accrual basis accounting system.

All the posting examples in this chapter assume you are using the accrual method because the expenses are being recognized before they are actually paid out. This is because payroll taxes from one month's payroll are generally not remitted to the federal and state governments until the following month. In other words, when you have employees the most accurate way to keep your books is to use the accrual method. This is also the surest way to avoid employment tax problems, as the taxes are posted to the liability accounts each payday and you know exactly how much you will have to pay out when the next Federal Tax Deposit is due.

In recent years, the IRS has established a system for paying tax liabilities electronically. The guide for using the Electronic Federal Tax Payment System (EFTPS) can be found in Appendix A of this book.

If you are not keeping your own books, your accounting firm can extend its monthly service to your business by doing your payroll, too. Of course, there will be an additional fee for this added service, but the firm will calculate taxes and advise you of the amounts you must remit to state and federal revenue departments. Remember, regardless of who actually handles the payroll for your thrift shop, as the owner you need to understand the process and the rules and regulations set by the IRS and your home state.

Not for Resale

Businesses that do not pay the correct amount of employment taxes in a timely manner are subject to substantial fines and penalties.

Reports and Returns

Let's begin by studying the tax reporting forms that must be filed quarterly or annually with the state or IRS.

Form 941, Employer's Quarterly Federal Tax Return—This form is due on the last day of the month following the end of a calendar quarter. For example, after the quarter ending March 31, the report is due on April 30. Employers that accrue $2,500 or more in employment taxes in a quarter must file this form and make advance Federal Tax Deposits (FTDs) using the monthly deposit schedule. A copy of Form 941 can be found in Appendix B.

Form 944, Employer's Annual Federal Tax Return—This form can be used by small businesses that accrue less than $2,500 in employment taxes each quarter. Employers must obtain prior approval from the IRS before this annual report can be used. A copy of Form 944 can be reviewed in Appendix B.

Form 940, Employer's Annual Unemployment (FUTA) Tax Return—This annual report can be used by all employers, but employers are only allowed to remit $500 with this tax return. If an employer accrues more than $500 in federal unemployment taxes during the year, those taxes must be deposited according to the monthly schedule dates for the quarter in which the limit is met or exceeded. The FUTA tax return and all taxes due for the prior year are due on or before January 31st of the next year. A copy of Form 940 is included in Appendix B. January 31st is also the deadline for employers to provide *W-2* forms to employees. Visit the IRS website (www.irs.gov) for information, instructions, and forms. W-2s can also be filed electronically.

def•i•ni•tion

A **W-2** form is an annual report of wages and taxes that employees must file with their individual tax returns.

State Withholding Tax Forms—The forms for reporting state taxes withheld from employees' wages vary from state to state, and it is up to the employer to contact the state revenue departments to obtain forms and instructions.

State Unemployment Tax Forms—Contact your state department of unemployment services to obtain information and forms if your state requires employers to pay into the unemployment fund.

The IRS has now made it possible for the employment tax forms 940, 941, and 944 to be filed online. The due dates for filing online are the same as for filing a hard copy by mail. One of the big benefits of filing online is that completing the form is automated with software that calculates the taxes. Online filing also allows the employer to authorize electronic funds transfers to pay any taxes due with the form. Preregistration with the IRS is required. To learn more about the program, go to www.irs.gov and access the following publications:

- 3112—the IRS e-file Application Package

- 3823—Employment Tax e-file System Implementation and User Guide and Revenue Procedure 2003-69

You can also call the help line at 1-866-255-0654.

Your state may also have programs that allow you to file tax forms electronically. Check online or by phone with your state taxing authorities.

While the IRS and individual states are making filing tax reports and paying taxes quicker and easier, the basic rules of reporting and remitting taxes have not become more lenient. Failure to file tax reports and pay the taxes due results in fines, penalties, and interest. Other than the option of filing an annual employment tax form rather than a quarterly report, small businesses do not get any special tax breaks or considerations. So if and when you hire employees or become an employee of your corporation—whether it's a nonprofit or a profit-making venture—educate

Not for Resale

If you file any tax form electronically, make sure you keep a hard copy of the form you filed for your records.

yourself on all the rules and regulations associated with federal and state employment taxes and follow them carefully.

Remember that there are books listed in Appendix A that should be read if you are going to do your own bookkeeping. These books also contain detailed information and instructions for payroll, payroll reports, and payroll taxes.

The Least You Need to Know

- ◆ Make up forms for volunteers to complete so you have easy access to their pertinent information.

- ◆ All employees must provide a valid Social Security number and proof of U.S. citizenship for the I-9 form that employers must keep on file with copies of employees' documents.

- ◆ Employees must complete a W-4 form to indicate marital status and the number of exemptions claimed for federal withholding taxes. Employers must also match the employees' contributions to FICA taxes. Obtain a copy of Circular E Employer's Tax Guide at beginning of each tax year.

- ◆ Employers must pay unemployment taxes to the IRS and most states. Taxes and reports must be filed according to the schedules established by the IRS and the state where you are located.

- ◆ Electronic payments and filings may require registration and applications. Visit www.irs.gov for information.

- ◆ Using a payroll service does not relieve the business owner of responsibility for filing tax returns and making tax payments on time.

Part 3

Improving Your Business Operation

You have successfully jumped all the hurdles and your thrift store is open and running. As soon as you get done patting yourself on the back for a job well done, you will want to start thinking about ways to make your store stand out in the community. You can do that initially by offering good merchandise at excellent prices, but to sustain the sparkling first impression you have established means that you will have to maintain and improve the way you run your store.

In these chapters, lots of ideas and suggestions will be presented to help you keep your store stocked with the best merchandise and help you, as the owner, become well thought of in your community. The more improvements you make to your store and to your public image and standing in the area where your store is located, the more profitable your business will become.

Chapter 14

Extra Services for Customers and the Community

In This Chapter

- ◆ Offering giveaways
- ◆ Making deliveries when possible
- ◆ Providing meeting space
- ◆ Setting up fund-raising events
- ◆ Community service events and special programs
- ◆ Handling warranties and returns

Building a high-profile and successful business means that your store must contribute to the community where it is located and reach out to other areas of the city as well. It must also go the extra mile to ensure customer satisfaction.

If you are running a nonprofit store, you are already contributing to the charity your business supports, but spreading *good will* to other causes and other community projects will increase your customer base and the money earned by your store.

def•i•ni•tion

Good will is the reputation a business has in its community for service and customer satisfaction. It is so important that you will often see "Good Will" listed on a company's financial statements with a monetary value.

Good will is just as important to a store that operates for profit. In fact, it may be even more important because the store does not have the reputation for helping the community that is automatically attached to a business supporting a charitable cause.

Free Gifts

There is nothing that attracts attention to a business like offering something free. This will get your customers talking and recommending your store to their family and friends. If you post a sign in your store window, anyone who passes by will be tempted to come inside for the free gift.

There are many businesses where you can buy an item to use as a free gift, but try to avoid the most common gifts like pens, pencils, and key chains with the store's name, address, and phone number printed on them. However, having these on hand for customers to take all the time is a nice reminder they will have of you and your business.

Not for Resale

If you get free gifts from outside sources, check out the items and make sure they are safe and appropriate for your customers. Even though someone else is handing out the free gifts, that person and the gifts directly impact you and your store.

If you know people in other businesses that perform a service, you can set up an area in your store for them to give your customers a free sample. For example, people in the cosmetics business often give free samples of cologne or lipstick. They can also do complimentary makeovers or give out coupons for free makeovers at a future date.

Balloon animals are popular with kids and adults. Find someone adept at doing this and give him the chance to show off for your customers. This will provide a cute gift and amusement for your customers and gives the performer a chance to book some party dates.

The gift doesn't always have to be something tangible. People of all ages love magic shows, and magicians are always looking for bookings. Dazzling your customers with their amazing feats is a good way for them to promote themselves.

Your giveaway can also be a discount on purchases, but it is best to give a set amount as a discount rather than a percentage of the sale. If you can afford it, "buy one, get one free" is always a good offer.

No matter how you decide to structure the customer giveaway, you should try to advertise it across the city by using some of the ideas you reviewed in Chapter 10.

If you are not a nonprofit entity, you can contact other charitable organizations in your city and offer to give them some type of assistance. For example, an organization that helps children could be invited to your shop on a particular day and be allowed to select free clothing for the kids.

> **Helping Hands**
>
> A giveaway to an established charity benefits your store by attracting new customers. The added perk is that the charity will help you by advertising the give-a-way to its supporters.

Bring It to Them

Thrift stores that carry large items such as furniture and appliances would be smart to have a truck and people who can deliver those items at no charge to the customer. While the expense of owning and maintaining a vehicle and extra people to do the deliveries will reduce your profits, the service will help you increase your customer base.

The vehicle will benefit your store in a number of ways, as it can be used for pickups and to help out other businesses in your area. Also, a panel truck with the name, address, and phone number of your business painted on both sides of it is a constant source of free advertising for your store.

Your delivery people do not have to be employees of your store. You can usually find workers who will do it for a set fee per delivery. Such workers are considered contract labor and there are some tax reports and other paperwork that will have to be completed for them, but you will not have the added expense of payroll taxes or other employee expenses.

> **Not for Resale**
>
> Contract laborers or outside service people are required to give you Tax Identification Numbers, and you may be required to report the total amount paid to them to the IRS.

It may also be possible for your store to find delivery people with their own vehicles if your store can't afford the expense of a delivery truck.

If you have customers who are able to pick up the large items they purchase from your store, you might consider giving them a small discount on the sale.

Delivering goods to your customers is an additional service you can offer that will pay for itself with the smiles of satisfied customers.

After-Hours Services

If you have an extra room connected to your store or just extra space in it, you can provide meeting space for organizations in your area.

You can offer the meeting space free or charge a modest fee to cover the cost of utilities. There are many small groups who like the idea of meeting in a set location on a regular basis. This relieves the members of having to travel to each other's houses or meet in noisy places like restaurants.

If you own a thrift store that carries a particular type of merchandise, you can look for groups that have an interest in the goods you sell.

For example, if your shop carries books, you can host events like book signings. Although you are selling used books, authors with new books being released will bring their own to sell in your store and even give you a percentage of the sales. That's because promoting a new book is all about finding new readers. The added benefit is that those readers who come to see the author will probably purchase some of your used books, too.

> **Added Value**
>
> Thrift stores that specialize in nursery items can probably find small groups that are made up of young parents. A shop that carries youthful clothing styles can host student study groups.

No matter what your store sells, you can offer meeting space to outside groups. This is something you can advertise with a discreet sign inside your shop or in your store window.

There are, of course, some precautions that need to be taken when allowing outside groups to meet in your store, whether you are charging them a fee or not.

Here are some of the guidelines for providing meeting space:

- Set a realistic schedule of one or two meetings per week.
- Set a time limit on the length of the meetings.

- You or a staff member must be in the store the whole time the meeting is taking place.

- Depending on your merchandise, set rules for bringing in food and/or drinks.

- Have a contact person for each group.

- Avoid political and activist groups.

Reaching out to the community in this way can be beneficial to your business, but establishing rules and limitations such as those listed will protect you and your store.

Consider keeping your store open for customers during the meeting times, especially if the meetings are being held in an extra room.

You can close out your cash register at the regular time if the meeting is going be held after business hours, but keep some change on hand for sales that may occur before or after the meetings. Keep in mind that members of the group will be walking through your store, where they're apt to find something they need.

Support a Cause

Fund-raising events do not have to be limited to nonprofit thrift stores. Any business can host a fund-raising event.

Some restaurants, for example, allow charity groups to dine at a specific date and time and donate a percentage of the food sales to the organization.

The restaurant even provides flyers that the group can distribute throughout the city, inviting people to take part in the one-night fund-raising event. The flyers are then turned in to the restaurant as a way of identifying the diners who are there to support the charity.

A thrift store can host a shopping party for a charity. Like the restaurant, a percentage of the sales resulting from this one- or two-day event is then donated to the charity.

You can also attach your event to an annual charity drive. Think about donating a percentage of your sales to the Muscular Dystrophy Association while the telethon is taking place. You can even bring your donation to the local station and get some on-air time to present it on behalf of your thrift store.

If a local charity is hosting a fund-raising event, find out how you can help them. Sometimes helping is as easy as donating a prize for a raffle or allowing them to hang a sign or poster in your store window. Providing a service to any charity means that their supporters will hear about you and your business.

If your thrift store is located in a shopping center, get the other businesses in your center involved in your fund-raising efforts and they will help you attract more people to your store and their own.

Consider a multiple-location event that is based on an annual fund-raiser for a group of thrift stores in California. It is called a "Poker Run." Participants pay a fee to enter the event and are given a map and instructions to all the stores taking part in the Poker Run.

Depending on the distance between the stores, people can walk, ride, or drive to each location, where they select a playing card from different decks, and then return to the starting point. The entrants who have drawn the best poker hands win prizes.

With a little imagination and ingenuity, the Poker Run can be modified and structured to fit any area and any number of participating merchants.

Not for Resale

The key to hosting successful fund-raising events is not to go overboard with them. Be selective and don't burden your customers and the public in general with too many in any one month or year.

Be Generous

The holiday season provides many opportunities for a smart owner to cash in on some free publicity and provide much-needed services to the community. Here are some ideas:

◆ Become a drop-off place for Toys for Tots and your store will probably be listed in the advertising campaign that covers all areas of your town or city.

◆ Invite the Salvation Army people to station a volunteer and a kettle in front of your store during the holiday season.

Don't limit your community service efforts to the holidays alone. The needs of your area don't stop and start; they are there all year long:

◆ Collecting food donations for the Community Food Bank on a regular basis is always a nice gesture, especially if your thrift store is located in an upscale area where your customers can afford the donations.

♦ Contact the Girl Scouts, Boy Scouts, or schools in your area and offer to let them set up tables in your store or outside it to sell cookies or other items to earn money for special projects.

♦ Organize a prom promotion for low-income high school students. Gather and store all the fancy dresses donated to your store during the year. A month or so before the prom, invite the high school girls to your store to pick out a dress for a really low price. If possible, get some beauticians and cosmetic representatives in the store during the event to advise the girls on hairstyles and makeup.

♦ If you are in a cold climate, organize a collection for blankets and warm clothing for the homeless. All of these items are needed and can be donated to a shelter in your area.

Any of these ideas can generate more income for your shop by attracting the attention of new customers. However, the main purpose is to make your store stand out as one that cares about the community that supports it.

All the suggestions mentioned in this chapter are simply that: suggestions for activities that will improve the public image of your store. As you learned earlier, it is important that you go into the community and find out what the needs are, and then choose the ones your business can endorse and support.

Generating More Ideas

There are lots of ways to get new ideas that will help you service your customers and your community. Remember that ideas cannot be copyrighted, so if you read about one that worked for someone else, feel free to try it for your business.

Here are a few ideas for programs you can develop that can be used by nonprofit or for-profit thrift stores:

♦ Develop a program that can be brought to schools in your area or be presented in your store about the benefits of recycling. Give it a new twist by showing the students unusual items you have for sale and having them come up with ways the item could be used in someone's household. You can even invite the students to bring in odd pieces from their own homes to add to the fun.

♦ Create a program with an artist or craft person that demonstrates how to refashion items that might be considered trash. For example, old adult T-shirts can be remade into tiny shirts or other apparel for babies and toddlers.

◆ Instead of clothing drives, do a school supply drive for students in your area. Remember that with budget cuts teachers often have to spend their personal funds on supplies for their students.

Reading about other businesses is vital to the success of your own. The library is full of books that will provide you with tips for advertising and promoting your store.

Then there is that vast, never-ending, unlimited source of information called the Internet. No matter what type of store you own, if you do an Internet search for key words, you are likely to find thousands of references to look at.

> **Helping Hands**
>
> If you go online and do a search for fund-raising events, you will find over 58 million references for companies, ideas, and plans that can help you establish special programs.

The National Association of Resale and Thrift Shops is probably the largest organization for thrift store owners. The organization has a website and a newsletter. Even if you're not a member, you can access articles from the newsletter written by members who have shared their ideas for fund-raising and other services to the community.

The Association of Christian Thrift Stores also has a website and sponsors an annual conference and a preconference workshop for thrift store owners.

Another site, www.thriftstoreplanners.com, has a number of areas with helpful information for thrift stores.

The Internet can also tell you about local thrift store associations in your area. Search those out and determine whether joining the organization will benefit you and your business.

In other words, finding new and different ways to service your customers and your community is as easy as clicking a few keys on your computer or paying a visit to your local library.

Handling Complaints

Warranties and returns are services that have always been associated with retail outlets. In fact, some shoppers feel that a retailer's policy of standing behind the products it sells is one of the best reasons to do business with that company.

In the past, the resale industry was not expected to provide any such services to its customers. However, times are changing. As you learned in an earlier chapter, the news media is always quick to report a potential problem with a toy that contains lead-based paint or an infant seat that does not meet current safety requirements.

You know that you must visit the website of the Consumer Product Safety Commission (www.cpsc.gov) often and receive e-mail alerts from them. If you have sold an item that is reported to have a problem, the smart thing to do is take the product back and refund the price of that item to the customer, or issue a credit that the customer can use to purchase other merchandise in your store.

 **Not for Resale**

Unhappy customers usually complain to their family, neighbors, and friends, and that starts a word-of-mouth campaign that can damage your reputation and cause your store to lose sales.

Remember that another way to avoid problems is to inspect the items that come into your shop before adding them to your inventory. This is especially important when you receive electronics or small appliances. Test these items before offering them for sale. A customer is not going to think an electric can opener is a bargain if he or she gets it home and finds that it doesn't work.

As far as clothes, linens, and decorator items are concerned, dealing in used merchandise often means the items are damaged in some way. This happens in retail outlets as well, and you can take a tip from the way many of them handle the problem.

Retail stores often have special tables where flawed or damaged items are sold at a reduced price. People looking for bargains will often buy a shirt with buttons missing or tears in the fabric. This is especially true if the shirt is of good quality and the markdown is sufficient to warrant replacing the buttons or sewing up the rip in the fabric.

So receiving goods that are damaged in some way doesn't mean that you can't offer them for sale. However, the items must be clearly marked as defective and placed in a special area of your store. Lastly, the reduced price must reflect a good value for the customer.

The other thing you can do with any goods that are damaged or need repairs is to donate those items to a charitable agency, such as Goodwill Industries.

As you've just learned, there are exceptions to every rule, but you can post a prominent sign in your store advising customers that all sales are final. If you provide sales receipts, that phrase should be printed on those as well.

The most important thing to remember regarding warranties and returns is that you must keep an open mind and listen to the customers' complaints, no matter what their perception of the problem turns out to be. Sometimes a customer just wants to be heard, and if you are willing to listen that alone could solve the problem for them.

Do try to rectify any problems or complaints. It is an extra service that will keep your customers happy and your cash register ringing up sales.

The Least You Need to Know

- Offering special discounts and free gifts will attract new customers to your thrift store.

- Delivering large items to customers promotes good will.

- Allowing small groups to meet in your store can be a service to your community. Shopping parties that benefit a charity are easy events to host.

- Establish educational or fun programs that can be done in your store or taken to schools in your area.

- Look for national and local associations that can help you run your store more successfully.

- Keeping your customers happy is an important part of any business.

Chapter 15

Finding the Best Merchandise

In This Chapter

- ◆ Going to yard sales, estate sales, and swap meets
- ◆ Attending going-out-of-business sales
- ◆ Establishing residential pick-ups
- ◆ Acquiring contents from storage units
- ◆ Utilizing drop-off boxes

As a thrift store owner you will constantly be on the lookout for merchandise for your business. Even a nonprofit entity may occasionally have to seek out items from other sources when donations are slow or sparse. Customers don't want to come into your shop and see empty shelves or racks.

While you may already have a list of places where resale items can be obtained, this chapter will give you some insights on getting the best deals and developing relationships that will make you a welcome visitor at any place where resale merchandise can be found.

Short Sales

Yard sales are held in lots of places other than people's yards. They can be in garages, parking lots, church halls, or other public buildings. They can be renamed rummage sales or white elephant sales. The term is now used loosely to describe any sale that offers items gathered from people's homes and included in a sale that only lasts one or two days.

Many church groups hold rummage sales as fund-raising events for causes sponsored by their parishioners. One of the reasons a sale sponsored by a church or other organization is so good is because the assembled merchandise is generally priced very low. Often the people pricing the merchandise have no idea of the true value of the items they are handling, making these sales a virtual gold mine for the thrift store owners. It's no wonder that the owners usually line up waiting to inspect the merchandise earlier than the advertised time for the sale to begin. The owners are all hoping to find one of those hidden gems among the piles of household goods and other items offered as rummage or white elephants.

One of the great things about a group event is that merchandise comes from so many different donors that the variety of goods is unlimited. Remember that many of these sales held by churches and other organizations occur on a regular basis, and often the same people donate their time to sell the goods. Consider the Friends of the Library that hold sales of used books every few months. If you have a special interest in books, you should think about joining the group and becoming part of the sale committee. You will make new friends, promote your shop, and get an advanced look at the books before they are offered to the public.

Experienced thrift store dealers bring their own baskets, boxes, or other containers to fill up at these large group sales. This allows them to move quickly through the sales area and scoop up any items they think they can sell at a profit in their shops. If you've ever been on the other side of one of these sales as a volunteer selling the goods, you know that the owners will also come up to you and ask, "How much for everything I've got in this box?" or "I'll give you $20 for what's in this basket." When people are selling things for 10 and 20 cents an item, $20 sounds pretty good and some owners make a very good deal for themselves.

Added Value

Any container that you bring to a sale should be one that allows the goods you put into it to be seen by the sellers, such as a laundry basket or a shallow box.

Sales at individual residences or a sale held by all the residents of a community such as a mobile home park or condo complex are usually not so apt to make a thrift store owner such a wonderful deal. That's because this type of seller tends to have some emotional attachment to some of the goods being sold. For example, consider an old army relic that a man's wife may have put on the sale table. The husband doesn't really want to part with it unless he thinks the buyer is offering a fair price. This doesn't mean you can't offer this person less than what the item is priced at; it just means you can't make your offer so low that the person feels insulted and refuses to sell it to you at all.

While you need to consider the feelings of any person you are trying to make a deal with, it is especially important to make friends with people who are not accustomed to selling their personal possessions. There are a number of underlying reasons that prompt people to put the things they once purchased or got for gifts on sale. Consider some of the following reasons why people hold yard sales:

♦ Moving to smaller quarters

♦ Making room for a new addition to the family

♦ Making room for a parent or sibling who needs help

♦ Trying to organize their households

♦ Needing the money for living expenses that can be generated by selling their personal items

All of these reasons have some emotional baggage attached to the sale of the items. Even a person who is just trying to rid his or her house of clutter may have special feelings about specific items.

An individual that you are purchasing goods from should receive the same courtesy and consideration that you extend to the customers who come into your shop. Everyone you meet has the potential of becoming one of your customers.

If your shop is located in an area with a mild climate, you will find yard sales to check out every weekend. If you reside in an area that has months of snow and ice, most of the

Not for Resale _____

When at a sale run by the owner of the goods, never utter disparaging remarks about the items. If you don't like what you see, simply thank the seller and leave. You never know when you might return to this seller and make a nice buy.

sales will be held in the warmer months. For dealers in those areas, you have to make the most of good weather and, like the squirrels, accumulate merchandise and store it away for the winter months.

Dealing with the Heirs

Most estate sales are held indoors, so they are not affected by the weather. Generally, they are held at the home of the previous owner or at an indoor facility owned by a relative or an agent who is handling the sale.

Sales advertised as estate sales may not always be true sales of a deceased person's possessions. The term has become associated with sales that offer better-quality merchandise because of the notion that items were still in use and would not be on sale if the owner had not died. However, sales designated as estate sales are always worth checking out because they often offer smaller lots of merchandise and sometimes contain wonderful buys for your shop. If the heirs are present, they could have some emotional attachment to the goods being sold at an estate sale, but many do not even attend the sale, leaving it up to an agent or broker to take care of it for them. Those who do attend or run the sale themselves have probably already gone through the deceased relative's possessions and taken what they liked before the sale.

Estate sales can also yield true antiques, and if you find an item that you think is old enough to be an antique at a good price, by all means buy it. This assumes that the item is in resalable condition. If you acquire it at a good price, you will probably not have any trouble making a nice profit on it, either by selling it in your shop or selling it to another dealer regardless of whether it is a true antique or not. While on the subject of estate sales and antiques, if you have customers who come into your shop looking for antiques, take down their names and numbers in the event you acquire an item they are interested in buying. This list of potential buyers for specific items can mean a quick resale and profit for your shop.

Not for Resale

Find a reputable dealer to appraise jewelry or other items you purchase at estate sales to determine their true value.

One of the common items you find at estate sales, in addition to furniture and household goods, is jewelry. Again, the jewelry may or may not be of real value, but if a piece is attractive and in good condition, it can be easily resold. While it is rare that diamonds will pass as rhinestones, it does happen. A resale shop in Arizona sold a ring that needed cleaning for $2.50 that turned out to be worth several thousand dollars.

Even real diamonds can occasionally lose their luster when not properly cleaned and stored.

Estate sales often prompt auctions, and if you are quick with figures, you can do well at an auction. Keep in mind that the bidding at an auction is often fast and furious, so if you can't think on your feet about the value of an item and how much you could resell it for, leave the auctions to others who enjoy the excitement and frenzy.

Added Value

Most auctions allow potential bidders to examine the goods before the auction starts, allowing you to determine whether you want to stay around for the bidding.

A Mix of Merchandise

Swap meets have evolved from places where individuals come to sell unwanted items to outdoor, and sometimes indoor, retail malls. Oh, there are still people with card tables selling odd dishes, linens, and clothing, but today more and more retailers have set up booths at swap meets to sell new merchandise.

Many dealers position themselves at the entrances to swap meet facilities and flag down sellers with used furniture or other items they are looking for as the sellers drive onto the swap meet property. For the sellers, it's a chance to make a quick sale of unwanted items. For the buyers, it's a chance to acquire merchandise without having to walk through all the booths and tables searching for it.

Swap meets in general can be fun and a way to find some genuine treasures for your store, but they are much more time consuming than visiting a place where all the used items are assembled in one place for viewing and selling. If you have staff to run your store while you hunt for merchandise, swap meets are okay, but consider your time and how valuable it is to you and your business.

Helping Hands

Swap meets may be a good place for nonprofit entities to sell donated items that are not good enough to display in their thrift stores, but still have some resale value.

Distressed Sellers

There are a number of retailers that purchase merchandise from manufacturers or other retail dealers who are about to file bankruptcy. If you have advance information on a business that is in financial trouble, you can make contact and find out if any of the merchandise will fit your needs and if the price is low enough to allow you to resell the goods at a profit.

Once the bankruptcy has been filed, a judge or referee is assigned to sell the merchandise of the debtor and the money is then distributed to the creditors. This may still allow you as a buyer to purchase merchandise at a reduced price. However, this is one of the primary ways dollar stores and other deep discount stores obtain their merchandise, and they buy in large lots. So a small shop may not have the resources to purchase large quantities of goods. Also, unless the bankrupt business is another thrift store, the items received from buying bankrupt stock will be new.

Not for Resale

Bankruptcy laws prohibit debtors from selling or transferring valuable assets in order to protect them from the bankruptcy court rulings. So proceed with caution when purchasing items from a distressed seller.

If you have a special interest in collectibles, furniture, or decorator items, checking out bankruptcy sales may allow you to acquire some unique items at low prices. Sometimes the stock of a bankrupt company is sold at auction, but the sale method depends on what it is and how much there is of it. It's a good idea to belong to a merchants' association in your area because advance news of other stores that are on the verge of financial collapse is usually circulated through these associations, and you may be able to purchase items before the bankruptcy.

While buying stock from a distressed business may be helpful, it is the individuals filing for bankruptcy that will be more likely to have the type of merchandise you need for your store. Non-businesspeople who file for bankruptcy are allowed to keep the necessities they require to live and start over again. They are not allowed to keep items that are considered luxuries, like excessive amounts of jewelry, electronic equipment, more than one television set, and various other items that the court decides to sell to pay off the individual's debts. Again, a bankruptcy referee is assigned to sell all the excess items, and thrift store owners often purchase these used items. Bankruptcies are a matter of public record. So if you are interested in obtaining merchandise for your store from financially distressed individuals, you can access information on recent bankruptcy filings by reading your daily newspaper. You should also become familiar with individuals and companies that handle the sales of items bankruptcy filers must give up.

Closings and Closeouts

The big difference between merchandise from a business that is going bankrupt and a business that is simply closing down or discontinuing certain merchandise is that bankruptcies are often secret until the day of the court appearance. Businesses that are closing generally advertise that fact and hold going-out-of-business sales.

Again, most of the merchandise obtained in closing-down or closing-out sales will be new, but no one says you can't mix new merchandise in with the used items. For example, you may want to buy some of the Christmas decorations and other holiday items from a business that is closing and keep them stored until the next Yuletide rolls around. You can then use those items for a special holiday event to draw more customers into your shop.

The thing to remember about going-out-of-business sales is that they can last a long time, and initially the discounts offered on the store's merchandise may not be good enough for a thrift store owner to purchase. As a thrift store owner, you always have to keep your eye on the profit margin and only take on items that will allow you to make a decent amount when they are resold.

So when a store that has merchandise you would like for your shop is going out of business, it's best to bide your time and wait for the final days before purchasing anything. Of course, if the store is individually owned rather than a large chain establishment, you can approach the owner in advance and try to make a good deal for the items you want to purchase.

> ### Helping Hands
>
> If your store supports individuals who need clothing, you may be able to make a big purchase from a store that's going out of business at a small price for the needy clients of your charity, or get the store to donate the clothes it is unable to sell before closing.

Unless a store operated by a large chain is closing down all of its stores, the prices on store closures in your area may not be all that good. That's because whatever the chain store in your area doesn't sell can be shipped to the remaining stores that are staying open in other parts of the country.

After-Sale Services

If your thrift store owns a vehicle or you have a personal vehicle that can be used for picking up merchandise, you will probably find many opportunities to acquire items that have not sold at yard sales or estate sales. Just as making deliveries to your customer is a nice added service you can offer, letting your community know that you are willing to haul away any items left after a sale is a smart way to add to your store's inventory.

When you visit a sale, whether you purchase anything or not, you can arrange to pick up unsold items at a specific time. If the people running the sale don't want to do a prearranged pick-up, you can leave your business card and tell them to call you if you they decide to accept your offer.

Granted, you may end up picking up a pile of junk, but there may be enough saleable items to make it worth your while. Even if there are not, you will be providing a service to the community at large and your neighbors in particular, and that will keep you and your store in a favorable light.

Not for Resale

Be sure to use the safety precautions outlined in Chapter 12 when picking up unsold items from people you do not know personally.

By visiting a sale first, you will have an idea of what is available, so if you don't see any items that could be resold in your store, you don't have to offer your after-sale pick-up service. If you only see one or two items with good resale value, you can purchase them on your initial visit and again do not offer the after-sale pick-up service.

The longer you visit sales in general, the more practiced you will become at spotting good values among the items that will not be profitable to acquire.

Abandoned Goods

In Chapter 12, much was written about the hazards of sorting through boxes and containers abandoned in storage facilities. However, despite the potential problems that handling these goods can present, it is an excellent way to obtain merchandise of all kinds for your thrift store.

There are people who earn a living by acquiring the contents of storage lockers and reselling them. Some do not have a thrift store, but take a chance on finding items that can be resold to dealers or on the ever-popular eBay site. Before you decide to use this method to obtain merchandise, you will have to do some research of storage facilities in your area.

Here are some of the questions you need to ask of the people or companies that operate storage facilities:

◆ What is the monthly rental fee?

◆ Do they have restrictions on what can be stored in their lockers?

◆ Does their contract clearly state when the contents of the locker will be considered abandoned?

◆ In addition to the back fees owed on the lockers, are there other fees charged to people claiming the abandoned contents?

Obviously, some of these questions are to protect you in the event that you take possession of items that the owners return to claim at a future date. It's a good idea to establish a relationship with any storage facility you are interested in working with. Perhaps you can make arrangements for them to call you when a locker or space has been abandoned.

Storage facilities can be a lucrative source of merchandise for your thrift store. Many lockers contain furniture as well as clothing, household items, bicycles, appliances, and electronic equipment. Depending on where you are located, competition to obtain these abandoned lockers can be fierce.

There have been reports of frightening and bizarre items that were found in abandoned storage lockers. The best way to avoid a real problem is to clean out a locker only when the storage facility has office staff or security on duty in the event you need assistance.

> **Added Value**
>
> You can call companies that construct storage facilities and find out when and where new ones are being built to establish a relationship as a vendor before a new site opens.

Unattended Donations

If you are a nonprofit thrift store that depends on donations to stock your store, you should consider having a donation drop-off box somewhere on your premises. A regular thrift store could also benefit from a drop-off donation box, if it is properly promoted. Many people wanting to dispose of unwanted items want a convenient location where they can drop off the items at any time of the day or night.

Red warning lights should now be flashing in your mind. It's true unattended drop-off boxes can be a source of problems. As mentioned in the safe-handling chapter, there's no way to stop people from dumping trash into the box. The best way to discourage people from doing this is to keep the box in a well-lit, well-traveled area, but that is not always possible.

Another safeguard is to make sure the opening is not large like those on city trash containers and that it has some type of safety latch to prevent children or animals from getting inside it. Of course, people will still bring large items and place them outside the box, so wherever the box is located, it must be checked on a daily basis.

There are companies that rent donation drop-off boxes, and you may want to rent one for a month or two to see what type of merchandise is deposited in the box. If you are not getting useful, resalable items, you can have the box removed from your premises.

In the western states, there is a company, CoolBox Portable Storage, that rents portable insulated containers. They also have containers that are air-conditioned, but obviously need an electrical outlet nearby in order for the air-conditioning to work. If you are located in a western warm-weather state like Arizona, California, or Nevada, you may want to check out this company's services and prices. Visit their website at www.getacoolbox.com.

Some thrift stores simply have a drop-off area where people can leave donated goods. If you plan on setting up such an area, it should be covered to protect furniture or other goods that can be damaged by rain when there are no staff people on hand to monitor the donations. These open areas are not advisable for stores located in colder climates, and keep in mind that items left in the drop-off area are at risk for theft or vandalism.

Now that you have read so many reasons why you shouldn't have unattended drop-off boxes or areas connected to your store, let's give you a reason for trying one or the other in your area. The cost to have a drop-off box is minimal and, despite the risks, there is a chance that you will obtain some valuable merchandise for your store. Remember that sorting through items in a drop-off box can be hazardous, so take the proper safety precautions.

As your store becomes established in your community, you will make many contacts and find different places to obtain good resale items.

The Least You Need to Know

◆ Group sales organized by churches and other organizations are a source for good resale items from a variety of households.

◆ Keep the following in mind: individuals who run yard sales are sometimes emotionally attached to the items they are selling; estate sales generally offer higher-quality items; and exploring swap meets can be very time-consuming.

◆ Bankruptcies are a matter of public record and are listed in the newspaper.

◆ Generally, only the last days of a going-out-of-business sale have deep discounts on the merchandise.

◆ Storage facilities are a good source of merchandise, but require advance planning and safety precautions.

◆ Drop-off boxes can be problematic, but sometimes yield valuable items.

Chapter 16

Determining the True Value of Resale Items

In This Chapter

- ◆ Discovering treasure
- ◆ Evaluating jewelry, books, and antiques
- ◆ Reviewing collectibles and dolls
- ◆ Working with appraisers, auctioneers, and dealers

In an earlier chapter, you learned about setting prices on the merchandise you are reselling in your thrift store. When you are dealing with the common items you will display on an ongoing basis, pricing is simply a matter of making sure you are providing a good value for the customer and factoring in a profit for yourself. This means that the goods are still in useful condition and the discounted price is substantially lower than the retail cost of the same items.

It is said that the value of an item is as much as a buyer is willing to pay for it. Keep that in mind as you review this chapter, because you are going to learn how to proceed when an extraordinary object falls into your hands. This chapter assumes that the piece has come to you anonymously and you don't know who it belonged to originally. Finders, keepers may be a motto you'd like to adopt, but honesty and integrity oblige you to return something of real value to its rightful owner if you know that it was not meant to be donated or sold to your store. If it's a gray area, use your own discretion.

Surprise Finds

Everyone is familiar with the red kettles that appear on street corners during the holiday season. Salvation Army volunteers, usually dressed like Santa, supervise the kettles and ring bells to alert people passing by. You know donations are simply dropped into the kettles and then the donor walks on. At the end of 2008 in Tucson, Arizona, the local Salvation Army center that supplies meals to the homeless was very low on funds and wondering if the people who depend on them for food would go hungry. Donations of all kinds were down, and that included the kettles with the street-corner Santas. Then, a few days before Christmas, several loose diamonds were found among the cash and change in one of the big red kettles. Of course, there was no way of knowing who had dropped the diamonds into the kettle or even if the person actually owned the donated jewels. The diamonds were sold and the Salvation Army food program was able to meet the need in the community and feed more homeless people than ever before.

Fortunately, charities often receive anonymous donations of exceptional value. It is also possible for thrift store owners who purchase merchandise at estate sales, auctions, swap meets, and other places to find a stunning surprise among the assorted clothing and household goods they have acquired. Such a marvelous find requires owners to plan ahead and be prepared to seek out professionals who will help them determine the true value of the item and handle the sale of it properly.

Let's face it: as an owner, you would not take a Van Gogh painting and hang it on the wall of your shop next to a paint-by-number work of art. You would find out the value of the Van Gogh and probably sell it through a qualified art dealer. Of course, before that could happen, you would have to know enough to recognize that the painting you acquired might be worth a good deal more than any of the other wall hangings in your shop.

Added Value

If you do not know a qualified art appraiser, you can contact the Appraiser's Association of America at www.appraisersassoc. org and fill out an online form to find a reputable one in your area.

If you don't know the difference between a Monet and a Picasso, you may want to consider doing some research or making friends with an art expert.

While most paintings are too large to get buried and overlooked in a box or other container, there are many smaller items that you may find as you sort through acquired merchandise. Let's take a look at some of the things you may come across that need to be researched and evaluated.

Gems of All Types

Necklaces, bracelets, pins, and rings are common items that thrift store owners acquire, either through donations or purchases. Most of this jewelry is of the costume variety, and while it may be attractive it is not worth a great deal of money.

But what if, like the Salvation Army, you came across a handful of diamonds or an emerald ring or a string of pearls? Before you put it on display in your jewelry case, you would want to know its true value. Even an uneducated eye can usually tell the difference between rhinestones and diamonds, a piece of green glass and an emerald, and plastic beads versus real pearls. So when you are sorting through jewelry, reserve a safe place where you can put any items that need further scrutiny.

A jewelry appraisal is the only sure way to know the actual value of precious stones and metals. That's because in every category of fine jewelry there are degrees of excellence. Often both an appraisal and a *lab certificate* are required to determine the value of gems.

def•i•ni•tion

A **lab certificate** is a grading report for gems that are not mounted in a setting.

Appraisals and lab certificates are both important reports used to place a value on gemstones, but they do not serve the same purpose. An appraisal can be done on any piece of jewelry whether it contains gems or not. A lab certificate documents precious stones and provides specific information about carat weight and dimensions as well as color and clarity grades. The lab report does not change unless the cut and/or appearance of the stone is altered. However, because the jewelry markets tend to fluctuate, the appraised value of jewelry can go up or down according to the current economic conditions.

Since you will be dealing with used items, it is recommended that you clean the jewelry before having it appraised. Removing built-up dirt and grime will help you determine the quality of the pieces and save the extra cost of the appraiser having to clean the jewelry. However, since you may be handling pieces that are both delicate and valuable, take heed of the following tips and warnings.

def·i·ni·tion

Real **scarabs** are beetles that the ancient Egyptians used as adornments because they believed the beetles to be a sign of good fortune. Colorful oval stones carved to represent the beetle are still used in jewelry today.

♦ Do not attempt to clean hair jewelry from the Victorian era; jewelry set with *scarabs*, butterflies, or other fragile materials; or jewelry with foil-backed stones.

♦ Do not clean antique jewelry with a patina finish.

♦ Clean jewelry pieces in a safe environment and use a small bowl that will catch any stones that may be dislodged during the cleaning process.

♦ Pearl strands, amber, jet, and ivory should only be cleaned by wiping carefully with a soft damp cloth.

♦ Clean gently by soaking in warm water with a little dishwashing liquid added, and then brush gently with a soft-bristled brush and rinse.

♦ Very dirty jewelry can be dipped in alcohol or sudsy household ammonia for a few minutes, then rinsed and wiped with a soft cloth.

♦ When in doubt, do not attempt to clean at all.

Small sonic or vibrating jewelry cleaning units sold for home use can be used to clean chains and other gold jewelry. The following is a list of some of the most common gemstones, with suggestions for cleaning them safely.

♦ Amber: Easily damaged by heat. Wipe or soak in soapy water. No sonic cleaning.

♦ Amethyst: Avoid strong heat and temperature changes. Soak in ammonia and brush. No sonic cleaning.

♦ Aquamarine: Acids can cause damage. Soak in ammonia and brush. Sonic clean cautiously.

♦ Cat's Eye: Sonic cleaning is okay.

♦ Coral: Organic material, soft and often dyed. Clean with soapy water and brush.

♦ Diamond: Soak in ammonia and brush.

♦ Emerald: Use extreme care. May be filled with oil or resins. Clean with soapy water and brush.

♦ Garnet: Sonic cleaning okay. Soak in ammonia and brush.

- Jade: Often has wax finish. Soak briefly in ammonia and brush.

- Lapis: May be dyed. Clean gently with soapy water and brush.

- Opals: Do not attempt to clean.

- Pearls: Clean gently with soapy water and brush.

- Quartz: Avoid strong heat and temperature changes. Soak in ammonia and brush.

- Ruby: Sonic cleaning okay. Soak in ammonia and brush.

- Sapphire: Sonic cleaning okay. Soak in ammonia and brush.

- Topaz: No sonic cleaning. Soak in ammonia and brush.

- Turquoise: No sonic cleaning. Soak in ammonia, rinse, and dry.

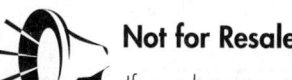

Not for Resale

If you have questions about cleaning any piece of jewelry, it is best to pay the extra cost and let the appraiser do the cleaning.

Like any business service you need, get recommendations from people you know and trust before handing valuable jewelry over to be appraised. If you can't get a recommendation, you can contact the National Association of Jewelry Appraisers (NAJA). Access their online directory to find a professional in your area by visiting the NAJA website at www.najaappraisers.com, or call at 718-896-1536.

When you get an appraisal, it should contain the following information:

- A cover document detailing what type of value is sought (market value, replacement value) and how the appraisal is to be used.

- The methods and resources used to place a value on the piece(s).

- A complete description of the piece(s) written so that the item(s) can be recognized with photographs.

- The date and location of the inspection and the effective date of the value.

- A statement by the appraiser that he or she has no financial interest in the piece(s) or that such interest is disclosed in the report. (In some cases a qualified appraiser may also be a dealer enlisted to help you sell the piece.)

- The appraiser's qualifications and signature.

Once you have established the value of the jewelry, you have several options you can use to sell it. You can use the services of a qualified jeweler, auction off the piece, or try selling it yourself to private parties or on eBay.

First-Edition Books

You learned earlier that the value of most used books is less than half of the original sale price printed on its cover.

Still, given their durability, books have always been passed from person to person and even from generation to generation. If you decide to carry books in your thrift store, you will undoubtedly handle many titles and sell them for low prices. If you are acquiring stock from donations, estate sales, and other types of sales, you will probably find boxes of books to sort and stock in your store. Paperback books have no special value, except to someone who wants to read them. However, the first edition of a hardcover book can be very valuable.

The first editions of classic books or those written by famous authors are the ones that collectors want to own and will pay sizeable prices to do so. If the book is signed by the author, the value increases substantially. So as you or one of your staff is sorting through hardcover books, take the time to open the books and look at the copyright page in the front for first editions. Finding even one in a thousand is usually worth the extra time it takes to examine the books.

The following phrases appear on the copyright page of a first edition:

- First Edition
- First Printing
- First Published
- Published
- First Impression

You may also find a series of numbers imprinted on the copyright page. Reading these numbers from left to right, the last number in the series is the print number. If that number is 1, the book is the first edition of that particular title. However, remember that even if the book is a first edition, it is only as valuable as the popularity and/or the prominence of its title or author.

Every book that is published has a first edition, and most are the only edition printed and not at all valuable. On the other hand, a second or third printing of a book signed by a famous author may have a much higher value than the price for which it was originally sold.

Let's assume that you have found a first edition written by a well-known author. The next thing to be considered is the ready availability of the book—or its scarcity. In the case of a best-selling author, millions of books are published and distributed and continue to be available through various channels for years, so the first edition price remains low. If the book is scarce, it is valuable, but how valuable depends on the condition of the book. If the book is damaged in some way, it will be worth considerably less than another in excellent condition.

Added Value

Guidelines explaining how specific publishers mark first editions can be found by visiting www.lazylionbooks.com/identifyingfirsts.

If you are interested in books and want to take the time to look for ones that have exceptional value, you should establish a relationship with a rare book dealer, who will either purchase the book outright from you or offer it for sale to his customers and take a commission on the sale of it.

Not for Resale

Get a written agreement outlining the terms between yourself and any dealers you engage to resell merchandise for you.

The following questions must be asked and answered before a rare book dealer can put a price on a book he or she is interested in acquiring or selling on your behalf:

- What is the current demand for the book? (This can vary depending on the demand and economics of a specific area.)

- What is the condition of the book?

- Is the book a first edition?

- Is the book signed by the author?

- How quickly have copies of this book sold in the past?

- How many copies of the book are currently on the market?

- How much money are all parties expecting to receive on the sale of the book?

Of course, like any special item you are hoping to sell, you can always bypass a dealer and attempt to resell the book yourself through the other avenues mentioned earlier. However, to do that you must research and answer the same questions the dealer would ask to determine the sale price of the book. Some of the information you need to gather is available on the Internet. There are many used and rare book dealers online that list their books and the prices of the books. You can also find a book appraiser to examine the book and set a value on it.

If you have more than a passing interest in books, you may want to subscribe to a magazine for book collectors. One of the most prominent is *Firsts*, and you can get more information about the publication by visiting their website at www.firsts.com. You will also find a list of books recommended for book collectors in Appendix A.

> **Added Value**
>
> One of the largest used book dealers online is AbeBooks. Visit www.abebooks.com to get a general idea of prices and the number of similar books on the market.

Examining the Old Stuff

You've already been advised not to specialize in antiques unless you have gained some knowledge and experience in that area. Of course, that doesn't mean that you shouldn't get as much as you can out a fortuitous find. Like a rare first edition, antiques that are in good condition are much more valuable than those that have flaws. Once again, you can find a qualified appraiser to put a value on any antiques you discover during the course of business, and that may be what you end up doing, but there are some preliminary steps you can take yourself before contacting an appraiser.

A close visual inspection of an object can detect any obvious signs of damage or wear and tear. If something is 100 years old or more, it's unreasonable to expect it to be in perfect condition, but the collectors who will pay the highest price for an object want it to be in mint or near-mint condition. The following suggestions for examining certain antique items will help you determine their condition:

> **Added Value**
>
> The Associated Antique Dealers of America have an online directory of qualified appraisers. Visit the association's website at www.antiquedealers.org.

- For china, glassware, and pottery, check for chips and cracks by carefully running your finger around all the edges.

- Tap ceramic items. They will emit a dull sound, rather than a nice ring, if they are cracked.

- Look for scratch marks from utensils on glass surfaces.

- Sick glass has a film on it. Wet the surface of the item to see if it is just dirty. After it dries, if the film reappears, it is "sick."

- Look for identifying porcelain marks on antique china from manufacturers like Lennox, Royal Copenhagen, and Limoges. A complete listing of markings and companies can be found online at www.antique-china-porcelain-collectibles. com/.

- Make sure all parts to an object are present and in good condition. Watch for a stopper that doesn't match the bottle it's in, or an odd cup or other piece in a set of china.

- For vintage clothing, make sure there are no stains, tears, or moth holes.

Another way to inspect antique items is the method used by many antique lovers, collectors, and dealers. Objects are examined under a long-wave *black light*. The ultraviolet light will detect flaws and repairs made to the item that are not visible otherwise.

The following is a list of things that will or will not show up on items inspected with a black light:

- Porcelain repairs will show up because modern paint and glue will glow under a black light.

- Cracks or other damage will show up on works of art under a black light.

- Old postcards, books, signs, and photos made before 1930 will not glow under a black light.

- Cloth objects containing modern fibers such as rayon and polyester will glow under a black light.

Testing items yourself will give you a pretty good idea of whether the objects are old enough to be antiques and whether they contain flaws or repairs that would diminish their value.

def•i•ni•tion

A **black light** or ultraviolet lamp emits electromagnetic radiation that causes objects to glow, but emits very little visible light.

Added Value

The Antiques Bible is an online reference that lists antiques by category. Access this valuable information by visiting www.antiques-bible.com.

There are many places where you can research the value of unusual or very old pieces. A list of reference books on a number of different antiques can be found in Appendix A of this book.

Dolls, Bears, and Ornaments

As you know, there are many categories of collectibles—and millions of people who acquire them. A collectible is not an antique, but that doesn't mean it won't garner a high price in the marketplace. Collections are sometimes donated to nonprofit thrift stores and acquired by regular thrift stores through estate sales and other sources. If you receive an entire collection of something, check out the value of the collection itself before you decide to sell the pieces individually. Again, there are many places online that will help you determine the value of a collection. And there are just as many places that will provide information on any single collectible items you obtain. There are also appraisers who specialize in collectibles.

> **Helping Hands**
>
> The International Society of Appraisers has an online form that will help find an appraiser in your area that specializes in the merchandise you need examined. Visit www.isa-appraisers.org, or call the society at 312-981-6778.

It's a good idea to familiarize yourself with the most popular brands of dolls, teddy bears, and ornaments that are sought after by collectors. The following is a list of manufacturers and items that people all over the world are willing to pay top dollar for:

- Boyds Bears
- Charming Tails
- Cherished Teddies
- D56 Villages, Snowbabies, and Snowbunnies
- Hallmark Ornaments
- Harmony Kingdom
- Hummels
- Longaberger
- Precious Moments
- Pocket Dragons

- Royal Doulton
- Walt Disney Classics

As you are sorting through merchandise for your store, keep an eye out for the above brands, and when you find one or even a collection of one of those brand names, put it aside for further consideration. Any collectible can be sold outright in your store or put aside to use for a special promotion of some kind. For example, Hallmark Ornaments can become the centerpieces of a Christmas sale.

Added Value _____

For more information on collectibles, visit Collectibles Database at www. collectiblesdatabase.com.

For Girls of All Ages

Dolls fall into the collectible category, but their place in the retail and resale markets is so huge, they really are in a classification all their own. While many are simply toys that little girls receive as gifts, many more are prized pieces in collections cherished by women of all ages. Perhaps it is the unlimited selection of dolls that makes them so appealing. From the simplest baby doll that is mass-produced to the one-of-a-kind dolls designed and created by famous celebrities, dolls can be a lucrative part of your thrift store offerings, and it is worth setting up a special place in your store to display them.

Again, it all starts with knowing which brands are most popular so they can be set aside for special handling. The following list contains the names of the most famous and popular collectible dolls:

- Adora
- American Girl
- Barbie and Ken
- Blythe
- Bratz
- Cabbage Patch
- Ginny
- Kewpie dolls

- Lee Middleton (creator and designer)

- Madame Alexander

- Robert Tonner (creator and designer)

- Strawberry Shortcake

Some of these brands, such as Ginny dolls and Kewpie dolls, are no longer being manufactured, which only makes them scarce and all the more valuable. Other dolls, like Barbie and Ken and Bratz, are still being mass-produced, but in a variety of styles that people continue to add to their collections. For these last two, they generally have to be still in the original packaging to have good resale value.

Robert Tonner is an award-winning doll maker and has created many famous dolls, such as Betsy McCall and Mary Endlebreit. As a fan of the power and might of super-heroes, he has also created a line of dolls called DC Stars, which appeal to boys as well as girls. Dolls by Robert Tonner sell for $60 to $200. So you can easily see how finding one of these dolls in good condition can result in a nice profit for your store.

Some valuable dolls are made of cloth, like the worry dolls that originated in Guatemala, based on the legend that little girls tell their worries to small dolls and then place them under the pillow so that by morning the little dolls would have taken all the worries away. These dolls usually come in sets of six with a cloth pouch where they can be kept to "sleep away worries" under a child's pillow. Some of these worry dolls are as inexpensive as $2 or $3, while others sell for more than $100. Again, finding a set of worry dolls can give your sales a boost.

Kachina dolls are usually carved out of wood, and each one represents a Native American dancer that—according to the tribes' folklore—has magical powers. To the Hopi and Zuni Indians of northern Arizona and New Mexico, the Kachinas are super-natural beings that help them in their everyday lives. The Kokopelli doll, for example, is the god of fertility.

Originally, these dolls were carved by the Native Americans, but now various doll designers and wood carvers are also creating them. If your store is located in the southwestern part of the country, Kachina dolls will be popular additions to your inventory. The price range for these dolls, depending on whether they are handcarved and authentically dressed, is between $20 and $2,800. Therefore, if you should acquire a Kachina doll, it is worth your time to research the doll and establish its value.

Added Value

A website that offers information and estimated values of all kinds of dolls is www.anythinggoesinc.net.

In general, most dolls in good condition have resale value, but it is the collectible dolls that you may acquire that should be researched and evaluated.

Selling Partners

Throughout this chapter, information has been given on ways you can determine the value of exceptional merchandise, as well as the options you have for selling the item(s). Information on appraisers and dealers has been provided, with professional organizations and associations that can help you locate a qualified person in your area. Selling items through auctions is another way to make a good profit on a valuable object you have acquired and do not want to sell in your store. You may go to auctions on a regular basis looking for general merchandise or a specific item for a customer. If you have a local auctioneer and place that you feel is reputable and fair, you can turn your exceptional items over to them to be included in their next auction. Be sure to establish the initial bidding price on the item so that you get the minimum price you desire.

> **Helping Hands**
>
> The National Auctioneers Association has an online form that you can complete and submit to receive recommendations for auctioneers in your area. Visit their website at www.auctioneers.org.

Another place you can go for information on appraisers, dealers, and auctioneers is your local Chamber of Commerce. While they probably won't recommend people, they should have a listing of the people and places that are doing business in your area. You can also talk to other thrift store owners and business associates, and get personal recommendations for people who can help you sell those treasures you find among the donations or general merchandise you purchase for your store. Establishing a good relationship with other local business people is good for you and good for them as well.

The Least You Need to Know

- Items of exceptional value should be put aside for further consideration. Remember that dirt and grime can conceal the true value of gems.

- When in doubt about cleaning gems, leave the job to a professional jeweler or appraiser. A lab certificate provides important information about gems.

- Use a black light to examine antique glassware, furniture, and other items to find hidden flaws.

◆ Look for the famous brand names on items in the collectible categories. Dolls of all types are in demand for collections.

◆ Contact professional membership organizations for recommendations for appraisers, auctioneers, and dealers.

Chapter 17

Your Place in the Community

In This Chapter

- ◆ Getting involved with community affairs
- ◆ Joining clubs and the Chamber of Commerce
- ◆ Utilizing tourist information centers
- ◆ Working with schools, churches, and other charitable groups

As you've learned, taking part in community affairs and hosting community events is a smart way to project a positive public image for yourself and your thrift store. At this point you may be thinking that there are not enough hours in the day to do everything that has been suggested in this book. Managers of nonprofit thrift stores will have staff members to help them run the store, giving them the extra time needed to do other work in the community. However, you also know it is even more important for the individuals running regular thrift stores to become known in the community in order to promote their businesses because they don't have the built-in support that a store supporting a charity can count on.

Keep in mind that making time to work in your community will help your store become successful, and therefore provide the extra income needed to hire employees to free up the time you need for any organizations you need to join. Working with organizations in your area also opens up the possibilities of hosting events on behalf of those groups that will again help the overall image and profitability of your store.

Support Community Projects

Every community has certain projects that the citizens of that area are working on. Some projects are as simple as installing a traffic light at a school crossing. Others—like creating a park, or building a school or a recreation center for seniors—require substantial funding. Look around your community and find out what people are trying to do to improve the area.

Getting involved even in a small way with a project that will improve your community is a good way to meet new people and show your neighbors that you are interested and concerned about the welfare of your area. Here are a few ways you can help without a big-time commitment:

◆ Offer free meeting space to the committee

◆ Put a poster in your window or flyers on your counter

◆ Make a donation to the cause

◆ Host a fund-raising event for the cause

Not for Resale

Avoid any projects that are political or controversial. This is especially important if your store is a nonprofit, tax-exempt corporation.

You have learned the value of doing some of these things in prior chapters. Remember that these are simple, standard ways you can help a cause. They can be utilized over and over again because they are things that are always needed and welcome, regardless of the project or the organization that is spearheading it.

Service Organizations

Most cities have a number of philanthropic organizations that need members to do the good works they sponsor. Joining the local chapter of an internationally known organization connects you with a high-profile group that generally has some members who are prominent in the area. Association with the group and the services it renders to the community will automatically give you a certain amount of prestige. Even if you are running a nonprofit thrift store, there are definite advantages to extending yourself to these other groups and supporting the work they do.

While there are many different organizations you can associate yourself and your store with, the ones we will look at have names that are instantly recognized and perform different services in the communities where they are located and in the world in general. Be aware that these organizations all have members that can help your business grow and prosper. This is the reason that banks, insurance companies, and other big businesses generally require their upper-level employees to join one or more of the following organizations.

Lions Clubs International

This club began in 1917 when Melvin Jones, a Chicago businessman, decided that local business clubs should expand their activities from purely professional concerns to programs that would improve their communities and the world at large. Jones's group, The Business Circle of Chicago, agreed, and an organizational meeting was held with other business groups. Later that year, a convention was held in Dallas, Texas, where the newly formed Lions Club created a constitution, bylaws, and a code of ethics and set forth objectives.

In 1925, Helen Keller spoke to the now international organization and challenged them to become "knights of the blind in the crusade against darkness." From then on, Lions Clubs have been servicing the blind and visually impaired. In addition to their aggressive SightFirst programs, the clubs also work with young people, work to improve the environment, build homes for the disabled, support diabetes education, conduct hearing programs, and through their foundation provide disaster relief around the world.

Membership in a Lions Club is by invitation, or you can start your own club. To join an existing club, simply find one in your area and call for meeting information. To start a new club, organize a group of friends or business associates and contact the Lions' membership team. The Lions have community clubs, cyberclubs that meet online, and special-interest clubs that can be based on your profession, a hobby, or anything else you care about.

The Lions have a number of different programs that may interest you, but it is their efforts in preventing blindness and helping the visually impaired that has brought them worldwide recognition. In 2004, when areas of Sri Lanka were devastated by a tsunami, more than 2.5 million people were displaced and thousands lost their eyeglasses and their ability to see clearly. Working together, Lions in Sri Lanka and Massachusetts collected more than 30,000 useable eyeglasses for the victims of the tsunami. The following is a list of visual services that Lions clubs provide:

♦ Recycling eyeglasses at 17 centers worldwide

♦ The support of Lions Eye Banks, which provide quality eye tissue for sight-saving surgeries, medical education, and eye research

♦ Screening the vision of hundreds of thousands of people every year

♦ Providing cataract surgeries and other eye-care services to those at risk of losing their sight

Your thrift store will probably accumulate eyeglasses on a regular basis. If you don't do anything else for the Lions Clubs, donate the used eyeglasses to be recycled.

Helping Hands
Your thrift store could set up and manage a donation center to collect used eyeglasses for a Lions Club in your area.

If the activities of the Lions Clubs International interest you, contact them for more information by visiting their website at www.lionsclubs.org. You can also write to the Lions Clubs International Headquarters, 300 West 22nd Street, Oak Brook, IL 60523 or call them at 630-575466.

Kiwanis International

The first Kiwanis Club was organized in Detroit, Michigan, in 1915. The original purpose of this Kiwanis Club was to promote the exchange of business between its members. While the first Detroit club was waiting for its state charter, some of the members distributed Christmas baskets to the poor. This caused division between the members, as some wanted to keep their focus on business concerns while others wanted to reach out and help the community. By 1919, the community service advocates won out.

Today, Kiwanis is international in scope and its mission is to save the world, one child and one community at a time.

If you are touched by the great need in the world to support children and young adults, joining a Kiwanis Club in your area will make you a part of this worldwide effort. The following objectives serve as a basis for the operations of all Kiwanis Clubs:

- Evaluating children's issues and community needs on an ongoing basis.

- Conducting service projects that respond to those needs.

- Maintaining a membership roster of businesspeople who have both the desire and the ability to serve their community.

In addition to attending weekly meetings, members assist the club's service projects. Most of these projects are motivated by the club's main program, titled Young Children, Priority One. This places an ongoing focus on the following global issues:

- Pediatric trauma

- Safety

- Child care

- Early development

- Infant health

- Nutrition

- Parenting skills

Kiwanis service projects can also address other community needs, such as stopping substance abuse, helping the elderly, promoting literacy, supporting youth sports and recreation, responding to disasters, and reaching out to help specific individuals in need.

The club's dedication to helping children develop into leaders has prompted the sponsorship of clubs for kids of all ages. K-Kids Clubs are for the elementary school level, Builders Clubs for middle school kids, Key Clubs for high school students, and Circle K Clubs for college students. There are also Aktion Clubs made up of mentally and physically disabled adults who are trained to perform community services.

The Kiwanis website says that a typical Kiwanis Club is a snapshot of the community, with members from all walks of life and at every step of the career ladder united in the work they do to benefit for the children and youth of their communities and the world. You can learn more about Kiwanis Clubs by visiting their website at www.kiwanis.org, or contact Kiwanis International, 3636 Woodview Trace, Indianapolis, IN 46268, or call 1-800-549-2647, ext. 411.

Helping Hands
Your thrift store may be able to help Kiwanis by collecting diapers or cans of formula for needy children.

Optimist International

By providing hope and positive vision, Optimists bring out the best in kids. Whether you are interested in joining an Optimist Club in your area or not, working to follow the creed of the members will help you run a business and your life in general.

Here are the things that a member of the Optimist Club promises to do:

♦ To be so strong that nothing can disturb your peace of mind.

♦ To talk health, happiness, and prosperity to every person you meet.

♦ To make all your friends feel that there is something in them.

♦ To look at the sunny side of everything and make your optimism come true.

♦ To think only of the best, to work only for the best, and to expect only the best.

♦ To be just as enthusiastic about the success of others as you are about your own.

♦ To forget the mistakes of the past and press on to the greater achievements of the future.

♦ To wear a cheerful countenance at all times and give every living creature you meet a smile.

♦ To give so much time to the improvement of yourself that you have no time to criticize others.

♦ To be too large for worry, too noble for anger, too strong for fear, and too happy to permit the presence of trouble.

While living by this creed can present huge challenges in your everyday life, it is well worth trying to follow. This emphasis on optimism goes back to the beginnings of this club that was started in 1911. This was a time of industrialization and *urbanization* that brought many new problems to society. The first official club was formed in Buffalo, New York, with the purpose of spreading a positive outlook on life.

def•i•ni•tion

Urbanization in the 1900s was the growth and development of cities that brought about significant lifestyle changes because of more people and more problems.

From the start, Optimist Clubs directed their efforts toward youth services. In 1923, the organization adopted the motto "Friend of the Delinquent Boy." However, these clubs also took their positive attitudes and resolve to make the world a better place into programs that helped the country during the war years and collected scrap metal and rubber. A club in Canada believing the children of war-torn countries could use a little cheer started the Chocolate Fund, which delivered more than two million bars of chocolate to British children. It was the only sweet these children knew during 10 years of fear and famine.

In the 1950s, Optimist Clubs learned of homeless boys sleeping on the streets and began the building of boys' homes throughout the country. In addition to reaching out to troubled youth, the Optimists created a program to honor and reward young people who are normally not publicly praised for their good deeds and accomplishments. Youth Appreciation Week began in 1955. Another significant program developed by the Optimists is the Childhood Cancer Campaign to establish awareness and support for children battling cancer. Other recent programs include the Optimist International Tournament of Champions for junior golfers and the Internet Safety Program to keep children educated and safe from predators.

If you join an Optimist Club in your area, you will share in the club's high hopes and expectations for the future. What better way to work toward a bright tomorrow than to prepare our youth to become productive, responsible members of society. To that end, Optimists conduct 65,000 community service projects each year, spending $78 million in their communities. It is believed that in any year six million kids are positively affected by the Optimist Clubs.

There is a lot more to learn about the Optimists and the programs they sponsor. If you're interested in this organization, visit their website at www.optimists.org. You can also contact them by phone at 1-800-500-8130, or by mail at Optimist International, 4494 Lindell Blvd., St. Louis, MO 63108.

Added Value

The Optimist philosophy for the future is one of their basic beliefs: to think only of the best, to work only for the best, and to expect only the best.

Rotary International

There are 33,000 Rotary Clubs in more than 200 countries, so wherever you are located, you should be able to find a Rotary Club to join and/or support. Rotary Clubs are nonpolitical, nonreligious, and open to all cultures, races, and creeds. The motto of the Rotary Club is "service above self"; their main objective is "service in the community, in the workplace, and throughout the world." As a thrift store owner you are already providing a needed service to your community, regardless of whether your store is run for profit or for a special cause.

More than 1.2 million businesspeople and community leaders are members of Rotary International, which provides humanitarian services, encourages high ethical standards in all vocations, and helps to build good will and peace in the world. The following is a list of the programs and service opportunities designed to help Rotarians meet the needs of their communities and people around the world:

♦ Global Networking Groups are open to all members and their spouses.

♦ Interact is a service organization for youth ages 14 to 18.

♦ Rotaract groups promote leadership, professional development, and service among young adults 18 to 30.

♦ Rotary Friendship Exchange encourages members and their families to make reciprocal visits to other countries, staying in each other's homes to learn about different cultures firsthand.

♦ Rotary Volunteers allow Rotarians and other skilled professionals to offer their services and experience to local and international humanitarian projects.

♦ Rotary Youth Exchange offers students ages 15 to 19 the chance to travel abroad for cultural exchanges of one week to a full academic year.

♦ World Community Service allows Rotary Clubs and districts from at least two countries to implement community service projects together.

As you can see by the different groups within Rotary, it is truly an international organization that supports the idea of people from different countries working together for the common good.

The Rotary Club of Chicago was formed in 1905 by Paul P. Harris and is considered the world's first service club. Harris, an attorney, started the club because he wanted to capture in a professional club the friendly spirit he had known in the small towns of his youth. The earliest meetings rotated among members' offices, and the name evolved from that practice.

As Rotary grew, expanding to six continents, the focus of the clubs changed from the professional and social interests of its members to servicing needy communities. The members pooled their resources and contributed their talents to this new purpose, based on a positive response to the following questions:

♦ Is it the truth?

♦ Is it fair to all concerned?

♦ Will it build good will and better friendships?

♦ Will it be beneficial to all concerned?

Like other service clubs, during the war years Rotary Clubs provided emergency relief to victims and called for a conference to promote international educational and cultural exchanges. This project has continued on through the years, as evidenced by the various cultural exchange groups listed previously. Through the years Rotarians have worked to meet society's changing needs, and currently sponsor programs that address issues such as environmental degradation, illiteracy, world hunger, and children at risk.

Professional people are welcomed into Rotary Clubs all over the world, and if you share an interest in the programs they sponsor or the cultural exchanges they provide, seek out a club in your area and become a member. If you would like more information, visit www.rotary.org. You can also write or call Rotary International at One Rotary Center, 1560 Sherman Avenue, Evanston, IL 60201 (847-866-3000).

Joining any one of these high-profile service-oriented clubs is a good way to service your community and establish valuable friendships with other business professionals. Interacting with the members of these organizations will probably help you as much as you will be helping others.

Added Value

An interesting event you could sponsor through your thrift store would be to have a Rotarian who has lived with a family in a foreign country speak about the experience and the cultural differences.

Connect with the Chamber

Most cities have a Chamber of Commerce; some even have more than one, depending on the ethnic makeup of the area. A Chamber of Commerce is not a government agency and does not receive public funding of any kind. This organization is supported by the membership dues paid by the businesses who realize the benefits of belonging to the Chamber in their area outweigh the costs of membership. A Chamber of Commerce is as strong as its members, and answers the needs of those members and all businesses in its locale by addressing the problems that could have an adverse affect on their operations. In addition, membership in the Chamber of Commerce can increase your store's visibility and exposure in the area.

The projects and accomplishments of a Chamber of Commerce vary with the area. Their efforts generally include the following:

◆ Sponsoring community events, such as fairs, rodeos, and health awareness seminars

◆ Lobbying for city and state laws to benefit business owners

◆ Establishing job training funds

◆ Working to establish viable public transportation

◆ Supporting measures to lower taxes on businesses and business property

◆ Establishing business expansion and retention programs

◆ Being available to answer questions and address the concerns of business owners

Depending on the area where your store is located, you should consider joining the Chamber of Commerce. Membership fees vary from city to city and state to state. Some chambers in large cities, like Chicago, have different levels of membership, with a tiered fee structure that allows businesses to choose how active they wish to be in the chamber's programs and decisions.

Becoming active in the Chamber of Commerce in your area is another way to make valuable contacts. Chamber programs are developed through member-run committees that work in the areas of community enhancement, political advocacy, governmental affairs, economic development, and member benefits. If these important issues are ones you would like to have a say in, contact your local Chamber of Commerce and join.

Tourist Information Centers

Although the tourist bureaus in your area are not organizations that businesses owners join, they are a valuable resource for some thrift stores. It is worth your time to go to the tourist information center in your town or city and introduce yourself and give them information about your store. Take along flyers or brochures that give your store's name and location and the type of merchandise that you carry. Believe it or not, people actually call these information centers and ask where they might find an inexpensive dress, coat, lamp, or a variety of other items. People also ask about obtaining souvenir items that represent the area, such as Kachina dolls made by Native American tribes. If your store stocks such items, that information should also be on your information sheets.

Tourist bureaus usually have a number of brochures on hand for people to take. Keep in mind that people who come to the centers for information are often new residents to the area. The tourist bureaus also place brochures at airports and other public places, and you may be able to get in on that, too. While this is not going to improve your image in the community, it could bring in some new customers.

Visit the Schools

If you have school-age children, getting involved in the parent/teachers association is a must. Schools always need help, and you will be performing a valuable service for your community and letting your children know their education is important to you.

In an earlier chapter, it was suggested that you prepare an educational program for the local schools on recycling, or anything else you can think of to present to students. Here's the upside of anything you do for a school: the teachers get to know you, other parents get to know you, and the parents who don't volunteer get to know you because their kids will tell them about you. In fact, other than the time commitment you must make to schools, there is no downside.

Remember that high school students can become regular customers of your thrift store. Volunteer for any activities you can handle, like chaperoning dances and trips, or as mentioned earlier, letting the students hold fund-raising events on your store's property.

Anything you do that helps kids helps their parents as well. Your dedication to the kids and the community will not go unnoticed.

> **Helping Hands**
>
> Put any extra donations or purchases of school supplies aside and hold a back-to-school sale at the end of summer.

Give Back to God

If you are an atheist who would never be associated with any type of church, don't read this section. If not, become active in the church of your choice. There's not a church on earth that doesn't need volunteers. Remember the St. Vincent de Paul Society discussed in Chapter 3? If you attend a Catholic church and are a thrift store owner, you are the perfect person to work with your church's St. Vincent de Paul conference.

Calls for help come into the St. Vincent de Paul conferences every day. Volunteers go out and make home visits to ascertain the exact needs of the clients. Many of those needs are things like clothes, linens, dishes, pots and pans, and other household items, and the St. Vincent de Paul thrift stores in the area may be too far away or not have what the client needs. You can offer the society workers discounts on the items they purchase for the clients or, depending on your situation, you can donate some things. So even if you don't have the time to become one of the conference members that makes visits, you will still be taking an active part in the organization and filling some of their needs.

Helping Hands
Since you are an expert in resale, you can organize a church rummage sale as a fundraiser. You will then get first look at all the items donated and be able to obtain stock for your store. You can also haul away all the leftovers.

Other churches have programs that you can take part in. Youth programs, help for the elderly, fundraising, and any schools connected to the church will be happy to have you work with them and for them. The important thing is to put yourself out there and let the parishioners know that you are a person they can count on.

Your religious affiliation makes no difference. Work for the church of your choice and give back to the community. Churches provide unlimited opportunities for doing charitable works, and at the same time, promoting your thrift store and yourself as a Good Samaritan.

Be a Philanthropist

Once you open yourself up to doing good works, you will have no problem finding groups that want and need your help. In fact, many of these charitable groups will seek you out. This is true even if you are a nonprofit entity supporting another cause, because that tells the other groups that you are a person who cares and your thrift store has been established to help others.

Think about the wonderful consequences of being known as a loving, caring person. You will have respect and admiration. Your thrift store will thrive, because people will want to support you because you are helping others. As mentioned in an earlier chapter, when you don the hat of a Good Samaritan, you will find others want to be associated with you and your good works. This often means simply shopping in your thrift store, and that is exactly why you go out into the community and connect yourself with a group or cause that is service oriented.

You may never have as much money as Bill Gates or Donald Trump, but you will be successful in business and in life. So when you open your thrift store, open your heart and mind to all the need that exists in the world and do your part to help out. Whether you work with one of the big international clubs or simply volunteer at a school, your efforts will be rewarded.

The Least You Need to Know

- Take part in community affairs that will improve your city or neighborhood. When you help kids, you help their parents, too.

- Study the international clubs and learn about the services they provide. Keep in mind that being a part of an international organization may require a good deal of time.

- Joining an international club will improve your image. International clubs have professional members that can help you as you help them.

- Local organizations work to improve business conditions.

- Give back to the church of your choice—you can always support more than one charity or group.

Part 4

Expanding Your Business

Success often means expansion, and given the great popularity and potential of thrift stores, moving up to a larger store or even opening a second or third store is a definite possibility.

These chapters present information that will help you decide when and how to deal with expansion. It is a move that must be carefully considered and timed right. Opening more stores means you will need more staff to run them and more merchandise to stock them. Suggestions for managing these and other issues connected to spreading out into other areas of the thrift business will also be presented.

Even if you don't want to move on to bigger things, you will find a lot of good advice and suggestions that can be used in your one and only store.

Chapter 18

Moving to a Larger Store

In This Chapter

- ◆ Knowing when to consider moving
- ◆ Determining what you need to move
- ◆ Realizing the advantages of a new store
- ◆ Taking customers with you

Moving on to a bigger space is not something that will happen overnight. As you have learned throughout this book, making your first store successful takes a lot of dedication and hard work. Unless you have staff to help you, it also means that you will have to put in a lot of hours to keep your store running smoothly, obtain new merchandise, and promote your business by establishing a good image in the community.

While doing all of these things may be time-consuming, they can also be enjoyable and rewarding. There is an old saying: If you want something done, ask a busy person. That's because people like those who run thrift stores take pleasure in being busy and productive. They are also dedicated to the causes they support, and are able to prioritize their jobs so that the most important things get done first.

Everyone knows that timing the moves you make in life is crucial to your success. In this chapter, you will learn how to determine when you are ready to move to a larger store and, more importantly, make sure that your current customers move right along with you.

Is It Time to Move On?

The first sign that you should consider moving to a larger space for your resale business is when you have too much and too little all at the same time. If you have too much merchandise and a lack of space to display it and store it, it's time to consider moving to a larger store. This assumes that your store is profitable and you have been able to hire people or schedule extra volunteers to fill in during the busiest times. Moving to a bigger store is not a decision that should be made hastily. There are ways you can cope with too much merchandise and too little display or storage space without the expense and work of moving.

You may be able to add storage space or expand your display area by using one or all of the following suggestions:

♦ Add more shelving to your display area

♦ Add more shelving to your storage area

♦ Add a storage building to your property

♦ Rent storage space

♦ Be more selective when acquiring new merchandise

♦ Remove large, slow-moving pieces from your display area to make room for faster-moving merchandise

♦ Rearrange and consolidate display and storage areas

♦ Have a sidewalk sale to move some of your merchandise outside for a while

Not for Resale

Sidewalk sales are only feasible if the weather is nice, and moving merchandise outside and then back inside at night can involve a lot of time and energy.

Some of these suggestions may work for you, others may not, depending on where your store is located. If you are renting space, you may not be able to add shelving to display areas or storage areas without prior approval from the landlord. There may not be room for an additional storage building on the property, and even if there is, you may not be able to get permission to erect another building. This is especially true if your store is located in a shopping mall. Also, a mall may rule out placing merchandise outside the confines of the store itself, so a sidewalk or mall walk sale may not be an option. However, some of the suggestions can solve the too little space problem, regardless of where your store is located or what restrictions your landlord has written into your lease.

Display Areas

You may be able to rearrange and consolidate the display and storage areas to make more efficient use of the space you have. There are actually people and companies you can hire to help you do this. Sometimes an objective eye and a different point of view can work wonders.

Removing large pieces from your display area can also work, provided your store carries larger merchandise like furniture and appliances. If it does and these items are real moneymakers, you may want to keep them and eliminate some other merchandise instead.

Lastly, you can stop acquiring merchandise until your stock is down to the point where everything fits again. If you are a nonprofit entity, this will not work well because you do not want to turn donors away. People who support your cause will keep bringing items to you, and if you stop taking them, you are taking the risk that they will never bring you anything again.

For the owner of a regular thrift store, the risk is that you will miss out on some lucrative items to sell. While you will not miss what you have never seen, some of the resources that you buy from on an ongoing basis may tell you what you have missed and stop calling you when good items become available.

Finding More Storage Space

You can always rent storage space. In fact, those same storage facilities with abandoned lockers that you clean out to obtain merchandise may have rental space available. You can also add a storage building to your backyard, if you have one. The downside of using a storage facility that is not adjacent to your store is that some merchandise will not be immediately available when and if a customer requests it. It will also necessitate moving the merchandise to and from the store and then to and from the storage building when it is needed.

If none of these suggestions work and you, your staff, and your customers are tripping over each other, moving to a larger store may seem like the only solution. If you have business partners, their views and opinions must be in line with yours before further steps are taken. If your business is incorporated, you will also have to bring the matter before your board of directors for approval. Of course, one of the first questions your partners and the board will ask is, do you have the funds to do it? So before you run out and start looking at other locations, everyone involved will have to take a long hard look at the store's financial reports.

Added Value

Any valuable merchandise stored in rented space should be insured for loss or damage. Talk to your insurance agent to see if your policy covers merchandise not stored on your property.

Financial Requirements

If you are using an outside accounting firm to do your books, it's a good idea to discuss your desire to move to a bigger store with the person who keeps your books. Your accountant can go over your current financial situation with you and tell you if you can afford a move and if you will be able to handle the added expenses that you will have to assume with a larger facility. Most of this boils down to the profitability of your current store.

If you are doing your own books, you will have to look back on the financial reports for the last year and determine your financial status for yourself, analyzing the profit margin yourself or with your partners and the board members of your corporation.

Here are the items you need to pay particular attention to when studying your financial reports:

- The balance in your checking account
- The balance in your savings account
- The value of your assets
- Your current liabilities
- The payments due on your liabilities each month
- The total of expenses for each month
- The amount of profit you make each month
- The increase in profits from month to month

Take at least six months' worth of financial reports, add the amounts on your reports for those six months for each of the listed items, and divide that amount by six to get an average per month. You do this because the monthly amounts can fluctuate from month to month, and you want a total amount for each that accurately reflects six months' worth of data. The whole idea for averaging these categories is to see if the net worth of your business and the profitability are sustained and increasing.

Let's look at the store's net worth first. Add the bank balances to the store's other assets and subtract the amount of all the liabilities. Your liabilities include any amounts you owe, including payroll taxes. If the value of the store's assets is more than the store's liabilities, you have a net worth. If the liabilities are more than the assets, you need to stay in your existing store until those liabilities are paid off or paid down enough that your store has a net worth. If you have a savings account with money in it, you are moving in the right direction, but may not be ready to move into a larger store.

> **Not for Resale**
>
> If the average amount you come up with for an asset or profit category is a minus figure, forget about moving at this time and try to make one of the space saving suggestions work.

Ongoing Profits

If your store has a net worth, move on to the bank balances, liability payments, and expenses. Add the balances in checking and savings, and subtract the expense total. Your expenses include rent, utilities, supplies, payroll and payroll taxes, and any other expenses that have been paid out over the last six months, like repairs or advertising expenses. Then subtract the amount of the total liability payments. Study the following sample to make sure you are doing this correctly.

Average Checking Account Balance	6,000
Average Savings Account Balance	1,000
	7,000
Average Monthly Expenses	–4,000
	3,000
Average Liability Payments	–1,200
Average Excess Profits	1,800

As you can see from the example, this store was able to pay all its bills and liabilities for the last six months and had money left over. That is good, but is it enough to consider moving the store to a larger location, where the expenses will probably be more than the current store? No. That's because although the store is profitable, making a profit that is $1,800 a month more than its liability payments and expenses, it is not making enough money to take on the extra costs of moving. If the bottom line was an amount great enough to cover all the current payments for at least three months, it would sustain the business during and after the move.

Added Value

The conservative approach is presented here to help you avoid financial problems, but always seek competent financial advice before making a final decision.

Keep in mind that moving to a new location often means reduced profits for the first few months, but the monthly bills and payments will not be reduced. You never want to jeopardize your livelihood or profitability by making a move without sufficient funds. It is possible based on the above example to get a bank loan to cover the move. But before you apply for a loan, you need to do some research and acquire more information.

Take the time to go out and look for another, larger location for your store. Once you have actually found a place, ask yourself the following financial questions:

- Is the new store large enough for continued growth?

- Could the rent be easily paid based on the old store's profits for the last six months?

- Are there extra fees or expenses that have to be paid before moving into this new store?

- Could the payments on a new bank loan liability be made without a problem at least for the first three months?

If you can answer yes to all of the above questions, and have a good credit rating and the collateral to secure a bank loan, moving may be a good option for you and your store. Again, seek counsel from trusted financial advisors.

Staffing Considerations

Staffing a larger store will probably not be problematic for a nonprofit corporation. In fact, the move will have had the support of the board as well as the other supporters of the charity your store funds. The board may have also approved the move of a regular thrift store, but since volunteers are not part of the package, some thought needs to be centered on employees.

First of all, if you have employees who have been working at the smaller store, you should have consulted them about the move. Not that they have a vote in whether to move or not, but they will have to decide if they want to move with you and the store to the new location. If you are moving to a space in the same area, the employees will probably not mind moving with you. However, if you are moving to the other side of town, you may lose an employee whose residence is near the old store.

> ### Helping Hands
>
> If you have valued employees or volunteers without transportation, try to make arrangements for them by setting up a car pool, or getting schedules for convenient public transportation.

Hopefully, you have picked a new location that is easily accessible via public transportation. That could be a big factor in the case of an employee who does not drive or have a car available. It could also be a factor in whether or not your customers follow you, but more on that later. For now, consider the possibility that you will have to either hire additional staff to run a larger store, or replace the staff you had helping you in the old store.

Since you already know hiring procedures and such, just think about whether the larger store could be run efficiently with your current staff. If it can, there is no problem. However, if it is much larger, you may need more help, not only to run the store, but to fill in for you while you are out finding additional merchandise to fill up the larger store. Even if you have been juggling excess merchandise for months before the move, with the extra room to display it and store it you must plan ahead for replacing it as it sells.

So before you open the doors to the new store, make sure you have enough competent people to run it. After all, a larger store will also hold more customers and you want to give them the same excellent service the customers at your old shop received.

Good Things About a New Space

While space may have been your biggest consideration in choosing a new location, hopefully you remembered all the reasons you chose the last location and made sure those amenities were attached to this new place. That includes adequate parking for the customers and a nice, stable neighborhood where everyone will feel safe and comfortable. Another thing you would have considered again is the amount of foot traffic and vehicle traffic that passes by the new store.

Added Value

Your new location is an opportunity to establish new relationships. Do that by attending meetings, visiting schools offering pickups, and doing all the other things you did to get established in the old location.

Perhaps one of the best things about being able to move into a larger store is that you are now experienced in all aspects of the thrift store business. You know where to get the best merchandise. You have learned how to set up your store and display the items attractively. If you are in an area with a different economic structure, you may want to adjust your prices to suit the neighborhood, but that's no problem because you know how to set prices that are fair and reasonable. You also know how to handle any special merchandise that comes your way so that you realize the most profit from it.

Your storage area in the new store is larger and better organized so that you can put your hands on any item stored there that a customer requests. All in all, the advantages of moving into a new store are many, and you have the experience and knowledge to make the most of them.

They Will Follow You

There are many ways you can ensure that you don't lose good customers when you move your store to a bigger location. If you have remained in the same area, they will probably just start coming into the new store to shop. Of course, you will have to give them plenty of advance notice of the move. In addition, you will have to update all your advertising materials. If you have a website, make sure to put a notice on the site that tells visitors where you are moving to and exactly when the old store will close and the new one will open.

Having a moving sale before leaving the old location is a good idea; having a grand opening for the new location is an even better idea. Again, now that you know the most effective ways to advertise and the type of events your new store can host, you will have no problem keeping the old customers and attracting new ones.

Your image in the community should be firmly established; your associates in the groups you have chosen to work with will help you spread the word about your new store, and even pitch in and help with any opening events you are planning. Starting over in a new, larger store can be even more exciting for you than opening your first store was. You will be mixing the old with the new, and at the same time facing new challenges and responsibilities.

As you know, thrift stores can have a distinct advantage over retail stores, where each one seems to have the exact same merchandise. Even if you travel across the country, you will find the chain stores offer the same things you can buy in the one near your home. The merchandise in thrift stores has variety and often has one-of-a-kind items that can't be easily found elsewhere. When you open your new store, remember that and display the unusual items prominently. Remember that many older resale items can be the source of lovely memories for both your new customers and the old friends who have followed you to your new location.

> **Helping Hands**
>
> While you're making new friends, do something for the old friends who supported the first store—a small gift or special discount will work.

The Least You Need to Know

- ◆ A lack of space is a good reason to consider moving to a larger store. Before giving up on the old store, try to make changes to free up more space.

- ◆ Your financial status has to be better than good to make a move feasible. Average your income and expenses for at least six months to get an accurate financial picture.

- ◆ Make sure your new location has all the customer conveniences of the old.

- ◆ Try to retain volunteers and employees in the move.

- ◆ Give your old customers plenty of advance notice about the move.

Chapter 19

Opening Additional Stores

In This Chapter

♦ Obtaining community support

♦ Evaluating financial and personal considerations

♦ Working with management and staff

♦ Finding a second location

♦ Stocking the shelves

Owning more than one store doubles, triples, or quadruples your work and responsibilities, but this is often the goal for people who are part of the resale industry. This is especially true of a nonprofit organization running a thrift store to support a cause. That's because the nonprofit entity usually finds that their original plan has to be expanded in order to keep answering all the related, underlying needs of the people they have sworn to help. This is evident by the histories of all the charitable groups and international organizations mentioned in prior chapters. Each of these nonprofit groups started out small supporting one cause, only to find that the one cause fostered other causes and greater needs, which led them to become international in size and scope.

If you are running a nonprofit thrift store, opening new stores might be a little easier because your corporation has supporters and volunteers who will assume some of the work and responsibilities with you. In this chapter, you will study the history and accomplishments of a nonprofit corporation that will serve as a model for expansion. Although a thrift store that supports an owner rather than a charitable cause may have to hire people to do some of the work, the advice and suggestions in this chapter will help that owner attain his or her goals for expansion.

A Worthy Cause

In the fall of 1979, Dr. Douglas Tustin and other community leaders formed a steering committee to examine the possibility of creating a hospice program in Placerville, California. In 1981, using an old hospital building for patients and administrative offices, a team of five volunteers serviced 26 patients in the hospice program called Snowline.

def•i•ni•tion

Respite visits are made to families caring for a terminally ill member to give the family a short break from the stress and strain of caring for the patient.

By the following year, The Friends of Hospice was in place. This group of women and men raised funds to support Snowline Hospice, which provided nursing, *respite visits*, limited chaplain and physician visits, and bereavement counseling for the family. Because their funds were limited, all staff members volunteered their time, even the on-call nurses, who were available for the patients 24 hours a day.

While donations were received from other hospitals, an informal group of women known as The Tea Group began working to raise additional funds to expand the hospice services. They created the Light A Life Holiday Tree Program, where lights on a holiday tree are lit in memory of loved ones. A box lunch program and an annual crab dinner were also added to the fund-raising activities.

As the number of people serviced by the Snowline Hospice grew, the need for additional services became apparent. Camp Harmony, a family grief camp, was established. The camp combines the study of nature's cycle of life and death with growth and the healing process. Snowline Hospice also began a pet visitation program, P.A.W.S. (Pooches and Warm Smooches). Volunteers and their trained pets made patient visits. Physicians have noted that dogs can lessen anxiety, alleviate depression, and enhance the healing process. Pets can often reach people when human relationships falter.

Despite funding from some major donors, the need for a permanent ongoing source of income prompted the supporters to open a thrift store in Placerville that sold general merchandise, and another nearby store that only sold furniture. To get these stores started, volunteers were stationed at the store locations weeks before they opened, accepting donations to stock the stores. These same volunteers were responsible for getting the first stores operational. After two months, a manager was hired to take over the running of the first general merchandise store and her first recommendation was that the store needed to move to a larger location.

The runaway success of the thrift stores gave Snowline a predictable source of funds. Shortly after the stores opened, Snowline Hospice was licensed as a hospice Medicare provider, allowing it to expand services again. Now, in addition to the nurses, physicians, chaplain, and respite volunteers, medical social workers, home health aides, and contract therapists were added to the team. With this licensure, Snowline was also able to provide patients with all their medications, durable medical equipment, and supplies.

Snowline is a prime example of a charitable organization that started out with one goal in mind—to provide hospice care—which evolved into a multitude of other services for the terminally ill and their families. Today, much of its funding comes from multiple thrift stores that are run by managers and staffed by volunteers. As a nonprofit organization, Snowline had the support of many people in the community, and that enabled it to open its first stores and eventually expand into the five stores that currently provide funds for the many services it provides.

> **Helping Hands**
>
> Offering a brand-new service that is needed in your community generally attracts many people to your organization who are willing and able to help you reach your goals.

Look to the Future

The decision to open a second or third store mainly depends on the level of success you have reached with your existing stores. If it has become all that you want it to be and then some, you may be ready to take everything you've learned and use it to create another store. Keep in mind, the two stores should not be treated like a pair of identical twins, but like fraternal twins. They will be alike in a number of ways, sharing many of the same qualities, but will still be different enough to be unique.

In the last chapter, you learned how to examine your finances to determine whether it was feasible for you to move to a larger store. That same type of financial analysis is necessary when you are considering the challenge of opening additional thrift stores. Here are a few guidelines to help you decide if expanding into multiple stores is a practical idea:

- Your profit margin is sufficient to bear the cost of opening and setting up another store.

- Your financial status is strong enough to obtain a bank loan if it is necessary to fund the opening of another store.

- There are areas of your city that don't have thrift stores.

- You see the need in your area for a thrift store that carries merchandise other than what you currently offer.

- You have an abundance of goods that could be transferred to a new store.

- You have people, employees, volunteers, or family members you can count on to help you with all the work necessary to open a new store.

- You are certain that opening an additional store will not put a financial strain on your existing store.

- You are certain that opening an additional store will not jeopardize your personal health and well-being.

Your financial assessment should also be based on the number of customers your first store is serving. Is your customer base growing at a steady rate? Are the values you offer on the goods you sell and the services you provide keeping your customers loyal to your store? Are your customers bringing in friends and relatives to shop in your store? If you can answer yes to these questions, the next question is: will you be able to sustain all of this in another store?

Added Value

Understanding what you do well in your existing store will help you establish additional stores that provide the same values and services.

If you have established your first store as a business that is respected in the community and you have worked to earn a good public image for yourself, your new thrift store will probably be enthusiastically welcomed. As soon as you decide that an additional store is what you want, begin putting the word out. Hopefully, you have continued to use all the promotional avenues available to you, like direct mailings, newsletters, and an Internet presence.

As you are aware, expanding your business is like starting over again. However, this new venture will benefit from everything you have learned from starting and running your first store. You can be cautiously optimistic and proceed as you did the first time, with careful concern and consideration for all the decisions that must be made.

Who Will Run It?

Since it is impossible for one person to be in two places at the same time, it is imperative that you have competent people to run the first store while you establish the second location. The second store needs your time and attention because, as noted above, there will be many tasks to perform and decisions to make that only you or one of your business partners can handle. Once the second store is open and running, it will probably still need your personal attention until it is established and turning a profit.

If you have business partners or family members to help you with the stores, you won't have to go out into the world looking for someone else. Again, a nonprofit organization will have volunteers and supporters like the ones who helped Snowline Hospice establish its stores. If you are not a nonprofit store and don't have partners and relatives you can trust to run your first store while you organize the second one, you will have to look for dependable help even before you look for a second location.

You have been all through the procedures for hiring employees, and the rules and regulations are the same for any person you hire regardless of the level of responsibility this person will assume. What is different is the fact that you probably won't have much time to work alongside this person to make sure that you have made a good choice and have hired someone you can trust to run your business.

 **Not for Resale**

No totally new employee should be left alone to run your business. If you can't be there yourself, assign another staff member or volunteer to work with the new hire.

There is a theory that says to test your management personnel you should go on vacation for at least two weeks. When you return, if your business is still running as well as it would with you present, your management is solid. If the thought of leaving your current employees or volunteers in charge while you go on vacation fills you with dread, it's a sign that you need to get more competent help.

Delegating authority may be difficult for you to do, but if your business is ready for expansion, it is something you will have to learn how to do. In Chapter 21 you will find some good suggestions on how to monitor managers and others who will assume some of your responsibilities. For now, remember that you must look for a person who will adopt your business philosophies and want to meet your expectations.

You will need a person with good people skills to service your customers. That person must also have the ability to understand the resale industry and the unique sales potential it offers. It won't hurt if the manager you hire also has a flair for displaying merchandise and the patience to deal with donors and vendors.

Finding and training the right person to run your existing store so that you have the time necessary to look for a new location and establish a new business in it may take some time. You also have to allow for a training period so that you can be certain the new hire is capable of all that you are entrusting to him or her. So before you rush out and find a new location, take whatever time is needed to make sure your current store won't suffer from your absence.

Where Will It Be?

Perhaps you have already found the perfect location for opening another store. If so, you should have already considered a number of things that will make this location work well for your new store. Because this is your second store, it is more important than ever to find a location that will fulfill all your needs. If you have not found the perfect location, start looking with the following things in mind:

- A location zoned for your type of business

- A location far enough from the existing location that it does not draw customers away from the first store

- A location that has all the amenities, such as good visibility and ample parking

- A location that is in a good area, but can be rented for a monthly fee you can afford

- A location that will not require costly remodeling to make it work

- A location where the population density is sufficient for the customer base you want to establish there

- A location that fits in with the image you have established for your first store and want to maintain in the new store

- A location that is served by public transportation

- A location with competitors nearby that will help to attract customers

- A location where vendors and your delivery trucks will have easy access

Buying a Building

Another option is to purchase property where your new store can be located. This option was not really discussed for your first store, as it generally requires a large cash outlay for a down payment. Renting space for a brand-new business venture is recommended because if it doesn't work for some reason, you can walk away from it easier. For example, one of the stores Snowline Hospice opened did not succeed because the overhead was greater than the profits. This can happen with any new business, but the success of the other Snowline Hospice thrift stores demonstrates that it is not a common occurrence in the resale industry. However, the fact that you have a track record in establishing one successful thrift store will make lenders more open to financing a mortgage on a second store if you are fortunate enough to find one that has all the components listed above.

> **Added Value**
>
> Don't forget the tax advantages of purchasing property that will allow you to deduct depreciation on the asset over a number of years.

Getting a Mortgage Loan

Purchasing property will probably entail shopping for a lender, and this may require that you prepare a business plan. Here are some elements of a good business plan:

- Executive Summary: objectives, mission, keys to success

- Company Summary: ownership, history, locations

- Products and Services: descriptions, sources

- Market Analysis Summary: target markets, trends, growth, industry analysis, main competitors

- Strategy: pricing, promotion, sales, sales forecasts

- Web Plan Summary: marketing strategy

- Management Summary: organization structure, management team, and personnel plan

◆ Financial Plan: financial indicators; break-even analysis; projected profit and loss, cash flow, balance sheet

If you don't feel you have the ability to write a business plan that will make lenders fight over who is going to give you money to purchase property, there are professionals that can be hired to write the plan for you. There are also many sample business plans you can access on the Internet. For information on a book that will guide you through the process, see Appendix A.

> ### Helping Hands
>
> A business plan template approved by many banks and the Small Business Administration can be downloaded as a pdf file by visiting www.bplans.com/ business_plans_template.

Since you have been through the process already, you know all the expenses that opening a new store requires. There are signs to install, furniture and fixtures to purchase, utility bills, and another advertising campaign for the grand opening. Even if you don't purchase property, you may need additional funds for any or all of these expenses related to your new store, and a business loan may be necessary to help you handle the initial costs.

Empty Shelves and Display Areas

One of the reasons you want to open an additional store may be because you have an abundance of merchandise and know you will be able to stock it well initially. If you do not have enough goods to stock an additional store, you will have to look at ways to acquire the extra merchandise you need.

Once you have decided on a location for your new store, you may want to advertise for donations and follow the lead of the Snowline Hospice thrift stores. As mentioned earlier, Snowline stationed a volunteer staff at the new location to accept donations for that store. Remember that this procedure can accomplish two things: it helps fill up the empty spaces at the new store and it serves as an introduction to the people in that area for the new store.

Once the new store is open, you will have to be able to gather enough stock to keep the shelves and display areas of all your stores filled with merchandise. This is another reason that you have to find competent people to work with you. Either they have to manage the store while you're out finding merchandise, or they have to know how to acquire the best merchandise for the least amount of money, or they have to know how to charm people into donating goods for the new store.

Of course, you can also take consignments or do trade-ins following the procedures presented in the next chapter. This allows you to obtain more merchandise with no up-front costs or very low costs to your business. Again, this requires more paperwork, but once you begin taking consignments, it's really a process that will sell itself to your customers and their families and friends.

As you add new locations, you really want to define your business model and create your stores as brand names. The woman in Tucson, Arizona, who opened one store to provide low-cost clothing to students on a budget now has stores all across the country. Her business grew and prospered because she gave it a definite focus and purpose that made it synonymous with trendy clothes at great prices. If your first store has already earned a reputation for specialty items, service to the community, or just exceptional values, you can carry that over to any store added to your business plan. You can also keep the basic structure you have created for your first store and modify it a little to make the additional stores stand out on their own.

Added Value

If your first store specializes in nursery items, your new store can move up to specialize in apparel for school-age kids.

Remember that at the very least, your second, third, or fourth store will have to live up to the reputation of the first store. At the same time, it will also have to offer some unique goods or services not found at the first store. The beauty of that is that customers will want to frequent all your stores to avail themselves of the different items each provides.

Lastly, before you make a final decision to expand your business, consult your board of directors and seek competent legal and financial advice. As you learned in Part 1 of this book, the key to success is research and proper, careful planning.

The Least You Need to Know

- Your image and reputation in the community will support plans to expand. In-depth analysis of your finances will be necessary to determine your growth potential.

- Consider the effect on your personal time and energy that opening and running another store will have.

- Good, dependable employees and staff must be in place in order to expand.

◆ The location for a second store requires even more research than your first one did.

◆ To purchase property, you probably need a lender and a business plan.

◆ A second store will require twice as much merchandise to stock it than the first store.

Chapter 20

Growing with Consignments or Exchange Credits

In This Chapter

- ◆ Establishing sales agreements
- ◆ Setting prices for consignment pieces
- ◆ Keeping reliable consignment records
- ◆ Exchange credits, trade-ins, ledger cards, and postings
- ◆ Determining credit amounts

Owning more than one store means that you have to acquire that much more merchandise. No matter how creative you are, filling up a lot of empty space in a store can be difficult. The other problem is that running multiple stores can take up a lot of time. Even if you have competent managers in place, you still have to supervise the managers and make sure that each business is operating properly. That means you will have less time to be out and about seeking merchandise, even though you need more of it. So now may be the time to start taking items on consignment, and it may also be the time to start an exchange credit program in your stores.

In this chapter, you will learn how to accept and sell merchandise on *consignment* and how to set up a system for exchange credits. Both will result in your obtaining more merchandise to sell, and both will allow you to get that merchandise with little or no up-front costs.

def•i•ni•tion

Consignment is the process of offering goods for sale through a broker or store for a prearranged fee to be collected by the seller when and if the goods are purchased by a third party.

Put It In Writing

There are many resale businesses that receive all their merchandise from people who want to sell their personal property but don't want to go through the hassle of placing an ad in the newspaper and dealing with potential buyers. That's also why there are real estate agents, auctioneers, and general brokers who sell other people's property for a fee. Sometimes these sellers require an up-front fee, but mostly they work on a commission basis. When they sell the house, car, furniture, jewelry, or other item, they receive a percentage of the sale price or a prearranged fee from the owner of the property.

For a thrift store, this is a way to obtain merchandise without having to pay for it when it is received. The owner of the property is entrusting it to the store in hopes that it will be sold. The owner of the thrift store is also hoping that the property will be sold so that he or she can collect a commission on the sale. While this sounds like a simple enough arrangement, there are issues that must be addressed to avoid problems.

Since the consignment item must have substantial value in order for the owner and the dealer to make a profit on the sale, the first issue is who is responsible in the event the item is lost or stolen. The location of the property may determine that. If you have a consignment item in your store that is damaged or stolen before you can sell it, a claim may have to be made to the insurance company that carries your theft and liability coverage. However, in some instances, insurance against loss or damage may remain the responsibility of the property's owner. This is especially true with very valuable items like

Not for Resale

Check the owner's insurance policy to be sure the item(s) will still be covered when in your possession.

antiques and jewelry that have an appraised value and are specifically listed on the owner's insurance policy. The important thing to remember is that this issue must be worked out before the property is transferred to your store.

Another issue that must be discussed and agreed upon before the consignment merchandise is taken into your possession is the sales price and the commission you will receive for selling the property. If it sounds like you need a signed agreement or contract before accepting consignments to offer for sale in your store, you're right. This document does not have to be a long, complicated legal agreement, but it does have to stipulate the following items:

- Names and addresses of all parties

- Description of the consignment item(s)

- The sale price of the item(s)

- The amount of the commission or fee to be paid to the seller upon the completion of the sale

- Information on insurance coverage on the item(s)

- The date the agreement goes into effect and the date it ends

- A cancellation clause

Obviously, the names and addresses of all parties have to be listed on the agreement as well as a description of the property that is being consigned to you. The projected sale price of the property can be a set amount, but it may be better for all concerned to establish a price range instead. This gives both parties some flexibility in negotiating a sale and allows you as the seller to reduce the price if buyers are passing on it because they feel it is too expensive. The price range clause also eliminates the need to redo the agreement if the original price is adjusted to meet the changes in the current market for that type of item.

As the seller, your commission will be collected on the amount received for the property. Therefore, it is only natural that you will strive to sell it for the higher end of the price range. On the other hand, if the item is gathering dust in your shop, you will have the option of selling it at the lower end of the price range rather than exercising the cancellation clause in your agreement.

 **Added Value**

When setting a price range on a consignment item, both parties must agree on the lowest amount that will be accepted when the property is sold.

The starting date of any agreement is the date it is signed by both parties. It is not necessary to have an ending date, but it may be beneficial to include one or specify a time frame for the agreement to be in effect. The agreement can always be renewed with a simple addendum, but this gives both parties an automatic out if the consigned property has not been sold by the time the contract expires. If a time limit is set on the sale of the property, then a cancellation clause is not needed. If no time limit is set, including the cancellation clause gives both parties the option of changing their minds. Usually a cancellation clause requires that either party give the other a written notice to end the agreement.

Although you can make up an agreement yourself, you may want to have an attorney do it for you to make sure all the issues are covered. This would involve a one-time fee to the lawyer making up the basic agreement, and once you have it, you can make copies and use it for as long as you need it, and as many times as necessary.

The paperwork involved in accepting consignment items is necessary, but once your agreement is drawn up, it becomes a simple procedure. Obtaining additional merchandise for no up-front costs is beneficial in a number of ways. You can pick and choose the merchandise you accept. You can also continue to sell all the goods you have gathered through other sources and simply use the consignment items to fill in any empty spaces in your store. It can also provide the variety that makes customers come in on a regular basis to see what new items you have added to your inventory.

Both Sides of the Sales Price

Before the consignment agreement can be completed and the item placed on sale in your shop, you and the property owner must agree on the asking price for the consignment piece. If you are dealing with an exceptionally valuable object, the owner should provide you with an appraisal to verify its value. However, most of the time you will be handling items that are in good condition, but are not priceless treasures. As you learned in Chapter 16, something that valuable requires a dealer that is an expert in that type of merchandise.

It is also possible that you will receive a group of items from one seller, such as a collection or an entire household of furniture. In the case of a collection, you and the owner must decide whether the collection is to be sold as one item or if it can be broken down into smaller lots. Sometimes collections cannot be split up, but often parts of the collection can be sold separately. As for furniture, an entire bedroom set will generally bring a higher price overall than the individual pieces would bring if sold separately.

The owner of the consignment piece probably already has a specific amount in mind for the item. If you agree with that amount or think it should be priced higher, there's no problem. Unfortunately, most of the time the owner's ideal price is higher than what you, as a dealer, know is realistic. Here is where your knowledge and experience in the marketplace comes into play. Most sellers will listen to you and go along with your recommendations if they are presented coolly and logically and backed up with

Helping Hands
Supporters of nonprofit thrift stores often leave collections of books or coins to the charity. It is generally wise to turn these collections over to a qualified dealer who can determine whether to sell them as is or break them up into smaller lots.

facts and figures. The more you deal in consignment pieces, the more adept you will become at negotiating the right prices for the merchandise you take into your store. After all, pricing an item too high will only mean it remains on a shelf or on your display floor until your agreement with the owner expires or is cancelled.

If your store specializes in a particular type of item, you may want to limit your consignment business to that specialty. Your interest in that category of merchandise will undoubtedly make you an expert in it and allow you to price the consignment pieces fairly and honestly.

You have already learned about a number of resources that you can consult when determining the value of goods. Research and your own experience will guide you accurately when setting prices on consignment items. Keep in mind that pricing the merchandise fairly will enable you to sell it and collect your fee or commission on the sale. You are getting the merchandise with no up-front cost, but in order to be profitable in this area of the resale business, you cannot waste your time and floor space displaying items that are overpriced and will never yield any income for your store.

Speaking about your income, when you set the fee for selling the consignment item, make sure the amount you are going to realize on the sale of the merchandise is sufficient to cover your expenses. Your fee or the percentage you charge for selling the merchandise can vary, depending on the item or items being sold. You can adjust your fee for items that require special handling, delivery, or advertising. You can also make provisions for these extra expenses when you make up the consignment agreement by stipulating that they will be paid by the owner, either in advance or when the item is sold.

Vendor Cards and Price Tags

Like everything involving money or potential income, dealing in consignments requires paperwork. You already know that you need a signed agreement with the owner of the consignment item. That agreement should be set up in a folder and filed alphabetically by the owner's last name. Keep those files in a fireproof cabinet or other secure location. In addition to this signed contract, you should set up an index card that can be easily accessed on every owner. Assign a number or some other identifying code to the owner and the property consigned to your store. If you are going to keep records of these cards in your computer system, you will have to use numbers that the system can recognize to access the individual cards or print out a report of all the cards in the system.

The following is a sample you can use to set up a card for your consignment vendors.

Name: George Moreno   **ID# 1001**

Address: **Commission**:
3235 E. Hay St.   20%
El Cajon, CA 92020

Phone: 619-555-5555

Consignment Item(s):   **Price**:

1-Walnut Table & Chairs $500.00

1-Lazy Boy Recliner   200.00

_____

_____

_____

Added Value

If you are charging different consignment fees on property belonging to the same seller, you may want to make up a separate card with a different ID number for each item to avoid confusion.

This same information can be entered into the computer on a vendor card. However, it is a good idea to keep 3×5 cards in a file box at the service counter in your store. You can make any special notations on the card. The price tags on the consigned items displayed in your store should contain the ID number assigned to the consigner, along with the price of the item. When an item is sold, simply scratch it off the card or mark it sold, with the date it was purchased. You can also write in any additional consignment items taken from that owner. Keeping accurate, easy-to-access records on all consigners and consignment items will help you avoid problems and errors.

Once a consigned item is sold, you can issue a check to the owner. The check will be for the net amount—that is, the sales price less the commission and any other expenses assigned to the owner in the consignment agreement. If you are handling a lot of consignment sales, you may want to establish a procedure where checks to the owners are only issued once a month. This will save you time and allow you to combine sales amounts for items for the same owner that were sold at different times of the month. If you are going to adopt this procedure, it should be mentioned in the original consignment agreement.

The simplest way to handle the checks written to consigners and the income derived from consignment sales is to add the following accounts to your bookkeeping system:

1. Consignments Payable in the Liability section of the Balance Sheet accounts

2. Commissions Earned in the Income section of the Profit and Loss accounts

Assume that your store has sold the walnut table and chairs posted on the vendor card for George Moreno. The transactions resulting from this sale would be posted as follows:

Account#	Account Title	Debit	Credit
2050	Consignment Payable		$400.00
4020	Commission Earned		100.00
1000	Cash in Checking	$500.00	
	Totals	500.00	500.00

You collected $500 and deposited that amount in your checking account. Your commission on the sale is 20 percent, or $100. That is your income on the sale. The balance of $400 is going to be paid out to George Moreno and is therefore posted to the liability account. That's because the $400 you collected on Moreno's behalf is not income for your store.

When the check is issued to George Moreno, that transaction would be posted as follows.

Account#	Account Title	Debit	Credit
1000	Cash in Checking		$400.00
2050	Consignment Payable	$400.00	

This entry clears the liability account of the dollar amount owed to the consigner and records the check written from your bank account.

Remember that one of the most important things about keeping consignment records is that they have to be updated every time a transaction occurs.

Merchandise for Trade or Credit

Another method that can be used to receive new merchandise is to establish a system for allowing customers to bring in items that you carry in your store. This works well for clothing, books, entertainment media, and merchandise for the nursery. It can be managed for larger items, if you desire to do that, but obviously larger merchandise may require special handling.

In Chapter 2, you learned about a clothing store that catered to college students. This store allows the students to bring in their used clothing and exchange it for store merchandise or credit. This is often called a trade-in policy because customers actually trade what they don't want or need for what they do want or need. Some businesses with an exchange system also pay cash outright to the customer for the merchandise they turn in to the store. Whether you do that or not is up to you. Just be aware that on-the-spot purchases require a good knowledge of the items being offered so that you can quickly determine how much to pay for the merchandise in order to resell it at a profit.

The following guidelines for accepting merchandise from customers will help you establish criteria for running a trade-in or exchange program in your store:

- Items should be in good condition
- Items should be currently marketable
- Items should not cause your store to be overstocked with that item

All of the above are necessary to turn a profit on most of the items you take in under the exchange or trade-in program. You can probably be a little more flexible with clothing exchanges, but if you already have 20 copies of a specific book that is not a bestseller, you are wise to pass on any additional copies of that title. Of course, you must be tactful and courteous so that the customer is not offended.

Bookkeeping Chores

Once again, accurate record keeping is crucial to the success of an exchange program. Many trade-ins and exchanges may work out to be even amounts. If you are doing an outright purchase of merchandise, you take the items and pay the customer on the spot, completing the transaction. This is posted into your accounting system the same way as any other purchase you make.

The record keeping comes in when you are offering credits to the customer in exchange for the merchandise he or she is turning in to your store.

Let's assume a customer brings in books, clothing, or other items you stock in your store and you agree to give the customer $50 in credit for those items. At this point, you would fill out a ledger card on the customer either by hand or in your computer system. The following sample is a suggestion of how that card would be completed.

Name: Sally Smith	ID# 5208		
Address: 10 N. First St. Tucson, AZ 85712			
Phone: 520-555-5555			
Date	**Debit**	**Credit**	**Balance**
10-2-10 25 books		$50.00	–$50.00

Now let's assume the customer does not take out any merchandise on that date, but returns the next week and purchases books.

The customer's ledger card would be updated as follows.

Name: Sally Smith		ID# 5208	

Address:
10 N. First St.
Tucson, AZ 85712

Phone: 520-555-5555

Date	Debit	Credit	Balance
10-2-10 25 books		$50.0050.00	
10-9-10 4 books	$20.00		−30.00

Added Value

The added advantage to keeping records on all exchanges is that it also provides you with the information needed to compile a mailing list of your customers.

Even if the customer does an even exchange the first time he or she comes into your shop, it is wise to fill out a ledger card anyway. That's because these customers usually become regulars to your shop and will not always do even exchanges.

As far as your bookkeeping system is concerned, to post exchange credits properly you will have to add a liability account for them and offset it with a purchase account. Because you have issued a credit that a customer can collect on, it is a liability on your books. Also, you will not make a profit on the books the customer takes in exchange credits. The following entries demonstrate how the transactions for Sally Smith would be recorded in your bookkeeping system.

Account#	Account Title	Debit	Credit
2060 Credits			$50.00
4400	Purchases	$50.00	
To Record Smith Exchange Credit			

Note that this transaction is a noncash transaction. If Smith had been paid cash for the books she brought in, the Cash in Checking account would have been credited to show the payment she received. These transactions simply record the inventory that was taken in and the credit that is due Smith. When Smith returns to the shop and takes merchandise using her credit to pay for it, her ledger card is updated as shown previously and the transaction is recorded as follows.

Account#	Account Title	Debit	Credit
2060	Exchange Credit	$20.00	
4000	Sales		$20.00

Although this is still a noncash transaction, the $20 is recorded as income because it reduces the $50 expense recorded as purchases.

Allowing customers to trade in merchandise and receive cash or exchange credits keeps them coming back to your store. It also provides you with a low-cost way to obtain new and different inventory, which in turn encourages other customers to frequent your store to see what has been added and changed. Lastly, it is just one more way to recycle products and contribute to the effort to save our planet for future generations.

How Much Credit Is Fair?

When issuing credits or paying out cash for trade-ins, you must walk a fine line. On one hand, you want to make sure the credit or cash you are paying out for the merchandise is high enough to be fair to the customer. On the other hand, the amount has to be low enough to allow you to make a profit on the deal when the merchandise is resold. That means you must keep up with the market for whatever type of goods you intend to take in through your exchange program.

While books have the original retail price imprinted on the covers, most of the other goods you will be dealing with will not give you such a surefire way of determining their value. However, the way most used book dealers operate their programs can give you an idea of how to handle exchange credits. If a book has a price of $10 on it, most used book store dealers will sell it for $5. That's half of the original price of the book. This, of course, assumes that the book is in good condition. Since the dealer knows that the book can be sold for $5, credits for similar merchandise are approximately

40 percent of that, or $2, allowing the dealer to make $3 when the book is resold, which is actually the net amount the customer who has traded in a book will pay for a replacement.

Not for Resale

If a customer balks at the amount of credit you are offering, don't offer him or her more than your standard amount. You don't want to set a precedent or have this customer spread the word that your credit amounts are not firm.

Taking a page from the book dealers, the formula is to estimate the original retail price of an item, deduct 50 percent, and offer the customer who is trading it in 40 percent of that amount. Again, this assumes that the merchandise is in good condition. This formula can be adjusted up or down depending on the merchandise, its condition, and the current prices and demand for this merchandise in the marketplace.

Remember that offering an exchange or trade-in program to your customers is not all about the profits you can earn; it's about offering something extra to the public, something that retail stores do not offer.

The Least You Need to Know

◆ Consignments require a written agreement.

◆ Appraisals may be necessary for high-priced consignment items.

◆ A price range rather than a set price is easier to negotiate.

◆ Offering exchange credits and trade-ins increases inventory and customer satisfaction.

◆ Bookkeeping records must be updated regularly on consignments and exchanges.

◆ Market research is necessary to set fair credit amounts and resale prices.

Chapter 21

Managing Multiple Stores

In This Chapter

- ◆ Delegating authority
- ◆ Setting up a system of checks and balances
- ◆ Organizing the stores
- ◆ Paying surprise visits to new stores
- ◆ Bookkeeping procedures

There are some real advantages to having more than one store, like increasing your base income. While that is the underlying reason for having multiple stores, there are other advantages that will allow you to save money, too. For one thing, you will be able to get more for your advertising dollars. When you run a special sale, you can include all your locations in whatever type of advertising or promotional materials you send out to individuals or the media. The stores can also help each other out by sharing merchandise acquisitions.

Of course, more stores also require more physical work and more paperwork. This chapter is about streamlining your business operations, finding qualified help, and lessening your workload. All of the suggestions presented are done so with the intention of making any additional stores you may open run as smoothly and efficiently as your first store.

Are They Trustworthy?

The very fact that you have decided to open and run a thrift store indicates that you are a take-charge person. While this is an attribute that all business owners must possess, it sometimes makes it difficult to let go of some of your jobs and responsibilities. However, expanding your business necessitates that you delegate a certain amount of authority to other people.

Obviously, you shouldn't entrust the business that supports you or a cause that is important to you to anyone you don't know or trust. If you have partners or family who are running the business with you, you may be able to depend on them to run an additional store. If not, you will have to search for other individuals and evaluate their experience and qualifications for the responsibilities you are turning over to them.

Although you have reviewed some hiring procedures in earlier chapters, it was assumed that those people would be working alongside you. This would allow you to supervise them and make sure they were competent and trustworthy before assigning any responsibilities to them that would affect the profitability of your thrift store.

Most people put their best foot forward when interviewing for a job. They also tend to leave out employment problems they've had in the past and only list positive information on their job applications. Unfortunately, it's not until after someone is working with you that you find out if the person is dependable and honest. However, if you are the owner of more than one thrift store, it may not be possible for you to work alongside of employees to determine if they actually possess the experience and qualifications listed on their job application.

When you are looking for a manager for one of your stores, the best way to find one is through a personal recommendation from someone you know and trust. Remember those organizations discussed in a prior chapter where you would be associating with other businesspeople? Those are the first people you may want to contact for recommendations when you are looking for a competent manager to work in one of your stores. If that doesn't turn up any good prospects, consider contacting an employment agency in your area. Most agencies prescreen applicants before sending them out on interviews.

Of course, you will have to take the time to interview people and then check them out yourself. Some employers require drug tests before hiring an employee; in an era when drug abuse is common, that's a good idea for you to consider. Some employers also run a credit check on potential employees, and that can be done discreetly through a credit bureau in your area for a fee.

While some people with a few credit problems are honest and dependable, people with too many unpaid debts tend to be unreliable and not so honest. Hiring someone with credit problems can also mean a lot of unwanted phone calls from collection agencies that seem to be able to track them down anywhere they work.

Consider that the person you hire to manage your store will be handling your cash and inventory, servicing your customers, and generally overseeing your business operation when you're not around. Take the extra time to check out potential employees and make sure the people you hire are as good as they seem and as competent as the information on their application indicates.

Owners and managers of nonprofit stores also need to be vigilant when letting volunteers assume responsibility. Although the volunteers are donating their time to the store, they are not always above reproach. While you probably wouldn't do drug testing or extensive background checks on volunteers, you should monitor them to make sure they are competent and trustworthy.

> **Added Value**
>
> If possible, promote from within your business operation. A good employee can become a good manager and a new employee can be hired for a lesser position.

Establish Safeguards

Before you hire a manager or anyone else to work in a store that you are not supervising on a full-time basis, you must work out a system of checks and balances for the store's operation. These are precautionary measures that you might want to use even if you are only running one thrift store, as they generally prevent costly errors and highlight problems.

The cash generated by your store depends on sales and on the availability of sufficient inventory. Depending on the size of your store or the number of stores you own, it is likely that you have volunteers or employees helping you with sales, stocking, accepting donations, and controlling inventory. While most people are basically honest and trustworthy, there are always those who use their intelligence and ingenuity for personal gain.

All you have to do is tune in to your local news channel to hear about the clever ways people cheat and steal. Of course, many of them get caught in the act; that's why their stories are on the news. However, there are many who get away with their plots and scams for years because they don't get greedy, and only steal small amounts over long periods of time.

The secret to protecting your business is to establish a set of procedures that will not insult the honest people, and at the same time, keep the dishonest people from trying to profit at your expense. Many thieves say that they were able to embezzle funds from their employers because the employers made it easy for them to do it.

Keep Track of the Cash

Someone other than the person who is running the cash register, ringing up sales, and paying out change must balance the cash drawer at the close of business each day. This is standard operating procedure for most retail stores and should be adopted by you for your store or stores. This assumes that someone other than you or a close family member is running the register.

Added Value

If you have multiple stores, you can stagger the closing hours of the stores, leaving enough time for you to visit each one and check out the register cash and receipts.

If you have a computerized cash register, you know that it will print out a report at the end of the day and the sales listed on that report can be used to check out the cash drawer. Don't get lazy. Always count all the money in the cash drawer and fill out a balance sheet like the one shown in Chapter 8.

If the cash in the drawer comes up short on more than one occasion, you need a new cashier or you need to spend a few days working with the cashier to determine what he or she is doing wrong. Even if the person is counting out the wrong change, you do not want him or her handling the cash in your store. Cashiers who work in places like casinos where an abundance of cash is handled are fired immediately if their cash count comes up short at the end of a workday. Verifying the cash against the daily sales is top priority, especially when you are running more than one store.

Next on the list of priorities is making the bank deposit every day. Never leave more than the required change fund in the cash register or on the premises of your store. All banks have night depository boxes where you can drop your daily bank deposits, even after the bank has closed for the day.

Keep the checkbook for your store in a safe or other secure place where no one else can get it. As you learned earlier, you and/or your spouse or business partners should be the only signers on any of your bank accounts. If your store doesn't have a secure place, keep the checkbook at your house. You have also learned that your checkbook must be updated every day so that you always know exactly how much is in the account. Don't keep excess funds in your checking account. Move the excess funds to your savings account.

If a bookkeeper or someone other than you pays the bills for the store, make sure that the checks all come to you for signing. You should make the time to go through the invoices to be paid each month and approve them for payment. If that is not possible, have the bookkeeper attach the invoice to the check that has been written to pay the bill and check each one to make sure the invoice is legitimate and paid correctly. Again, make sure the checkbook is updated properly and all the checks are accounted for on a daily basis. If you do this every day, it will only take a few minutes and can save you a multitude of problems.

Not for Resale

One of the most common ways people cheat is to make up phony invoices to be paid or make out checks to themselves for nonexistent services.

If a check has to be voided, rip off the signature line on the check, fold it, and staple it to the back of the check register that has been marked "void" for that check number. The following are a few more precautions that you can put into place for your store or stores:

- ◆ Have mail go to a P.O. box so that financial information on bank accounts and credit cards cannot be accessed by anyone but you. You can use the same box number for all your stores.

- ◆ Shred any convenience checks sent by credit card companies.

- ◆ Shred any offers for new credit card accounts that come in the mail.

- ◆ Never sign a blank check.

- ◆ When in doubt about an invoice for products or services, verify it before paying the bill or signing the check.

Most of the suggestions are simply a matter of paying attention to what is going on in your business operation. When you are running more than one store, you can get really busy, but it may be better to turn other jobs over to volunteers or employees that do not involve cash or profits to give you time to keep a watchful eye on those crucial elements yourself.

Controlling Inventory

For a nonprofit thrift store that gets all its stock from donations, controlling inventory may not seem necessary. However, anytime valuable merchandise is handled by your thrift store you should take extra precautions to make sure it is kept secure. A locked display case can be used to display small items like jewelry or collectibles, and special sales slips should also be used when anything of exceptional value is sold through your thrift store. Both of these procedures should be used by all thrift store locations to keep valuable items from being lost or stolen.

In addition, for the thrift store or stores operated for profit, some sort of inventory control is necessary. If you are a general merchandise store with lots of clothing and small items, doing a physical inventory on a regular basis is very time-consuming, but if you are paying for the merchandise that is stocking your store, it is necessary to take a physical inventory once or twice a year. In the meantime, there are other ways you can monitor what is going in and out of your store. These other ways require some things that you should be doing anyway, and that's keeping your store and your goods organized and neat.

In prior chapters, the importance of having neat, orderly display and storage areas has been stressed. You've also learned that you should walk your store at least once a day to make sure that nothing is amiss or out of place. You are probably displaying all the clothing in one area and all the household goods in another. Keeping those displays neat allows you to see at a glance if there are fewer items than there should be on a shelf or rack. Choose one or two categories of goods a week and count them and then check your sales figures to see if reductions in inventory are justified by the week's receipts.

Your storage area should be organized by category as well, and it should be checked on a regular basis. Again, taking a quick count of different items each week will give you a good idea of the popularity of certain merchandise and train you to recognize any unexplained reductions in quantity.

When sorting merchandise, make a note of anything of extraordinary value and pay attention to where it is placed in the storage area or on the display floor and monitor it. When it is no longer visible, check and make sure it was sold for the correct amount.

Keep in mind, you know your stores and the merchandise in them better than anyone else, so you can probably come up with other security procedures that will monitor and protect your assets.

Similar Set-Ups

Obviously, the success of your first store has led to the opening of other stores. Different sizes and designs of the buildings that house your stores may make it impossible to carry over the same layout in each one of them. The neighborhoods and areas where the stores are located will also dictate the overall design of each one. However, keep in mind that grocery stores and other large retail outlets often use the same layouts and designs in all their stores. This gives their customers a level of comfort in that they don't have to search for the department or the items they have come in to purchase. The variation should come in the way the merchandise is presented within a familiar setup.

You should also carry over any extra services or conveniences from your first store into the new store. This includes a few chairs for elderly shoppers to rest on, bathrooms and dressing rooms, and a play area for the kids. The merchandise you offer that taps into your special interests, like antiques, jewelry, or books, should also be included in your new store's display areas. If you have been listening to your customers at the old store and absorbing both the positive and negative comments, you will have a pretty good idea of how your new store should be set up. After all, no matter how many stores you own, it's still all about customer satisfaction.

Helping Hands
A nonprofit store can take any merchandise that it isn't moving in the first store and use it for a special sale or a giveaway to the customers at the new store.

For your own convenience, set up the storage area at the new store or stores as much like the first store as possible. This continuity will help you when putting away additional merchandise you have acquired and finding any merchandise quickly and easily that is requested by a customer. While you're not trying to make your new store a clone of the old one, you are striving to make it as customer- and staff-friendly as the old one. It probably took you a long time to get the first store set up to function efficiently, and now you can use that experience to make your second or third store run smoothly from the beginning.

Pop In Unexpectedly

In addition to showing up at closing time to verify and balance the day's receipts, you should make a point of visiting all your stores on an irregular basis. Don't get in the habit of just coming in at the same time every day. Vary the time and length of your visits so that the employees and/or volunteers are never sure exactly when you will show up. You're not actually trying to catch them doing something wrong, but you are trying to keep your store running the way it would be run if you were there all the time.

Remember the old adage, "When the cat's away, the mice will play." It's human nature to slack off when the boss is not around, and that is to be expected; but if employees are never sure just when the boss is going to pop in, they are more likely to stay focused on making the business run smoothly.

The following guidelines are things you should look at when you make an unexpected visit to one of your stores:

- The overall appearance of the store

- The overall appearance of the storage area

- Check the number of sales made that day

- Check on the office supplies

- Check on the bathroom facilities

If the overall appearance of the store and the storage areas are as neat and orderly as you would like them to be, it tells you that your staff members are taking care to keep them that way.

If the overall appearance of either or both areas is not good, check the sales for the day. This will tell you how busy the store has been this day—if it has been busy, it tells you why the display area and storage area are not in perfect order. The staff has been too busy waiting on customers to tend to them, and as you know, servicing customers comes before straightening up, which can be done after the shop is closed.

Added Value

Your store should have a sheet that employees or volunteers can use to let you know that supplies of any kind need to be replenished.

Take a quick look at the office supplies and any other supplies used on a regular basis to see if anything needs replenishing.

You should always check the bathroom facilities in your store when you visit. Make sure they are clean and well stocked with tissue, soap, and paper towels.

These things that you check on when you visit your store will make your impromptu visits seem more like you are looking out for their comfort, rather than checking up on employees. As long as you are there, you can also offer to relieve them of their duties so they can take a quick break.

Keeping the Books

Although your stores are all owned by the same entity, which may be the corporation you created for your business operation, it is best to keep a separate set of books for each individual thrift store, especially at the beginning. That means opening a separate checking account and setting up a separate bookkeeping system for each store. While this may sound like more work, it is actually easier than trying to consolidate all stores under one bank account and one accounting system.

The other reason to keep the books separate is that it makes it simpler to monitor the progress of the new store and determine whether it is profitable or not. You can also keep a closer eye on the assets and liabilities of each store, giving you a clearer perspective of its overall condition. Last but not least, keeping the books separately avoids confusion.

At the end of the tax year, the two financial statements will have to be merged, but that is a simple matter of adding the end-of-year financial information together to get a combined total of all stores covered by the parent corporation.

Software Concerns

This doesn't mean that you need a separate computer and a separate accounting software program for each store. Most software programs allow you to set up what is called multiple companies and run as many as you like through the same established bookkeeping procedures. It is advisable to differentiate the stores by numbering them or giving each its own name. Some owners use the same name for all stores, but identify them by their addresses—for example, Smart Saver Thrift Shop on Main and Smart Saver Thrift Shop on Congress. However you want to do that is fine.

Added Value

Capitalize on the good reputation of your first store by carrying the name over to any additional stores you open, even though your books may show the name differently.

Outside Accountants

The fact that your business is doing well enough to allow you to open additional stores may also indicate that you should turn your books over to a professional accounting firm. This is one of those chores you can delegate to someone else, freeing up time for you. It is advisable to keep doing all the banking and bill paying yourself, or hiring an employee to do it for you. This allows you to continue overseeing all sales, vendor invoices, and payouts for all your stores.

Some accounting firms will post all your transactions, balance your bank statements, write checks for your bills, do your payroll and tax reports, and issue financial statements. If you want to use these services, that is okay. However, remember that you are still responsible for the financial status and well-being of your business operation.

You must always monitor your checkbook, review and approve any bills to be paid, sign checks and verify their accuracy, and last but not least, study your financial statements as soon as they are issued. This has been said many times in this book, but it can't be stressed enough. Never give a third party total control of your books and bank accounts.

It's fine to seek help and turn some of the workload over to a professional, but as the owner of the business or an officer of the corporation, you are ultimately responsible for every financial transaction that takes place. This covers the day-to-day handling of cash receipts, bank deposits, bills, payroll, tax reports, and remittance of payroll taxes and other taxes related to your business operation.

Before bringing your books to a professional firm at the end of the month, make sure the following information is entered into the checkbooks for each store:

- The date and amount of all sales receipts deposited into the bank. If you are using different sales categories for your books, each category must be entered separately with the correct amount included for that particular deposit.

- The date and amount of any adjustments made to your checking account for credit card fees or other bank fees.

- Every check stub must be completed with the information needed to post the payment to the correct account in the General Ledger.

- A dated list of any regular or electronic transfers from the checking account to the savings accounts.

- A dated list of any electronic transfers for liability payments or other expenses taken directly from your checking account.

Making sure that all the necessary information is recorded in the checkbook will save the accountant who is doing your books time. Since accountants bill by the hours they spend working on your books, it will also save you money on accounting fees.

Again, if you turn your books over to an outside accountant, be sure to scrutinize the financial statements that are issued. Any questions about the statements should be directed to the accounting firm for answers and explanations. You should also analyze your sales figures and the expenses that are being paid out every month. If your profit margin is not as good as you think it should be, this analysis will help you improve it.

Consider the celebrities who have trusted their accountants and managers to handle all their finances, only to find themselves in deep trouble with IRS and unpaid debts. So keep your focus and keep control of your finances, both business and personal.

The information in this chapter may cause you to think twice about trusting anyone you hire or even meet on the street. Over and over in this book, you have been told to get recommendations for vendors, accountants, lawyers, and employees before you trust anyone with your money or your business.

Hopefully, you realize that you can trust most people and will be able to lessen your workload by turning certain jobs and responsibilities over to them. The majority of people you will come in contact with are good people, basically honest and trustworthy. The information in this chapter is presented to help you find those good people and avoid the few who are not to be trusted.

Rely on your own common sense and instincts to help you find good, reliable people to work with and help you make all your business ventures successful.

The Least You Need to Know

- Managing multiple stores requires you to delegate authority to others. Make sure you do background checks on potential employees.

- Set up a system of checks and balances for handling cash transactions. Always keep control of your checking account, and establish procedures for monitoring your inventory.

- Surprise visits to your stores will tell you if they are being managed properly.

- Review your financial statements as soon as they are issued.

- Keep your financial records updated and in order.

Chapter 22

Reviewing Your Choices and Options

In This Chapter

- ◆ Planning and research
- ◆ Getting down to business
- ◆ Improving your business operation
- ◆ Expanding your business
- ◆ Knowing the bottom line

All the choices and options presented in this book are meant to be guidelines for starting and running a thrift store. Hopefully they have given you an insight into the vast world of resale and an idea of how to create and develop your own vision into a successful business within this growing industry.

As you move forward with the desire to own your own thrift store, you will undoubtedly find that you can modify the information you have read in this book. Your own perceptions, and most of all your own creativity and imagination, will spring forward and take all that you have learned and mold it into your own personal business plan. Your own business plan may not be something that can be transferred to a formal set of documents, but rather the dream of the future that lives within you.

In this chapter, you will review the highlights from the preceding text to help you condense all you have learned and enable you to decide on your place in an industry that offers opportunity, challenge, and a chance to make a real difference in your community.

The Best-Laid Plans

Research and advance planning are necessary for any venture you pursue in life, but especially important for starting a business. Even a business like a thrift store that has lower start-up costs and is considered recession-proof must be studied and analyzed before you jump into it with both feet. There are different ways to go about formulating your initial plan, but some research, guidance, and forethought are necessary no matter how you decide to proceed.

Remember that all thrift stores answer a need in the community where they are located, regardless of the economic or ethnic makeup of that community. There are those in growing numbers who are concerned about the environment and want to do their part to keep it clean by purchasing used products. This is in addition to the people who shop in thrift stores because they need to find goods at a reduced price to survive. Then there are those who shop in thrift stores just for the fun of it. This brings us to the ongoing challenges facing thrift store owners, and that is finding and stocking usable merchandise that can be offered at reduced prices. This is coupled with the enjoyment of finding the unusual and unique and the potential of uncovering something of exceptional value and quality.

While start-up costs for thrift stores are generally lower than they are for other new businesses, there are costs to be considered. Some of those expenses will be dependent on where you want your store to be located. It is important that you take the time to research that area and estimate costs so that you will know how much revenue it will take to open a store in your area.

Helping Hands
Your initial plans should include a way to accept donations or acquire other low-cost merchandise for your store.

Another advantage of opening a thrift store is the opportunity to be your own boss, but understand the time and energy involved in doing that. If you have family and friends who are interested in the resale industry, you may want to form a partnership to lesson the workload and the financial requirements.

A lot of thought should be given to the type of thrift store you want to own. Do you want to handle general merchandise or do you like the idea of tapping into the market for something that holds a special interest for you? Perhaps you would like to keep all your options open and plan on offering general merchandise as well as specializing in one of the niche markets such as books, craft items, trendy upscale fashions, antiques, or nursery items. When you are dealing in resale, there is no limit to what you can sell in your store. Just make sure that you have sufficient knowledge about any specialized items you carry so that you can make good choices for yourself and your customers. If you don't know about a product, use the Internet, find books on the subject, or find an expert to advise you.

Get out into your community and obtain firsthand knowledge about the needs that exist there. Once you have zeroed in on a cause you think your thrift store should support, learn all you can about the charity and its needs. If you are going to sponsor a new nonprofit cause, keep in mind that the needs of a new charity tend to grow and spread over time. Therefore, your advance planning needs to include ways to find additional funding and resources to keep up with the demand for services.

Look to the existing nonprofit thrift stores in your area for guidance and think about adopting some of their proven techniques into your business model. Once you have settled on a charity to sponsor, it is likely that others who share your concern for this group will come forward to help you.

If you have decided to become a nonprofit store, consider the different ways you can move forward toward your goal. Attaching your store to an existing nonprofit organization brings your business under the protection of their charitable umbrella. However, starting your own nonprofit organization may be the best way to work independently and accomplish all that you plan on doing.

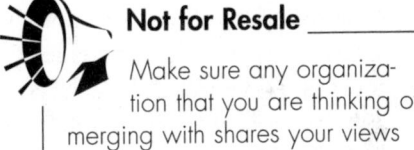

Not for Resale

Make sure any organization that you are thinking of merging with shares your views and plans for the future.

The recommended structure for your nonprofit business is to become a nonprofit corporation. While this type of business entity takes more time and effort to establish, it provides the most advantages for a thrift store that will be supporting a charity. Once you have gathered people to serve on the board of your corporation, you can contact the corporation commission in your state to begin the process. As you may recall, the process includes drafting a mission statement that sets forth the purpose and goals of your organization and preparing Articles of Incorporation and bylaws.

Once your nonprofit corporation has a name and is licensed by your state, you can apply for tax-exempt status to the IRS and your state taxing authorities. During the process of becoming a nonprofit entity, you may want to consult a legal advisor to help you through all the necessary steps.

Incorporating is also recommended for a thrift store business that is going to be operated for profit. However, there are other faster, easier ways to organize your business, especially if you intend to start out small. The following list of other business structures was discussed in detail in Chapter 5:

Added Value

There are a number of organizations and resources you can use to help with the process of incorporation.

- ◆ Sole Proprietorship

- ◆ Partnership

- ◆ Limited Liability Company

- ◆ S Corporation

Remember that running your business as a sole proprietor or a partnership puts your personal assets at risk if the business should encounter problems. A limited liability company can be formed to offer a measure of protection for your personal assets. An S Corporation is a smaller version of a regular corporation and generally protects the owners' personal assets as well as a regular corporation. All of the above entities can hire employees and claim the expenses related to employees and taxes on their annual tax returns.

Before deciding on a business structure, review the tax consequences for each one. The tax liability on the profits from all the business structures listed above are filtered down to the primary owners or partners in the organization and must be included on their personal tax returns. A regular corporation also files a tax return and pays tax at the corporate rate. Generally, the owner/manager of the thrift store is an employee of the corporation that has been responsible for his or her payroll taxes. At the end of the year, the corporation issues a W-2 to all employees to be used for their personal tax returns.

The important thing to remember when organizing your business is to use the structure that will work best for you over time. Although you can change the way a business is initially formed—that is, a sole proprietor can become a limited liability company or a corporation—it is smart to think ahead and choose the structure that will serve you best as your business grows and prospers. As soon as your business entity is created, go to the bank of your choice and open an account and acquaint yourself with the business services you will need for your store, such as credit and debit card processing.

Running the Business Successfully

You may have started scouting out potential locations for your thrift store while you were going through the process of structuring the business entity. Once you have all the legal work done, you are ready to settle on the perfect location for your first thrift store. The type of merchandise you are going to offer in your shop will determine many of the attributes your store must have. In addition, locations that provide other important amenities, such as visibility, a crime-free area, and customer convenience should be given priority over other cheaper locations that do not have everything you need and want for your store. Keep in mind that your personal investment in this business will be huge, and you shouldn't shortchange yourself by opting for a location that will not provide the conveniences and attractiveness that will bring customers into your shop.

You should be working with a real estate agent who does not have any connection with the owner of the store you decide to lease, so that the agent can negotiate the best lease terms for you.

If you have any questions about the lease that your agent does not answer to your satisfaction, it would be wise to bring in your own legal advisor to review the terms and conditions of the lease agreement.

After you have agreed on the lease terms, you will begin gathering merchandise for the store and purchasing furniture and fixtures. Since you are in the business of selling used merchandise, you may want to look into buying used shelving, display racks, and other equipment for your store, which is one way to cut down on the start-up costs. The one item you should not skimp on is a good electronic cash register.

Have a sign erected on your store as soon as possible so that anyone who passes by will be aware of the new business that is going to be opening soon. If your shop has display windows, they should be set up first with the best merchandise you have to offer, another preopening form of promotion.

If you are a nonprofit, you can call on volunteers to help you set up the store and get it ready for business. Partners or family members who are part of the business can also be pressed into service. If you don't have any of these people to help you and staff the store initially, you may have to hire an employee or two.

Not for Resale

Be sure to check the references of all potential employees to avoid hiring people who may cause you problems down the road.

Added Value

Make a checklist of all the things that have to be done and decided before your store opens to help you organize your thoughts and get everything done on time.

On-the-job training for yourself, volunteers, and others can take place while you get your store ready to open. All thrift stores should be open to receiving donations of merchandise in some way or another while the store is being organized and set up. This may mean organizing your storage areas first so that you have a convenient place to put donations or merchandise you acquire from other sources.

While your setup is in progress, you must begin making some important decisions on things like your store hours, inventory acceptance and control, pricing merchandise, scheduling of employees or volunteers, and basic sales procedures. Remember that you will already be paying rent on your store, so set a timetable for yourself and stick to it.

One of the most important tasks you will have to complete before your store opens is setting up a good bookkeeping system. If you are using the services of an accountant or other financial advisor, get his or her professional recommendations for a system you can manage yourself or an accounting firm that can do the books for you. Keep in mind that there are a number of good computerized software programs you can use to do your own bookkeeping. However, don't attempt to run one of these programs without reviewing the basic information provided in Chapters 8 and 9 of this book.

Part of your daily routine must be balancing the sales against the cash register printout and the cash drawer at the close of business every day and recording those sales figures in your bookkeeping system. It is highly recommended that you, as the owner of the store, perform this task yourself and keep control of the checkbook used for your store.

The secrets of keeping an accurate set of accounting records are being organized and following the steps outlined in the earlier chapters in the order given, establishing a good filing system, and updating your checkbook and financial records as often as possible. It is also imperative that your checking account balance be verified with the balance reported on your monthly bank statement at the end of every month. If you do not feel you can keep the books for your store yourself, either hire an experienced bookkeeper to do it for you, or hire an accounting firm to do it on a monthly basis.

Regardless of who does your bookkeeping, you are ultimately responsible for the financial condition of your store. If you are not issuing the financial statements yourself, take the time to review and analyze them.

At the end of the tax year, there are adjustments that may have to be made for tax purposes. Consult a competent tax accountant to make sure your business is getting all the credits and tax deductions that it is entitled to claim on its tax return. Remember that even a tax-exempt nonprofit corporation may still have to file tax reports with the IRS.

Not for Resale

The bookkeeping data in your computerized program should be backed up at least once a month to protect it from being lost if a power failure or other incident wipes out the information on the computer's hard drive.

With your store set up and the proper procedures in place, you can turn to more enjoyable items on your to-do list. The first of these should be advertising and promotion for your store's opening. You have many options you can use to let the public know about your new thrift store. They include all of the following:

- ◆ Direct mailings
- ◆ Internet site
- ◆ Connecting a charity event to your opening
- ◆ Public service announcements for the charity event
- ◆ Newspaper ads
- ◆ Radio and TV ads

Some of these options are more cost-effective than others, but all of them will work if done properly. Seek the help of family and friends to spread the word about your store. If you are a nonprofit store, enlist the aid of all the volunteers and supporters of your charity group.

Once your store is open for business, you will find a whole new set of duties that must be handled and procedures that must be established. At this point, everything you do must eventually result in some form of customer satisfaction. It starts with the merchandise you accept from donors or acquire from other sources. The items must be in good reusable condition and you must price them fairly for you and the customer. You want to provide the best values possible to the customer while making a profit on every sale. Remember that the donor who brings in unsuitable items may also be a customer, so treat everyone with courtesy even if what they want to give you is going directly to the garbage can when they leave the store.

Helping Hands

IRS rules allow donors to set the value on donated items, so all you have to do is give them a receipt if they request one.

The displays in your store should be as appealing as possible, and mixing in some brightly colored decorator items where they will provide some spark to an otherwise drab area is recommended. In addition, make sure your store is always neat and clean and the outside areas are properly maintained and as safe as possible. Offering extra services to customers will be appreciated and will result in good word of mouth for your store.

A big part of customer satisfaction begins when you sort through potential merchandise for your store. Everything that passes through your hands must be handled safely and be examined to make sure that it will not pose a threat to an employee or a customer. In Chapter 12, you read about the precautions you must take when dealing with hazardous materials and the rules established by the Consumer Product Safety Commission on recalled products. Always check out any item that could present a problem to a customer if placed on your sales floor. Subscribe to the updates issued by CPSC to keep abreast of changes in the law and new reports of products reported to be unsafe. This is especially important if your shop deals in children's items, as this is a category that receives constant scrutiny for defects and safety concerns.

Familiarize yourself with recycling programs in your area to dispose of unwanted donations. For electronic equipment that is no longer working or useful, remember that there are a number of manufacturers who take those items in trade or pay a small amount for turning them in.

Still, having customer service uppermost in your mind, you know that the volunteers and employees you have staffing your store may have to be trained to deal effectively with everyone who passes through the entrance. Volunteers are an added benefit of running a nonprofit store. Employees are an expense to a store run for profit and require additional paperwork for you. However, a good employee can make up for the expenses of salary and payroll taxes by allowing your store to service many more customers than you could manage on your own.

The additional paperwork that applies to payroll taxes can be handled by a payroll service if you don't have the time to do the reports required by the federal and state authorities. However, remember that you are ultimately responsible for making sure the reports are accurate and the tax deposits are remitted in a timely manner. Today, the IRS offers a number of options for making tax deposits. Study those options and decide which one will work best for you.

Employees and volunteers can both help you keep your business growing and profitable. At the very least, they can give you the time you need to do necessary work outside your store and even allow you the luxury of a vacation now and then.

Not for Resale

Be sure to acquire all the documents needed for the IRS and the U.S. Dept. of Immigration when hiring a new employee.

Getting Older and Better

The longer you manage a thrift store, the more adept you will become at making it run smoother and recognizing areas that may benefit from improvements. You'll also learn that anything you do that brings more customers into your store will increase sales and that type of improvement is an ongoing necessity. Let's review some of the suggestions that were presented in earlier chapters and let your imagination create ways to use these promotional ideas in new ways:

◆ Free gifts or other giveaways

◆ Special discounts

◆ Programs and seminars to entertain and educate

◆ Fund-raising events

You know that you don't have to be a nonprofit store to help your community or the charities in the area. You can also offer things like meeting space for groups, and if you have a truck offer free pickups and deliveries for your customers or people who want to donate goods to your store.

Lastly, you have to listen to the comments of your customers and be prepared to address their needs. Sometimes this could result in your store taking back an item that the customer returns or issuing a credit for an item that the customer claims is unsatisfactory. Although returns and warranties are not generally a part of customer service in the resale industry, you should be open to making exceptions now and then.

Helping Hands

Make friends with school and church personnel in your area and be willing to help them out with discounts and programs you can sponsor.

Joining national and local business associations will foster ideas for other promotions and extra services that will keep your customers coming back to your store again and again.

Another thing that will keep a steady stream of customers coming into your store is the quality of the merchandise you carry. Keeping your store stocked with the best resale items is going to be an ongoing challenge, and at the same time one of the most fun things you do for your business. Even a nonprofit store that relies on donations must occasionally search out other sources of goods. Chapter 15 listed a number of places where good merchandise can be found and purchased at low prices. Keep that list handy to remind yourself to check out these places on a regular basis.

As you go along, you will develop a sense of what places offer the most for the least amount. You will also learn how to forego sources that require a lot of time, such as swap meets.

As you search for goods for your thrift store, there is always the possibility that you will uncover an item of exceptional value. Acquiring an item like this can be an unexpected source of revenue for your store. However, as you have learned, unless you have knowledge and experience with an item, you have two choices. You can take the time to become knowledgeable about that category of merchandise, or you can seek out someone who is an expert in that area and ask for help. Appraisals are probably the best way to determine the true value of an object of exceptional value, like diamonds and antiques. Other items with questionable value, like collectibles and rare books, can be researched and even turned over to other dealers to be sold or auctioned.

Many options were presented on determining the true value of merchandise in Chapter 16. Take heed of the suggestions and advice so that you can derive the most profit out of any treasure you acquire.

One of the best ways to improve the image of your thrift store is to make yourself known to the community as a person who is concerned about its needs and is willing to give time and energy to worthy causes in the area. Becoming a part of an internationally known organization that sponsors the type of programs that interest you will help you establish a personal image that will help your business thrive. Finding the time to go out into the community and work with an international group, a local church or school, or even the Chamber of Commerce may be difficult, but it is a necessary part of building a good reputation for yourself and your business. It is also a surefire way to increase your profits and open the door to bigger and better things.

Bigger Stores, and More of Them

Keeping your store well stocked is important, but if there comes a time when you can't walk through the aisles without bumping into things and your storage area is overflowing, it may be time to think about moving to a bigger store. Of course, this is only feasible if your profits are good but not increasing because you don't have enough space to display more merchandise.

However, there are two things to be considered before running out to look for a bigger store:

1. Can you make more space in the existing facility by rearranging things or adding to your display areas and storage areas?

2. Is your profit margin good enough to cover the expenses of rent on a larger store and moving everything there?

The first question is an easy yes or no. If the answer is no, then you need to move on to the second question, requiring an analysis of your financial situation before it can be accurately answered. The formula for doing this is presented in Chapter 18.

If you then determine that your business can afford the move and the expenses of a larger store, you can start looking for a new, bigger location.

Keep in mind that all the customer conveniences and amenities of the existing store must be matched or improved in the new location. It is also important that your new location allows you to service your current customers and retain any volunteers or employees who staff your store.

Moving is never easy, but the prospect of getting more space and increasing your customer base will make it worthwhile. Opening additional stores in your area or other parts of the city is another option you may want to consider. In that case, you could keep the smaller store and solve the space problem there by moving some of the merchandise to the new store.

Added Value

Make up flyers to have in your old store that announce the new location, the date you are moving, and perhaps a discount for your old customers who bring the flyer into the new location.

If you have established a good reputation for yourself and your store, expanding your business will be supported by the community you serve. However, even more consideration has to be given to your financial condition, and in addition you must consider whether you will be spreading yourself too thin by taking on the work and responsibility of additional stores.

Along with the financial backing you need, the key to making this type of expansion work is the backup support you have from your staff of volunteers or employees. So the next big question then becomes: Do you already have people in place who can assume some of your duties and responsibilities while you turn your attention to a brand-new project? If so, you can begin making plans to own multiple stores.

Once again, as it was with your first store, you have to find the perfect location. At this point, you may even consider purchasing property to house your second store.

Added Value

The property you want to purchase can be used as collateral for a loan as long as you have enough money for a down payment on it.

If you don't have the funds needed to buy property and stock the new store, you can explore the possibility of outside financing. Your success with the first store will make lenders more open to lending you money to finance the second store. However, you should gather your advisors around you and come up with a good business plan to bring to lenders, since you may need a sizable loan to carry out your new project.

With more than one store to stock, you may now want to tap into a way to obtain merchandise at little or no cost to your business. This is possible by taking merchandise to sell on consignment or taking merchandise in exchange for store credit or trades. If you are interested in doing either or both of these, you will need to follow the guidelines presented in Chapter 20 of this book. Keep in mind that in handling consignment merchandise, an agreement that spells out the terms of the sale and the commission you will collect must be prepared and signed by you and the original owner. A separate area of your bookkeeping system may also have to be set up to keep financial records of consignments and exchange credits.

Not for Resale

Keeping a separate set of books for each store is one way to avoid confusion and keep track of how each store is doing financially.

Managing more than one store requires that you delegate authority to volunteers and employees. This is something that may have to be done over time unless you already have people you can trust to run your business like you do. The people you choose to take over for you must be thoroughly checked out. You must also set up a system that allows you to monitor your managers and alerts you to any problems that may occur.

Most people are basically honest, but you will probably want to work with new people for a while to make sure they have the attributes described on their resumés.

Final Words

Deciding to open and run a thrift store may require drive, determination, energy, and financial backing. As you have learned, there are many decisions and tasks that have to be handled before and after your store is opened. The bottom line is where you will find the profit or loss reported for your store. The bottom line is also used to describe the final outcome of a venture. As you work your way toward your goals, focus on the bottom line that is your final outcome, the vision you have of your store. Keeping your eye on the bottom line will encourage you to keep going and negotiate the bumps and curves you will find on your road to success.

The Least You Need to Know

- Your initial research and planning will move you forward with understanding and organization.

- Establishing simple, easy-to-follow business procedures will help you, your staff, and your customers.

- Working to improve your store and your image in the community is the best form of promotion.

- Expansion should be done cautiously after determining that you have the finances to make it work.

- Keep your goals in mind to motivate you when things don't go as planned.

Resources

The following books provide additional information on the topics presented in the chapters of this guide.

Chapter 4

Mancuso, Anthony. *How to Form a Nonprofit Corporation*. USA: NOLO, 2007.

Grubman, Gary M. *The Nonprofit Handbook: Everything You Need to Know to Start and Run Your Nonprofit Organization*. USA: White Hat Communications, 2008.

Larson, Rolfe. *Venture Forth! The Essential Guide to Starting a Moneymaking Business in Your Nonprofit Organization*. USA: Fieldstone Alliance, 2002.

Chapter 5

Diamond, Michael R. *How to Incorporate: A Handbook for Entrepreneurs and Professionals*. USA: Wiley, 2007.

Chapters 6 and 8

Costa, Carol. *Teach Yourself Bookkeeping in 24 Hours.* USA: Alpha Books, Penguin USA, 2008.

Addison, Wesley, and Carol Costa. *Teach Yourself Accounting in 24 Hours, 2nd Edition.* USA: Alpha Books, Penguin USA, 2006.

Chapter 16

Ellis, Ian C. *Book Finds, 3rd Edition: How to Find, Buy, and Sell Used and Rare Books.* USA: Perigree Trade, 2006.

Zempel, Edward M. *First Editions: A Guide to Identification.* USA: Spoon River Press, 2001.

Editors of Schroeders Publications. *Schroeders Antiques Price Guide.* USA: Schroeders Publications, 2008.

Miller, Judith. *Miller's Antiques Price Guide 2009, 30th Edition.* USA: MITCH, 2008.

Miller, Judith, and Mark Hill. *Miller's Collectibles Price Guide 2009.* USA: MITCH, 2008.

Herlocher, Dawn. *Collectible Dolls.* USA: Krause Publications, 2008.

Chapter 19

Berry, Tim. *Plan as You Go.* USA: Entrepreneur Press, 2008.

Important Information from the Consumer Product Safety Commission

The following questions and answers are from the section of the Consumer Product Safety Commission Improvement Act (CPSIA) that applies to Resellers of Children's Products, including Thrift Stores, Consignment Shops, and Charities:

Question: I run a small shop that sells new and used clothes, jewelry, shoes, and toys for children. Do I need to test the products I sell?

No, you are not required to test. However, retailers and resellers (including those who sell on auction websites) cannot knowingly sell children's products that do not meet the requirements of the law. You can protect yourself by screening for volatile products. But more importantly, as a businessperson, you do not want to be selling products that have the potential to cause harm to anyone, especially a child. Sellers should avoid products likely to have lead or phthalates, or do not meet mandatory toy standards (see Table A.1 for a general guide to commonly resold products).

It is now against the law to sell a recalled product. Remember to check the list of recalled products on the CPSC website (www.cpsc.gov), as a number of children's products have been recalled.

Question: How can I determine if something has lead in it before I sell it?

Resellers, in particular, need to make sound business decisions about the products they sell. As a practical matter, you must do one of the following:

- Test the product.
- Refuse to accept or sell the product, which will mean disposing of it if you already have it in your inventory.
- Use your best judgment based on your knowledge of the product.
- Contact the manufacturer about questionable products.

It would make sense to test, rather than discard, any suspect children's products that have a high resale value. You may want to hire a qualified, trained person in your area who can quickly screen all of your suspect products with a handheld device called an x-ray fluorescence (XRF) machine.

You should not rely on commercially sold lead testing kits. CPSC staff have determined that the kits are prone to give "false positive" or "false negative" results.

Commonly Resold Children's Products and Materials

Recalled Products: Illegal to sell *any* recalled product (for adults as well as children). Before taking into inventory or selling a product, check the CPSC website for dangerous recalled products, including cribs, play yards, strollers, high chairs, toys with magnets, toys that are choking hazards, and other products.

Books—"ordinary" children's titles (e.g., paperbacks and hardbacks): OK to sell if printed after 1985.

Cheap children's metal jewelry: Best to test. Contact the manufacturer or do not sell.

Unpainted/untreated wood toys: OK to sell.

Painted wooden or metal toys: Best to test. Contact the manufacturer, or do not sell.

Toys with soft plastic that are made for infants: Should be OK to sell if made for sale after February 10, 2009. If older (or if the date of manufacture is unknown), check with manufacturer or do not sell.

Dyed or undyed children's clothing made from natural, untreated cotton, silk, wool, hemp, flax, linen, and other untreated natural materials including coral, amber, feathers, fur, and leather: OK to sell.

Clothes with rhinestones, metal or vinyl snaps, zippers, closures, or appliqués: Best to test. Contact the manufacturer, or do not sell.

Surgical steel; precious metals such as gold (at least 10 karat} and sterling silver (at least 925/1000}; precious and semiprecious gemstones (excluding a list of stones that are associated in nature with lead}; natural or cultured pearls: OK to sell.

Toys that are easily breakable into small parts, including dolls and stuffed toys that have eyes, noses, or other small parts that are not securely fastened: Best not to sell (for children under 3); could present a choking hazard.

Question: How can I tell if a product contains a prohibited phthalate?

As with lead, you are not required to test your products for phthalates or to certify that they do not contain prohibited phthalates. There is no easy way to tell whether a product contains a phthalate or what kind of phthalate it contains. Unlike lead, where there is a reliable screening tool (the x-ray fluorescence machine), there is not yet a screening device to detect the presence of phthalates.

Be wary of certain products: very soft vinyl or plastic toys (excluding latex or silicone), or other children's products where the plastic is soft enough to enable an infant to grasp it more readily, may contain phthalates. Your safest course is not to sell or accept these products unless you know they don't contain phthalates.

Question: Can I sell vintage children's books and other children's products that are collectibles?

Yes. Used vintage children's books and other children's products sold as collector's items would not be primarily intended for children, because of their value and age. Therefore, they do not fall into the definition of children's product and do not need to comply with the lead limits.

Question: Do bikes that are not intended primarily for children 12 and under need to comply with the lead limits?

No. The lead limits in the CPSIA only apply to products intended or designed primarily for children 12 and under. The lead limits apply only to those bikes which, by nature of their size, design or other similar factors, indicate that they are intended or designed primarily for children. Thus, a bike with a 24" wheel size or smaller would generally be considered a children's bike and would need to comply.

Question: What happens if I sell a product in violation of the CPSIA or other applicable laws?

The commission's response to a violation of the law varies depending upon the circumstances, including the nature of the product defect, the number of products, the severity of the risk of injury associated with the product, and the type of violation. The commission's goal is to help you to avoid future violations and protect your customers, not to put you out of business.

Electronic Federal Tax Payment System

EFTPS is a service provided free by the U.S. Department of the Treasury that enables business and individual taxpayers to make all their federal tax payments electronically 24 hours a day, 7 days a week through the Internet or phone.

With EFTPS, you have two payment methods that are interchangeable: the Internet and phone.

You can use both of these methods to pay your personal or business federal taxes, 24 hours a day, 7 days a week. There is nothing special to learn; whichever method you use, you will be prompted for the information required to make a payment.

Because you enter all the information via the Internet or phone, you can check the accuracy of the information you report. Plus, you'll receive an EFT (Electronic Funds Transfer) Acknowledgment Number as a receipt for your payment instructions.

No one has access to your account except you. The combination of your Taxpayer Identification Number (Employer Identification Number or Social Security number) and a Personal Identification Number (PIN) gives you the security you need. And with EFTPS payments made online, you have the added security of an Internet Password.

Pay anytime day or night … from your office, your home, even if you're on vacation. You may check the status of any payment you have made using EFTPS in the last 16 months via the Internet at www.eftps.gov.

Schedule ahead of time … with the payment scheduling feature of EFTPS, you can schedule payment instructions in advance: up to 365 days for individuals, up to 120 days for businesses. If you are on vacation or busy, schedule your payments and on the selected dates your payment instructions will be carried out … without worry … conveniently and on time. This is especially useful for Form 1040-ES estimated tax payments that are due quarterly.

Here's how it works:

1. At least one calendar day prior to your tax due date, before 8:00 P.M. EST, you access EFTPS via the Internet or phone. EFTPS will prompt you for the necessary information to complete your tax payment.

2. The system processes your instructions, and when accepted you receive an immediate EFT Acknowledgment Number that you should keep for your records, in case of any questions at a later date.

Once your tax payment instructions are accepted, EFTPS will initiate a debit transaction against your designated bank account on the date you indicated when you made your instructions.

The funds will be transferred to the Treasury's account and the tax data will be reported to the IRS to update your records.

Cancel a Payment

You can simply and easily cancel a payment via the Internet or phone up to two business days in advance of the scheduled payment date.

Check Your Payment History

You can check 16 months of your EFTPS payment history at www.eftps.gov, or you can call EFTPS Customer Service. You will be able to check when your payments have been made, and if you use the Internet, have a print-out for your files.

Get Help

EFTPS Customer Service has live representatives available to answer any questions you may have about your payments. EFTPS Customer Service is open 24 hours a day, 7 days a week. Call 800-555-4477 for businesses, 800-316-6541 for individuals.

Express Enrollment for New Businesses

Any business requesting a new EIN and indicating it will have Federal Tax Deposit obligations is automatically pre-enrolled in EFTPS.

- Business taxpayers receive notification in the mail that they are pre-enrolled, along with their EFTPS PIN.

- They activate their enrollment by calling a secure 800 number and entering bank account information.

Enroll Today!

Join the millions of business and individual taxpayers already enrolled in EFTPS. To enroll, visit the EFTPS website at www.eftps.gov; or to receive an Enrollment Form, call EFTPS Customer Service.

Once you enroll, you will receive a Confirmation Package, Personal Identification Number (PIN), and instructions on obtaining your Internet Password—then you will be ready to begin using EFTPS.

Where to Donate or Recycle Electronics

Old computers and other electronic products can be donated or recycled by the following manufacturers and/or retailers:

AT&T Reuse and Recycle

This program allows you to bring unwanted cell phones, personal data assistants (PDAs), and other accessories, regardless of the manufacturer or carrier, to an AT&T-operated store or participating authorized dealer store near you.

Website: www.wireless.att.com

Best Buy

Drop off old cell phones, rechargeable batteries, and ink-jet cartridges at the free recycling kiosks located just inside the door of every Best Buy store.

Website: www.bestbuy.com/recycling

Dell

RECONNECT (specific cities within California, Michigan, New Jersey, North Carolina, Pennsylvania, and Texas only) is a comprehensive electronics recovery, reuse, and environmentally responsible recycling partnership between Goodwill Industries and Dell, Inc..

Website: www.dell.com/recyling

eBay

Rethink Initiative provides information, tools, and solutions that make it easy to find new users for idle computers and electronics, and responsibly recycle unwanted products.

Website: www.ebay.com

Hewlett-Packard

HP runs a trade-in and recycling program for hardware, laserjet supplies, and inkjet supplies called Hewlett-Packard/Compaq Asset Recovery Services.

Website: www.hp.com

Intel

Students Recycling Used Technology (StRUT) provides technology-based education for K–16 students through the process of refurbishing donated equipment for schools in the Silicon Valley, Arizona, and Oregon.

Website: www.intel.com

LG Electronics

Consumers can participate in a free mail-in recycling program (the link to the prepaid label appears after accepting the terms of use and privacy policy) for old cell phones and their accessories (any make or model). Box up your old phone and accessories, print out the prepaid mailing label from their website, and mail in the phone for recycling.

Consumers also can return and recycle any product (such as televisions, monitors, audio equipment, videocassette players and recorders, DVD players and recorders, combination TV/VCR and TV/DVD units, set-top boxes and accessories associated with those products) that have the LG, Zenith, or Goldstar brand name.

Website: www.lge.com

Motorola

Consumers can visit Motorola's website to print out postage-paid mailing labels and send in any unused phones or accessories.

Motorola also created the Race to Recycle program, an innovative fund-raising opportunity for K–12 schools that allows them to earn extra money by recycling old mobile phones.

Website: http://motorolarecycling.com

NEC Display Solutions

Total Trade Program

Website: www.necdisplay.com

Nokia

Nokia offers a free mail-in recycling program for old cell phones through its website. Additionally, consumers can pick up a prepaid shipping envelope at any of the Nokia flagship stores in Chicago and New York.

Website: www.nokia.com/werecycle

Office Depot

Tech Recycling Boxes ($5–$15, depending on size) are available at participating stores. You can fill the boxes with as many used consumer electronics (cell phones/PDAs, computers, televisions, etc.) as will fit and drop the unsealed boxes off at any Office Depot store to be recycled. Every store has kiosks where consumers can drop off used cell phones, batteries, and accessories.

Website: www.officedepot.com

Samsung

A mail-in recycling program is in place for customers who want to recycle Samsung cell phones and accessories. Simply box up your old phone and accessories, print out the prepaid mailing label from the website, and mail in the phone for recycling.

Website: www.samsung.com/recyclingdirect

Sony

Take Back Recycling Program

Notebook Trade-In Program

Website: www.sony.com/recycle

Sony Ericsson

Consumers can preprint shipping labels from their website and mail in old devices (any make or model) free of charge.

Sony Ericsson also offers an event-based cell phone recycling program. For more information on setting up a cell phone recycling program in your area, visit their website.

Website: www.sonyerickson.com

Sprint

Spring has two cell phone recycling programs for consumers:

- The Sprint Buy Back program offers customers an account credit for returning eligible Sprint and Nextel models of phones.

- The Sprint Project Connect program is available to all consumers. It accepts wireless phones, batteries, accessories, and connection cards for recycling, regardless of make, model, condition, or service provider. You can participate in either program at no charge by visiting Sprint's website or a Sprint retail store.

Website: www.sprintrecycling.com

Staples

Eco-Easy offers consumers in-store recycling of computers, monitors, printers, desktop copiers, and other electronic waste for a fee of $10 per item.

All Staples stores offer in-store collection bins where consumers can drop off cell phones, PDAs, chargers, other handheld electronics, and ink and toner cartridges for recycling ($3 rebates are available for some eligible toner cartridges).

Website: www.staples.com

T-Mobile

The handset recycling program offers both in-store drop-off locations and a mail-in recycling option for cell phones, PDAs, and accessories. To use the mail-in option, simply box up your mobile device and accessories, print out the prepaid mailing label from the website, and mail in the phone for recycling.

Website: www.t-mobile.com

Toshiba

Recycling and Trade-In Program

Website: www.reuse.toshiba.com

Verizon

The Verizon Wireless Hopeline program collects no-longer-used wireless phones and equipment in any condition from any service provider. The used phones are either refurbished for reuse or recycled. Used phones can be returned to any Verizon Wireless retail store across the country.

Website: ecofriendlytip.com

Wireless phones and equipment donations can also be sent to:

Verizon Wireless Hopeline
c/o ReCellular Inc.
2555 Bishop Circle W.
Dexter, MI 48130

Appendix B

Sample Forms

The forms in this section are all covered in this book and are included here to give you a better idea of the information needed to complete them and if necessary, file them with the IRS or other federal, state, or local authorities.

Chapter 4

Secretary of State
Business Programs Division

1500 11ᵗʰ Street, 3ʳᵈ Floor
Sacramento, CA 95814

Business Entities
(916) 657-5448

Organization of California Nonprofit, Nonstock Corporations

California nonprofit, nonstock corporations organized for religious, charitable, social, educational, recreational or similar purposes are formed pursuant to the Nonprofit Corporation Law, commencing with California Corporations Code section 5000. The three primary types of nonprofit corporations, namely, religious, public benefit and mutual benefit, are described below.

A.   A corporation organized to operate a church or to be otherwise structured for primarily or exclusively religious purposes is a nonprofit **Religious** corporation.

B.   A corporation organized primarily or exclusively for charitable purposes and which plans to obtain state tax exempt status under California Revenue and Taxation Code section 23701(d) and/or federal tax exempt status under Internal Revenue Code section 501(c)(3) or organized to act as a civic league or a social welfare organization and which plans to obtain state tax exempt status under California Revenue and Taxation Code section 23701(f) and/or federal tax exempt status under Internal Revenue Code section 501(c)(4) is a nonprofit **Public Benefit** corporation.

C.   A corporation organized for other than religious, charitable, civic league or social welfare purposes and planning to obtain tax exempt status under provisions other than California Revenue and Taxation Code sections 23701(d) and 23701(f), Internal Revenue Code section 501(c)(4), or not planning to be tax exempt at all, is a nonprofit **Mutual Benefit** corporation.

The attached samples have been drafted to meet minimum statutory requirements. The samples may be used as a guide in preparing documents to be filed with the Secretary of State. You must determine the type of nonprofit corporation to be formed and follow the applicable sample. It is suggested that you seek private counsel for advice regarding the proposed corporation's specific needs, which may require the inclusion of special article provisions. The Secretary of State does not provide a standardized form due to the many possible drafting variations.

Where to File

Documents can be hand delivered to any office location for over-the-counter processing between the hours of 8:00 am and 4:30 pm, Monday through Friday (excluding holidays) or mailed to the Sacramento office. The mailing address and office locations are as follows:

Sacramento Office
Business Entities Section
1500 11ᵗʰ Street, 3rd Floor
Sacramento, CA 95814
(916) 657-5448

Fresno Regional Office
1315 Van Ness Avenue, Suite 203
Fresno, CA 93721
(559) 445-6900

Los Angeles Regional Office
300 South Spring Street, Room 12513
Los Angeles, CA 90013
(213) 897-3062

Mailing Address
Document Filing Support Unit
P O Box 944260
Sacramento, CA 94244-2600

San Diego Regional Office
1350 Front Street, Suite 2060
San Diego, CA 92101
(619) 525-4113

San Francisco Regional Office
455 Golden Gate Avenue, Suite 14500
San Francisco, CA 94102
(415) 557-8000

To facilitate the processing of documents mailed to our Sacramento office, a self-addressed envelope and a letter referencing the corporate name as well as your own name, return address and telephone number   should also be submitted. Please refer to our Business Entities Mail Processing Times web page at http://www.sos.ca.gov/business/bpd_processing_times.htm for current mail processing times.

Note: The regional offices are only able to process organizational documents delivered in person. Please refer to our Regional Offices web page at http://www.sos.ca.gov/business/regional.htm for detailed information regarding the submission of documents to the regional offices.

Secretary of State **Information**
ARTS-NONPROFIT (REV 01/2008)

Page 1 of 2

Application for Public Benefit Corporation

Fees

The fee for filing Articles of Incorporation for a nonprofit, nonstock corporation is $30.00. There is an additional $15.00 special handling fee for processing a document delivered in person to the Sacramento office or to any of the regional offices. The special handling fee must be remitted separately for each submittal and will be retained whether the document is filed or rejected. The preclearance and/or expedited filing of a document *within a guaranteed time frame* can be requested for an additional fee (in lieu of the special handling fee) for documents that are delivered in person to the Sacramento office. Please refer to the Secretary of State's website at http://www.sos.ca.gov/business/precexp.htm for detailed information regarding preclearance and expedited filing services. The special handling fee or preclearance and expedited filing services are not applicable to documents submitted by mail.

Payments for documents submitted:

- by mail to Sacramento can be made by check or money order.
- in person, over-the-counter in Sacramento can be made by check, money order, cash, or credit card (Visa or MasterCard).
- in person, over-the-counter in any of the four regional offices can be made by check, money order, or credit card (Visa or MasterCard). Regional offices are not able to accept cash.

Checks or money orders should be made payable to the Secretary of State.

Copies

The Secretary of State will certify up to two copies of the filed document without charge, **provided that the copies are submitted to the Secretary of State with the document to be filed**. Any additional copies submitted will be certified with payment of $8.00 per copy. **Note:** If forming a nonprofit *public benefit* corporation, one additional copy must be provided for the Secretary of State to forward to the Office of the Attorney General as required by California Corporations Code section 5120(d).

Franchise Tax Requirements

A nonprofit corporation is a taxable entity and subject each year to an **$800** minimum California franchise tax **unless** the corporation has applied for tax-exempt status and the Franchise Tax Board determines the corporation qualifies for tax-exempt status. Therefore, until such a determination is made, the corporation must file a return and pay the associated tax every year until the corporation is formally dissolved.

After filing its Articles of Incorporation with the Secretary of State, the nonprofit corporation may apply for tax-exempt status in California by mailing an Exemption Application (FTB Form 3500), along with an endorsed copy of the Articles of Incorporation and all other required supporting documentation, to the Franchise Tax Board, P.O. Box 942857, Sacramento, California 94257-4041. Form 3500 can be accessed from the Franchise Tax Board's website at www.ftb.ca.gov or can be requested by calling the Franchise Tax Board at 1-800-338-0505. For further information regarding franchise tax exemption, refer to the Franchise Tax Board's website or call the Franchise Tax Board at (916) 845-4171. Questions regarding franchise tax requirements must be directed to the Franchise Tax Board.

Additional Resources

All corporations are subject to state and federal tax laws and may be subject to additional requirements depending on the type of corporation and/or the type of business conducted. Please refer to our Business Resources web page at http://www.sos.ca.gov/business/bpd_links.htm for a list of other agencies you may need to contact to ensure proper compliance. Note: The Secretary of State <u>does not</u> license corporations. For licensing requirements, please contact the city and/or county where the principal place of business is located and/or the state agency with jurisdiction over the activities of the corporation.

Organization of California Nonprofit, Nonstock Corporations

INSTRUCTIONS:

Articles of Incorporation must be drafted to include all the provisions required by the California Corporations Code. Articles of Incorporation may include other provisions as permitted under California law (e.g., the name and address of each initial director). The attached sample meets the minimum statutory requirements and should only be used as a guide in preparing Articles of Incorporation. The document should be typed with letters in dark contrast to the paper. Documents not suitable for reproduction will be returned unfiled. Note: The file date of Articles of Incorporation is generally the date the document complying with applicable law is received in the Secretary of State's office.

Article I: The articles must include a statement of the name of the corporation.

Note: The name must be exactly as you want it to appear on the records of the California Secretary of State.

Article IIA: **Mutual Benefit Corporation:** This exact statement is required by the California Corporations Code and should not be altered.

Public Benefit Corporation: This exact statement is required by the California Corporations Code and should not be altered except to include the applicable purpose description.

Religious Corporation: This exact statement is required by the California Corporations Code and should not be altered.

Article IIB: A statement describing the specific purpose may be included and, in fact, must be included if the corporation is organized for public purposes or if the corporation intends to apply for state franchise tax exemption.

Article III: The articles must include the name of the initial agent for service of process.[1]

- If an individual is designated as agent, include the agent's business or residential **street** address in California (a P.O. Box address is not acceptable). Please do not use "in care of" (c/o) or abbreviate the name of the city.

- If another corporation is designated as agent, do not include the address of the designated corporation.

Note: Before another corporation may be designated as agent, that corporation must have previously filed with the Secretary of State a certificate pursuant to California Corporations Code section 1505. **A corporation cannot act as its own agent** and no domestic or foreign corporation may file pursuant to Section 1505 unless the corporation is currently authorized to engage in business in California and is in good standing on the records of the California Secretary of State.

Article IV and Article V (where applicable): The Franchise Tax Board requires this language before state tax exemption may be granted.

Execution: The articles must be signed by each incorporator, or by each initial director named in the articles. If initial directors are named, each director must both sign and acknowledge the articles. Note: If initial directors are not named in the articles, the individual(s) executing the document is the incorporator(s) of the corporation. The name of each incorporator or initial director should be typed beneath their signatures.

---

[1] An "agent for service of process" is an individual (director, officer or any other person, whether or not affiliated with the corporation) who resides in California or another corporation designated to accept service of process if the corporation is sued. Note: The agent must agree to accept service of process on behalf of the corporation prior to designation.

MUTUAL BENEFIT SAMPLE

ARTICLES OF INCORPORATION

I

The name of the corporation is _____ *[NAME OF CORPORATION]* _____ .

II

A. This corporation is a nonprofit **Mutual Benefit Corporation** organized under the Nonprofit Mutual Benefit Corporation Law. The purpose of this corporation is to engage in any lawful act or activity, other than credit union business, for which a corporation may be organized under such law.

B. The specific purpose of this corporation is to _____

_____ .

III

The name and address in the State of California of this corporation's initial agent for service of process is:

Name _____

Address _____

City _____ State **CALIFORNIA**   Zip Code _____

IV

Notwithstanding any of the above statements of purposes and powers, this corporation shall not, except to an insubstantial degree, engage in any activities or exercise any powers that are not in furtherance of the specific purposes of this corporation.

_____
[Signature of Incorporator]

[Typed Name of Incorporator], Incorporator

If an individual is designated as the initial agent for service of process, include the agent's business or residential street address in California (a P.O. Box address is not acceptable). If another corporation is designated as the initial agent for service of process, do not include the address of the designated corporation.

This sample is provided to be used as a guideline ONLY in the preparation of the original document for filing with the Secretary of State.

Secretary of State **Sample**
ARTS-MU (REV 01/2008)

ARTICLES OF INCORPORATION

PUBLIC BENEFIT SAMPLE

I

The name of the corporation is _____ *[NAME OF CORPORATION]* _____ .

II

A. This corporation is a nonprofit **Public Benefit Corporation** and is not organized for the private gain of any person. It is organized under the Nonprofit Public Benefit Corporation Law for:

(   ) **public** purposes.

or   (   ) **charitable** purposes.

or   (   ) **public and charitable** purposes.

B. The specific purpose of this corporation is to _____

_____ .

III

The name and address in the State of California of this corporation's initial agent for service of process is:

Name _____

Address _____

City _____ State **CALIFORNIA**   Zip Code _____

IV

A. This corporation is organized and operated exclusively for **charitable** purposes within the meaning of Internal Revenue Code section 501(c)(3).

B. No substantial part of the activities of this corporation shall consist of carrying on propaganda, or otherwise attempting to influence legislation, and the corporation shall not participate or intervene in any political campaign (including the publishing or distribution of statements) on behalf of any candidate for public office.

V

The property of this corporation is irrevocably dedicated to **charitable** purposes and no part of the net income or assets of this corporation shall ever inure to the benefit of any director, officer or member thereof or to the benefit of any private person. Upon the dissolution or winding up of the corporation, its assets remaining after payment, or provision for payment, of all debts and liabilities of this corporation shall be distributed to a nonprofit fund, foundation or corporation which is organized and operated exclusively for **charitable** purposes and which has established its tax exempt status under Internal Revenue Code section 501(c)(3).

_____
[Signature of Incorporator]

[Typed Name of Incorporator], Incorporator

If an individual is designated as the initial agent for service of process, include the agent's business or residential street address in California (a P.O. Box address is not acceptable). If another corporation is designated as the initial agent for service of process, do not include the address of the designated corporation.

This sample is provided to be used as a guideline ONLY in the preparation of the original document for filing with the Secretary of State.

Secretary of State **Sample**
ARTS-PB (REV 01/2008)

RELIGIOUS SAMPLE

ARTICLES OF INCORPORATION

I

The name of the corporation is _____ *[NAME OF CORPORATION]* _____ .

II

A. This corporation is a **Religious Corporation** and is not organized for the private gain of any person. It is organized under the Nonprofit Religious Corporation Law exclusively for religious purposes.

B. The specific purpose of this corporation is to _____

_____ .

III

The name and address in the State of California of this corporation's initial agent for service of process is:

Name _____

Address _____

City _____   State **CALIFORNIA**   Zip Code _____

IV

A. This corporation is organized and operated exclusively for **religious** purposes within the meaning of Internal Revenue Code section 501(c)(3).

B. No substantial part of the activities of this corporation shall consist of carrying on propaganda, or otherwise attempting to influence legislation, and the corporation shall not participate or intervene in any political campaign (including the publishing or distribution of statements) on behalf of any candidate for public office.

V

The property of this corporation is irrevocably dedicated to **religious** purposes and no part of the net income or assets of this corporation shall ever inure to the benefit of any director, officer or member thereof or to the benefit of any private person. Upon the dissolution or winding up of the corporation, its assets remaining after payment, or provision for payment, of all debts and liabilities of this corporation shall be distributed to a nonprofit fund, foundation or corporation which is organized and operated exclusively for **religious** purposes and which has established its tax exempt status under Internal Revenue Code section 501(c)(3).

_____
[Signature of Incorporator]

[Typed Name of Incorporator], Incorporator

If an individual is designated as the initial agent for service of process, include the agent's business or residential street address in California (a P.O. Box address is not acceptable). If another corporation is designated as the initial agent for service of process, do not include the address of the designated corporation.

This sample is provided to be used as a guideline ONLY in the preparation of the original document for filing with the Secretary of State.

Secretary of State **Sample**
ARTS-RE (REV 01/2008)

YOUR RETURN MAILING ADDRESS

NAME:

ADDRESS:

CITY:

STATE: ZIP CODE:

LOS ANGELES REGISTRAR-RECORDER/ COUNTY CLERK

FICTITIOUS BUSINESS NAME STATEMENT

TYPE OF FILING AND FILING FEE (Check one)

☒ Original- **$23.00** (FOR ORIGINAL FILING WITH ONE BUSINESS NAME ON STATEMENT) ☒ New Filings- **$23.00-**
☒ Refile- **$18.00** (NO CHANGES IN THE FACTS FROM ORIGINAL FILING)   (CHANGES IN FACTS FROM ORIGINAL FILING-REQUIRES PUBLICATION)
$4.00- FOR EACH ADDITIONAL BUSINESS NAME FILED ON SAME STATEMENT, DOING BUSINESS AT THE SAME LOCATION **$4.00-** FOR EACH ADDITIONAL OWNER IN EXCESS OF ONE OWNER

The following person(s) is (are) doing business as:

*1._____ 2._____

Print Fictitious Business Name(s)

**_____

Street address of principal place of business   Mailing address if different

City   State   Zip   **COUNTY**   City   State   Zip

Articles of Incorporation or Organization Number (if applicable): AI #ON_____

*** **REGISTERED OWNER(S):**

1._____   2._____

Full Name/Corp/LLC   Full Name/Corp/LLC

Residence Address (P.O. Box not accepted)   Residence Address (P.O. Box not accepted)

City   State   Zip   City   State   Zip

If Corporation or LLC – Print State of Incorporation/Organization   If Corporation or LLC – Print State of Incorporation/Organization

3._____   4._____

Full Name/Corp/LLC   Full Name/Corp/LLC

Residence Address (P.O. Box not accepted)   Residence Address (P.O. Box not accepted)

City   State   Zip   City   State   Zip

If Corporation or LLC – Print State of Incorporation/Organization   If Corporation or LLC – Print State of Incorporation/Organization

IF MORE THAN FOUR REGISTRANTS, ATTACH ADDITIONAL SHEET SHOWING OWNER INFORMATION

**** **THIS BUSINESS IS CONDUCTED BY: (Check one)**
☒ an Individual   ☒ a General Partnership   ☒ a Limited Partnership   ☒ a Limited Liability Company
☒ an Unincorporated Association other than a Partnership   ☒ a Corporation   ☒ a Trust   ☒ Copartners
☒ Husband and Wife   ☒ Joint Venture   ☒ State or Local Registered Domestic Partners   ☒ a Limited Liability Partnership

***** The registrant commenced to transact business under the fictitious business name or names listed above on _____

(Insert N/A above if you haven't started to transact business)

I declare that all information in this statement is true and correct.
(A registrant who declares as true information which he or she knows to be false is guilty of a crime.)

REGISTRANTS/CORP/LLC NAME (PRINT) _____ TITLE_____

REGISTRANT SIGNATURE _____ **IF CORP OR LLC, PRINT NAME**_____

If corporation, also print corporate title of officer. If LLC, also print title of officer or manager.

This statement was filed with the County Clerk of LOS ANGELES on the date indicated by the filed stamp in the upper right corner.

NOTICE – IN ACCORDANCE WITH SUBDIVISION (a) OF SECTION 17920, A FICTITIOUS NAME STATEMENT GENERALLY EXPIRES AT THE END OF FIVE YEARS FROM THE DATE ON WHICH IT WAS FILED IN THE OFFICE OF THE COUNTY CLERK, EXCEPT, AS PROVIDED IN SUBDIVISION (b) OF SECTION 17920, WHERE IT EXPIRES 40 DAYS AFTER ANY CHANGE IN THE FACTS SET FORTH IN THE STATEMENT PURSUANT TO SECTION 17913 OTHER THAN A CHANGE IN THE RESIDENCE ADDRESS OF A REGISTERED OWNER. A NEW FICTITIOUS BUSINESS NAME STATEMENT MUST BE FILED BEFORE THE EXPIRATION.

THE FILING OF THIS STATEMENT DOES NOT OF ITSELF AUTHORIZE THE USE IN THIS STATE OF A FICTITIOUS BUSINESS NAME IN VIOLATION OF THE RIGHTS OF ANOTHER UNDER FEDERAL, STATE, OR COMMON LAW (SEE SECTION 14411 ET SEQ., BUSINESS AND PROFESSIONS CODE).
I HEREBY CERTIFY THAT THIS COPY IS A CORRECT COPY OF THE ORIGINAL STATEMENT ON FILE IN MY OFFICE.

DEAN C. LOGAN, LOS ANGELES COUNTY CLERK   BY:_____, *Deputy*

Rev. 01/01/08   P.O. BOX 53592, LOS ANGELES, CA 90053-0592   PH: (562) 462-2177   WEB ADDRESS: LAVOTE..NET

Fictitious Business Name Statement and Instructions

YOUR RETURN MAILING ADDRESS

NAME:

ADDRESS:

CITY:

STATE: ZIP CODE:

COPY of Document Recorded

Has not been compared with original. Original will
be returned when processing has been completed.
LOS ANGELES COUNTYREGISTRAR-RECORDER

FICTITIOUS BUSINESS NAME STATEMENT

TYPE OF FILING AND FILING FEE (Check one)

☒ Original- $23.00 (FOR ORIGINAL FILING WITH ONE BUSINESS NAME ON STATEMENT) ☒ New Filings- $23.00
☒ Refile- $18.00 (NO CHANGES IN THE FACTS FROM ORIGINAL FILING)   (CHANGES IN FACTS FROM ORIGINAL FILING-REQUIRES PUBLICATION)
$4.00- FOR EACH ADDITIONAL BUSINESS NAME FILED ON SAME STATEMENT, DOING BUSINESS AT THE SAME LOCATION **$4.00-** FOR EACH ADDITIONAL OWNER IN EXCESS OF ONE OWNER

The following person(s) is (are) doing business as:

*1._____ 2._____

Print Fictitious Business Name(s)

**

Street address of principal place of business   Mailing address if different

City   State   Zip   **COUNTY**   City   State   Zip

Articles of Incorporation or Organization Number (if applicable): AI #ON_____

*** REGISTERED OWNER(S):

1._____   2._____

Full Name/Corp/LLC   Full Name/Corp/LLC

Residence Address (P.O. Box not accepted)   Residence Address (P.O. Box not accepted)

City   State   Zip   City   State   Zip

If Corporation or LLC – Print State of Incorporation/Organization   If Corporation or LLC – Print State of Incorporation/Organization

3._____   4._____

Full Name/Corp/LLC   Full Name/Corp/LLC

Residence Address (P.O. Box not accepted)   Residence Address (P.O. Box not accepted)

City   State   Zip   City   State   Zip

If Corporation or LLC – Print State of Incorporation/Organization   If Corporation or LLC – Print State of Incorporation/Organization

IF MORE THAN FOUR REGISTRANTS, ATTACH ADDITIONAL SHEET SHOWING OWNER INFORMATION

**** THIS BUSINESS IS CONDUCTED BY: (Check one)

☒ an Individual ☒ a General Partnership ☒ a Limited Partnership ☒ a Limited Liability Company
☒ an Unincorporated Association other than a Partnership ☒ a Corporation ☒ a Trust ☒ Copartners
☒ Husband and Wife ☒ Joint Venture ☒ State or Local Registered Domestic Partners ☒ a Limited Liability Partnership

***** The registrant commenced to transact business under the fictitious business name or names listed above on _____

(Insert N/A above if you haven't started to transact business)

I declare that all information in this statement is true and correct.

(A registrant who declares as true information which he or she knows to be false is guilty of a crime.)

REGISTRANTS/CORP/LLC) NAME (PRINT) _____ TITLE_____

REGISTRANT SIGNATURE _____ **IF CORP OR LLC, PRINT NAME**_____

If corporation, also print corporate title of officer. If LLC, also print title of officer or manager.

This statement was filed with the County Clerk of LOS ANGELES on the date indicated by the filed stamp in the upper right corner.

NOTICE – IN ACCORDANCE WITH SUBDIVISION (a) OF SECTION 17920, A FICTITIOUS NAME STATEMENT GENERALLY EXPIRES AT THE END OF FIVE YEARS FROM THE DATE ON
WHICH IT WAS FILED IN THE OFFICE OF THE COUNTY CLERK, EXCEPT, AS PROVIDED IN SUBDIVISION (b) OF SECTION 17920, WHERE IT EXPIRES 40 DAYS AFTER ANY CHANGE
IN THE FACTS SET FORTH IN THE STATEMENT PURSUANT TO SECTION 17913 OTHER THAN A CHANGE IN THE RESIDENCE ADDRESS
OF A REGISTERED OWNER. A NEW FICTITIOUS BUSINESS NAME STATEMENT MUST BE FILED BEFORE THE EXPIRATION.

THE FILING OF THIS STATEMENT DOES NOT OF ITSELF AUTHORIZE THE USE IN THIS STATE OF A FICTITIOUS BUSINESS NAME IN VIOLATION OF THE RIGHTS OF ANOTHER
UNDER FEDERAL, STATE, OR COMMON LAW (SEE SECTION 14411 ET SEQ., BUSINESS AND PROFESSIONS CODE).
I HEREBY CERTIFY THAT THIS COPY IS A CORRECT COPY OF THE ORIGINAL STATEMENT ON FILE IN MY OFFICE.

DEAN C. LOGAN, LOS ANGELES COUNTY CLERK   BY:_____, Deputy

Rev. 01/01/08   P.O. BOX 53592, LOS ANGELES, CA 90053-0592   PH: (562) 462-2177   WEB ADDRESS: LAVOTE..NET

INSTRUCTIONS FOR COMPLETION OF STATEMENT

Business and Professions Code Section 17913:
* Where one asterisk appears in the form:
  (a) Insert the fictitious business name or names
  (b) Only those businesses operated at the same address and under the same ownership may be listed on one statement

** Where two asterisks appear in the form:
  (a) If the registrant has a place of business in this state, insert the **street address and county** of his or her **principal** place of business in this state
  (b) If the registrant has no place of business in this state, insert the **street address and county** of his or her **principal** place of business outside this state and file with the Clerk of Sacramento County (B&P 17915)
  (c) Mail Box and Post Office Box Numbers **are not acceptable** as a business address when used alone without a street address

*** Where three asterisks appear in the form:
  (a) If the registrant is an **individual**, insert his or her full name and residence address
  (b) If the registrants are **husband and wife**, insert the full name and residence address of both the husband and the wife
  (c) If the registrant is a **general partnership, copartnership, joint venture, limited liability partnership, or unincorporated association other than a partnership**, insert the full name and residence address of each general partner
  (d) If the registrant is a **limited partnership**, insert the full name and residence address of each general partner
  (e) If the registrant is a **limited liability company**, insert the name and address of the limited liability company, as set out in its articles of organization on file with the CA Secretary of State, and the state of organization
  (f) If the registrant is a **trust**, insert the full name and residence address of each trustee
  (g) If the registrant is a **corporation**, insert the name and address of the corporation, as set out in its articles of incorporation on file with the CA Secretary of State, and the state of incorporation
  (h) If the registrants are **state or local registered domestic partners**, insert the full name and residence address of each domestic partner

**** Where four asterisks appear in the form:
  (a) Check whichever of the terms listed on the front of the form best describes the nature of the business

***** Where five asterisks appear in the form:
  (a) Insert the date on which the registrant first commenced to transact business under the fictitious business name or names listed, if already transacting business under that name or names
  (b) Insert N/A if you have not yet commenced to transact business under the fictitious business name or names listed

Business and Professions Code Section 17914
The statement shall be signed as follows:
  (a) If the registrant is an individual, by the individual
  (b) If the registrants are husband and wife, by the husband or wife
  (c) If the registrant is a general partnership, limited partnership, limited liability partnership, copartnership, joint venture, or unincorporated association other than a partnership, by a general partner
  (d) If the registrant is a limited liability company, by a manager or officer
  (e) If the registrant is a trust, by a trustee
  (f) If the registrant is a corporation, by an officer
  (g) If the registrant is a state or local registered domestic partnership, by one of the domestic partners

Business and Professions Code Section 17915
The fictitious business name statement **shall** be filed with the clerk of the county in which the registrant has his or her **principal place** of business in this state or, if the registrant has no place of business in this state, with the Clerk of Sacramento County. Nothing in this chapter shall preclude a person from filing a fictitious business name statement in a county other than that where the principal place of business is located, as long as the requirements of this subdivision are also met.

Business and Professions Code Section 17917
Publication for Original, New Filings (renewal with change in facts from previous filing), or Refile
  (a) Within 30 days after a fictitious business name statement has been filed, the registrant shall cause it to be published in a newspaper of general circulation in the county where the fictitious business name statement was filed or, if there is no such newspaper in that county, in a newspaper of general circulation in an adjoining county. If the registrant does not have a place of business in this state, the notice shall be published in a newspaper of general circulation in Sacramento County. The publication must be once a week for four successive weeks and an affidavit of publication must be filed with the county clerk where the fictitious business name statement was filed within 30 days after the completion of the publication.
  (b) If a refiling is required because the prior statement has expired, the refiling need **not** be published, unless there has been a change in the information required in the expired statement, provided the refiling is filed **within** 40 days of the date the statement expired.

Business and Professions Code Section 17922
Abandonment of Fictitious Business Name
  (a) Upon ceasing to transact business in this state under a fictitious business name that was filed in the previous five years, a person who has filed a fictitious business name statement **shall** file a statement of abandonment of use of fictitious business name. The statement shall be executed and published in the same manner as a fictitious business name statement and **shall** be filed with the county clerk of the county in which the person has filed his or her fictitious business name statement.

Business and Professions Code Section 17930
Any person who executes, files, or publishes any statement under this chapter, knowing that such statement is false, in whole or in part, shall be guilty of a misdemeanor and upon conviction thereof shall be punished by a fine not to exceed one thousand dollars ($1,000).

Chapter 8

```
              SMART SHOPPER THRIFT SHOP
                  CHART OF ACCOUNTS


     1000      Cash in Checking                    Asset
     1010      Cash in Savings                     Asset
     1100      Accounts Receivable                 Asset
     1110      Inventory                           Asset
     1200      Buildings                           Asset
     1210      Accumulated Depreciation-Buildings  Asset
     1220      Land                                Asset
     1300      Furniture & Fixtures                Asset
     1310      Accumulated Depreciation- F & F     Asset
     1330      Equipment                           Asset
     1340      Accumulated Depreciation-Equipment  Asset
     2000      Accounts Payable                    Liability
     2010      Bank Loan Payable                   Liability
     2020      Credit Card Payable                 Liability
     2100      Sales Tax Payable                   Liability
     2200      Federal Withholding Tax Payable     Liability
     2210      Social Security Tax Payable         Liability
     2212      Medicare Tax Payable                Liability
     2220      State Withholding Tax Payable       Liability
     2230      SUTA Payable                        Liability
     2240      FUTA Payable                        Liability
     3040      Retained Earnings                   Equity
     4000      Sales                               Income
     4100      Interest Income                     Income
     4200      Cost of Sales                       In come
     6000      Salaries and Wages                  Expense
     6030      Officers' Salaries                  Expense
     6100      Advertising                         Expense
     6120      Auto Expense                        Expense
     6125      Bank Fees                           Expense
     6130      Depreciation Expense                Expense
     6140      Dues & Subscriptions                Expense
     6145      Equipment Rental                    Expense
     6150      Insurance Expense                   Expense
     6160      Interest Expense                    Expense
     6165      Legal & Accounting                  Expense
     6170      Miscellaneous Expense               Expense
     6175      Office Expense                      Expense
     6180      Rent                                Expense
     6185      Repairs & Maintenance               Expense
     6200      Supplies                            Expense
     6250      Taxes-Payroll                       Expense
     6255      Taxes-Other                         Expense
     6300      Utilities                           Expense

     This is a sample Chart of Accounts for information only.
```

Sample Chart of Accounts

Chapter 9

| SCHEDULE C
(Form 1040)

Department of the Treasury
Internal Revenue Service (99) | **Profit or Loss From Business**
(Sole Proprietorship)
▶ Partnerships, joint ventures, etc., generally must file Form 1065 or 1065-B.
▶ Attach to Form 1040, 1040NR, or 1041.   ▶ See Instructions for Schedule C (Form 1040). | OMB No. 1545-0074
2008
Attachment
Sequence No. **09** |

| Name of proprietor | Social security number (SSN) |

| **A** Principal business or profession, including product or service (see page C-3 of the instructions) | **B** Enter code from pages C-9, 10, & 11 ▶ |

| **C** Business name. If no separate business name, leave blank. | **D** Employer ID number (EIN), if any |

E Business address (including suite or room no.) ▶
City, town or post office, state, and ZIP code

F Accounting method: **(1)** ☐ Cash   **(2)** ☐ Accrual   **(3)** ☐ Other (specify) ▶

G Did you "materially participate" in the operation of this business during 2008? If "No," see page C-4 for limit on losses   ☐ Yes   ☐ No

H If you started or acquired this business during 2008, check here . . . . ▶ ☐

Part I Income

1	Gross receipts or sales. **Caution.** See page C-4 and check the box if:		
	• This income was reported to you on Form W-2 and the "Statutory employee" box on that form was checked, or	▶ ☐	**1**
	• You are a member of a qualified joint venture reporting only rental real estate income not subject to self-employment tax. Also see page C-4 for limit on losses.		
2	Returns and allowances		**2**
3	Subtract line 2 from line 1		**3**
4	Cost of goods sold (from line 42 on page 2)		**4**
5	**Gross profit.** Subtract line 4 from line 3		**5**
6	Other income, including federal and state gasoline or fuel tax credit or refund (see page C-4) . .		**6**
7	**Gross income.** Add lines 5 and 6 . . . . ▶		**7**

Part II Expenses. Enter expenses for business use of your home **only** on line 30.

8	Advertising	**8**		18	Office expense	**18**	
9	Car and truck expenses (see page C-5).	**9**		19	Pension and profit-sharing plans	**19**	
				20	Rent or lease (see page C-6):		
10	Commissions and fees . .	**10**		**a**	Vehicles, machinery, and equipment .	**20a**	
11	Contract labor (see page C-5)	**11**		**b**	Other business property . . .	**20b**	
12	Depletion	**12**		21	Repairs and maintenance . .	**21**	
13	Depreciation and section 179 expense deduction (not included in Part III) (see page C-5)	**13**		22	Supplies (not included in Part III)	**22**	
				23	Taxes and licenses	**23**	
				24	Travel, meals, and entertainment:		
				a	Travel	**24a**	
14	Employee benefit programs (other than on line 19) .	**14**		**b**	Deductible meals and entertainment (see page C-7) .	**24b**	
15	Insurance (other than health) .	**15**		25	Utilities	**25**	
16	Interest:			26	Wages (less employment credits) .	**26**	
a	Mortgage (paid to banks, etc.) .	**16a**		27	Other expenses (from line 48 on page 2)	**27**	
b	Other	**16b**					
17	Legal and professional services	**17**					

28	**Total expenses** before expenses for business use of home. Add lines 8 through 27 . . . . ▶	**28**	
29	Tentative profit or (loss). Subtract line 28 from line 7	**29**	
30	Expenses for business use of your home. Attach **Form 8829**	**30**	
31	**Net profit or (loss).** Subtract line 30 from line 29.		
	• If a profit, enter on both **Form 1040, line 12,** and **Schedule SE, line 2,** or on **Form 1040NR, line 13** (if you checked the box on line 1, see page C-7). Estates and trusts, enter on **Form 1041, line 3.**	**31**	
	• If a loss, you **must** go to line 32.		
32	If you have a loss, check the box that describes your investment in this activity (see page C-8).		
	• If you checked 32a, enter the loss on both **Form 1040, line 12,** and **Schedule SE, line 2,** or on **Form 1040NR, line 13** (if you checked the box on line 1, see the line 31 instructions on page C-7). Estates and trusts, enter on **Form 1041, line 3.**	**32a** ☐ All investment is at risk. **32b** ☐ Some investment is not at risk.	
	• If you checked 32b, you **must** attach **Form 6198.** Your loss may be limited.		

For Paperwork Reduction Act Notice, see page C-9 of the instructions.   Cat. No. 11334P   Schedule C (Form 1040) 2008

IRS Form Schedule C (Form 1040) Profit or Loss from Business

Schedule C (Form 1040) 2008   Page **2**

| Part III | Cost of Goods Sold (see page C-8) |

33 Method(s) used to
value closing inventory: **a** ☐ Cost   **b** ☐ Lower of cost or market   **c** ☐ Other (attach explanation)

34 Was there any change in determining quantities, costs, or valuations between opening and closing inventory?
If "Yes," attach explanation . . . . ☐ Yes   ☐ No

35 Inventory at beginning of year. If different from last year's closing inventory, attach explanation . .	**35**	
36 Purchases less cost of items withdrawn for personal use	**36**	
37 Cost of labor. Do not include any amounts paid to yourself	**37**	
38 Materials and supplies	**38**	
39 Other costs	**39**	
40 Add lines 35 through 39	**40**	
41 Inventory at end of year	**41**	
42 **Cost of goods sold.** Subtract line 41 from line 40. Enter the result here and on page 1, line 4 . .	**42**	

| Part IV | Information on Your Vehicle. Complete this part **only** if you are claiming car or truck expenses on line 9 and are not required to file Form 4562 for this business. See the instructions for line 13 on page C-5 to find out if you must file Form 4562. |

43 When did you place your vehicle in service for business purposes? (month, day, year) ▶ . . . . / . . . . / . . . . .

44 Of the total number of miles you drove your vehicle during 2008, enter the number of miles you used your vehicle for:

a Business . . . . **b** Commuting (see instructions) . . . . **c** Other . . . .

45 Was your vehicle available for personal use during off-duty hours? . . . . ☐ Yes   ☐ No

46 Do you (or your spouse) have another vehicle available for personal use?. . . . . ☐ Yes   ☐ No

47a Do you have evidence to support your deduction? . . . . ☐ Yes   ☐ No

  b If "Yes," is the evidence written? . . . . ☐ Yes   ☐ No

| Part V | Other Expenses. List below business expenses not included on lines 8–26 or line 30. |

. . . .	
. . . .	
. . . .	
. . . .	
. . . .	
. . . .	
. . . .	
. . . .	
48 Total other expenses. Enter here and on page 1, line 27	**48**	

Schedule C (Form 1040) 2008

SCHEDULE SE **(Form 1040)** Department of the Treasury Internal Revenue Service (99)	**Self-Employment Tax** ▶ **Attach to Form 1040.** ▶ **See Instructions for Schedule SE (Form 1040).**	OMB No. 1545-0074 **2008** Attachment Sequence No. **17**

Name of person with **self-employment** income (as shown on Form 1040)	Social security number of person with **self-employment** income ▶

Who Must File Schedule SE

You must file Schedule SE if:

- You had net earnings from self-employment from **other than** church employee income (line 4 of Short Schedule SE or line 4c of Long Schedule SE) of $400 or more, **or**
- You had church employee income of $108.28 or more. Income from services you performed as a minister or a member of a religious order **is not** church employee income (see page SE-1).

Note. Even if you had a loss or a small amount of income from self-employment, it may be to your benefit to file Schedule SE and use either "optional method" in Part II of Long Schedule SE (see page SE-4).

Exception. If your only self-employment income was from earnings as a minister, member of a religious order, or Christian Science practitioner **and** you filed Form 4361 and received IRS approval not to be taxed on those earnings,**do not** file Schedule SE. Instead, write "Exempt—Form 4361" on Form 1040, line 57.

May I Use Short Schedule SE or Must I Use Long Schedule SE?

Note. Use this flowchart **only if** you must file Schedule SE. If unsure, see *Who Must File Schedule SE,* above.

```
                    ┌──────────────────────────────────────────┐
                    │   Did you receive wages or tips in 2008?   │
                    └──────────────────────────────────────────┘
        No                                                    Yes

┌─────────────────────────────────────┐      ┌─────────────────────────────────────┐
│ Are you a minister, member of a     │ Yes  │ Was the total of your wages and tips │ Yes
│ religious order, or Christian       │─────▶│ subject to social security or        │────▶
│ Science practitioner who received   │      │ railroad retirement (tier 1) tax plus│
│ IRS approval not to be taxed on     │      │ your net earnings from               │
│ earnings from these sources, but    │      │ self-employment more than $102,000?  │
│ you owe self-employment tax on      │      └─────────────────────────────────────┘
│ other earnings?                     │                      No
└─────────────────────────────────────┘
        No                                   ┌─────────────────────────────────────┐
                                             │ Did you receive tips subject to      │ Yes
┌─────────────────────────────────────┐ Yes │ social security or Medicare tax      │────▶
│ Are you using one of the optional   │────▶ │ that you did not report to your      │
│ methods to figure your net          │      │ employer?                            │
│ earnings (see page SE-4)?           │      └─────────────────────────────────────┘
└─────────────────────────────────────┘                      No
        No
                                   No  ┌─────────────────────────────────────┐
┌─────────────────────────────────────┐ ◀──│ Did you report any wages on Form     │ Yes
│ Did you receive church employee     │ Yes │ 8919, Uncollected Social Security    │────▶
│ income reported on Form W-2 of      │────▶│ and Medicare Tax on Wages?          │
│ $108.28 or more?                    │     └─────────────────────────────────────┘
└─────────────────────────────────────┘
        No

┌─────────────────────────────────────┐      ┌─────────────────────────────────────┐
│   You may use Short Schedule SE below│      │ You must use Long Schedule SE on page 2│
└─────────────────────────────────────┘      └─────────────────────────────────────┘
```

Section A—Short Schedule SE. Caution. Read above to see if you can use Short Schedule SE.

1a	Net farm profit or (loss) from Schedule F, line 36, and farm partnerships, Schedule K-1 (Form 1065), box 14, code A	**1a**	
b	If you received social security retirement or disability benefits, enter the amount of Conservation Reserve Program payments included on Schedule F, line 6b, or listed on Schedule K-1 (Form 1065), box 20, code X	**1b** (	)
2	Net profit or (loss) from Schedule C, line 31; Schedule C-EZ, line 3; Schedule K-1 (Form 1065), box 14, code A (other than farming); and Schedule K-1 (Form 1065-B), box 9, code J1. Ministers and members of religious orders, see page SE-1 for types of income to report on this line. See page SE-3 for other income to report	**2**	
3	Combine lines 1a, 1b, and 2	**3**	
4	**Net earnings from self-employment.** Multiply line 3 by 92.35% (.9235). If less than $400, **do not** file this schedule; you do not owe self-employment tax . . . . ▶	**4**	
5	Self-employment tax. If the amount on line 4 is: • $102,000 or less, multiply line 4 by 15.3% (.153). Enter the result here and on **Form 1040, line 57.** • More than $102,000, multiply line 4 by 2.9% (.029). Then, add $12,648 to the result. Enter the total here and on **Form 1040, line 57**	**5**	
6	**Deduction for one-half of self-employment tax.** Multiply line 5 by 50% (.5). Enter the result here and on **Form 1040, line 27** . . . **6**		

For Paperwork Reduction Act Notice, see Form 1040 instructions.   Cat. No. 11358Z   **Schedule SE (Form 1040) 2008**

IRS Form Schedule SE (Form 1040) Self-Employment Tax

Schedule SE (Form 1040) 2008   Attachment Sequence No. **17**   Page **2**

Name of person with **self-employment** income (as shown on Form 1040)	Social security number of person with **self-employment** income ▶	

Section B—Long Schedule SE

Part I Self-Employment Tax

Note. If your only income subject to self-employment tax is **church employee income**, skip lines 1 through 4b. Enter -0- on line 4c and go to line 5a. Income from services you performed as a minister or a member of a religious order **is not** church employee income. See page SE-1.

A If you are a minister, member of a religious order, or Christian Science practitioner **and** you filed Form 4361, but you had $400 or more of **other** net earnings from self-employment, check here and continue with Part I . . . . . . ▶ ☐

1a Net farm profit or (loss) from Schedule F, line 36, and farm partnerships, Schedule K-1 (Form 1065), box 14, code A. **Note.** Skip lines 1a and 1b if you use the farm optional method (see page SE-4) — **1a**

b If you received social security retirement or disability benefits, enter the amount of Conservation Reserve Program payments included on Schedule F, line 6b, or listed on Schedule K-1 (Form 1065), box 20, code X — **1b** ( )

2 Net profit or (loss) from Schedule C, line 31; Schedule C-EZ, line 3; Schedule K-1 (Form 1065), box 14, code A (other than farming); and Schedule K-1 (Form 1065-B), box 9, code J1. Ministers and members of religious orders, see page SE-1 for types of income to report on this line. See page SE-3 for other income to report. **Note.** Skip this line if you use the nonfarm optional method (see page SE-4) **2**

3 Combine lines 1a, 1b, and 2 . . . . **3**

4a If line 3 is more than zero, multiply line 3 by 92.35% (.9235). Otherwise, enter amount from line 3 — **4a**

b If you elect one or both of the optional methods, enter the total of lines 15 and 17 here . . — **4b**

c Combine lines 4a and 4b. If less than $400, **stop;** you do not owe self-employment tax. **Exception.** If less than $400 and you had **church employee income,** enter -0- and continue. . . . . . ▶ **4c**

5a Enter your **church employee income** from Form W-2. See page SE-1 for definition of church employee income **5a**

b Multiply line 5a by 92.35% (.9235). If less than $100, enter -0- **5b**

6 **Net earnings from self-employment.** Add lines 4c and 5b **6**

7 Maximum amount of combined wages and self-employment earnings subject to social security tax or the 6.2% portion of the 7.65% railroad retirement (tier 1) tax for 2008 . . . . . . **7** 102,000 00

8a Total social security wages and tips (total of boxes 3 and 7 on Form(s) W-2) and railroad retirement (tier 1) compensation. If $102,000 or more, skip lines 8b through 10, and go to line 11 . . . . . . **8a**

b Unreported tips subject to social security tax (from Form 4137, line 10) **8b**

c Wages subject to social security tax (from Form 8919, line 10) . . . **8c**

d Add lines 8a, 8b, and 8c **8d**

9 Subtract line 8d from line 7. If zero or less, enter -0- here and on line 10 and go to line 11 . ▶ **9**

10 Multiply the **smaller** of line 6 or line 9 by 12.4% (.124) **10**

11 Multiply line 6 by 2.9% (.029) **11**

12 **Self-employment tax.** Add lines 10 and 11. Enter here and on **Form 1040, line 57** **12**

13 **Deduction for one-half of self-employment tax.** Multiply line 12 by 50% (.5). Enter the result here and on **Form 1040, line 27** . . **13**

Part II Optional Methods To Figure Net Earnings (see page SE-4)

Farm Optional Method. You may use this method only if **(a)** your gross farm income[1] was not more than $6,300, **or (b)** your net farm profits[2] were less than $4,548.

14 Maximum income for optional methods **14** 4,200 00

15 Enter the **smaller** of: two-thirds (⅔) of gross farm income[1] (not less than zero) **or** $4,200. Also include this amount on line 4b above **15**

Nonfarm Optional Method. You may use this method **only** if **(a)** your net nonfarm profits[3] were less than $4,548 and also less than 72.189% of your gross nonfarm income,[4] **and (b)** you had net earnings from self-employment of at least $400 in 2 of the prior 3 years.

Caution. You may use this method no more than five times.

16 Subtract line 15 from line 14 . . . . **16**

17 Enter the **smaller** of: two-thirds (⅔) of gross nonfarm income[4] (not less than zero) **or** the amount on line 16. Also include this amount on line 4b above **17**

[1] From Sch. F, line 11, and Sch. K-1 (Form 1065), box 14, code B.

[2] From Sch. F, line 36, and Sch. K-1 (Form 1065), box 14, code A—minus the amount you would have entered on line 1b had you not used the optional method.

[3] From Sch. C, line 31; Sch. C-EZ, line 3; Sch. K-1 (Form 1065), box 14, code A; and Sch. K-1 (Form 1065-B), box 9, code J1.

[4] From Sch. C, line 7; Sch. C-EZ, line 1; Sch. K-1 (Form 1065), box 14, code C; and Sch. K-1 (Form 1065-B), box 9, code J2.

Schedule SE (Form 1040) 2008

Form **4562**	**Depreciation and Amortization**	OMB No. 1545-0172
Department of the Treasury Internal Revenue Service (99)	**(Including Information on Listed Property)** ▶ See separate instructions. ▶ Attach to your tax return.	20**08** Attachment Sequence No. **67**
Name(s) shown on return	Business or activity to which this form relates	Identifying number

Part I Election To Expense Certain Property Under Section 179
Note: *If you have any listed property, complete Part V before you complete Part I.*

1	Maximum amount. See the instructions for a higher limit for certain businesses	**1**	$250,000
2	Total cost of section 179 property placed in service (see instructions)	**2**	
3	Threshold cost of section 179 property before reduction in limitation (see instructions) . . .	**3**	$800,000
4	Reduction in limitation. Subtract line 3 from line 2. If zero or less, enter -0-	**4**	
5	Dollar limitation for tax year. Subtract line 4 from line 1. If zero or less, enter -0-. If married filing separately, see instructions	**5**	

(a) Description of property	**(b)** Cost (business use only)	**(c)** Elected cost
6		

7	Listed property. Enter the amount from line 29	**7**	
8	Total elected cost of section 179 property. Add amounts in column (c), lines 6 and 7	**8**	
9	Tentative deduction. Enter the **smaller** of line 5 or line 8	**9**	
10	Carryover of disallowed deduction from line 13 of your 2007 Form 4562	**10**	
11	Business income limitation. Enter the smaller of business income (not less than zero) or line 5 (see instructions)	**11**	
12	Section 179 expense deduction. Add lines 9 and 10, but do not enter more than line 11 . . .	**12**	
13	Carryover of disallowed deduction to 2009. Add lines 9 and 10, less line 12 ▶	**13**	

Note: *Do not use Part II or Part III below for listed property. Instead, use Part V.*

Part II Special Depreciation Allowance and Other Depreciation (Do not include listed property.) (See instructions.)

14	Special depreciation allowance for qualified property (other than listed property) placed in service during the tax year (see instructions)	**14**	
15	Property subject to section 168(f)(1) election	**15**	
16	Other depreciation (including ACRS)	**16**	

Part III MACRS Depreciation (Do not include listed property.) (See instructions.)

Section A

17	MACRS deductions for assets placed in service in tax years beginning before 2008	**17**	
18	If you are electing to group any assets placed in service during the tax year into one or more general asset accounts, check here . . . . ▶ ☐		

Section B—Assets Placed in Service During 2008 Tax Year Using the General Depreciation System

(a) Classification of property	**(b)** Month and year placed in service	**(c)** Basis for depreciation (business/investment use only—see instructions)	**(d)** Recovery period	**(e)** Convention	**(f)** Method	**(g)** Depreciation deduction
19a 3-year property						
b 5-year property						
c 7-year property						
d 10-year property						
e 15-year property						
f 20-year property						
g 25-year property			25 yrs.		S/L	
h Residential rental property			27.5 yrs.	MM	S/L	
			27.5 yrs.	MM	S/L	
i Nonresidential real property			39 yrs.	MM	S/L	
				MM	S/L	

Section C—Assets Placed in Service During 2008 Tax Year Using the Alternative Depreciation System

20a Class life					S/L	
b 12-year			12 yrs.		S/L	
c 40-year			40 yrs.	MM	S/L	

Part IV Summary (See instructions.)

21	Listed property. Enter amount from line 28	**21**	
22	**Total.** Add amounts from line 12, lines 14 through 17, lines 19 and 20 in column (g), and line 21. Enter here and on the appropriate lines of your return. Partnerships and S corporations—see instr.	**22**	
23	For assets shown above and placed in service during the current year, enter the portion of the basis attributable to section 263A costs . .	**23**	

For Paperwork Reduction Act Notice, see separate instructions.　　Cat. No. 12906N　　Form **4562** (2008)

IRS Form 4562 Depreciation and Amortization

Form 4562 (2008) Page **2**

Part V **Listed Property** (Include automobiles, certain other vehicles, cellular telephones, certain computers, and property used for entertainment, recreation, or amusement.)

Note: *For any vehicle for which you are using the standard mileage rate or deducting lease expense, complete* **only** *24a, 24b, columns (a) through (c) of Section A, all of Section B, and Section C if applicable.*

Section A—Depreciation and Other Information (Caution: *See the instructions for limits for passenger automobiles.***)**

24a Do you have evidence to support the business/investment use claimed? ☐ Yes ☐ No	24b If "Yes," is the evidence written? ☐ Yes ☐ No

(a) Type of property (list vehicles first)	(b) Date placed in service	(c) Business/ investment use percentage	(d) Cost or other basis	(e) Basis for depreciation (business/investment use only)	(f) Recovery period	(g) Method/ Convention	(h) Depreciation deduction	(i) Elected section 179 cost
25 Special depreciation allowance for qualified listed property placed in service during the tax year and used more than 50% in a qualified business use (see instructions)					25			
26 Property used more than 50% in a qualified business use:								
		%						
		%						
		%						
27 Property used 50% or less in a qualified business use:								
		%				S/L –		
		%				S/L –		
		%				S/L –		
28 Add amounts in column (h), lines 25 through 27. Enter here and on line 21, page 1. .						28		
29 Add amounts in column (i), line 26. Enter here and on line 7, page 1.							29	

Section B—Information on Use of Vehicles

Complete this section for vehicles used by a sole proprietor, partner, or other "more than 5% owner," or related person.

If you provided vehicles to your employees, first answer the questions in Section C to see if you meet an exception to completing this section for those vehicles.

	(a) Vehicle 1		(b) Vehicle 2		(c) Vehicle 3		(d) Vehicle 4		(e) Vehicle 5		(f) Vehicle 6	
30 Total business/investment miles driven during the year (**do not** include commuting miles)												
31 Total commuting miles driven during the year												
32 Total other personal (noncommuting) miles driven												
33 Total miles driven during the year. Add lines 30 through 32												
34 Was the vehicle available for personal use during off-duty hours?	Yes	No	Yes	No	Yes	No	Yes	No	Yes	No	Yes	No
35 Was the vehicle used primarily by a more than 5% owner or related person?												
36 Is another vehicle available for personal use?												

Section C—Questions for Employers Who Provide Vehicles for Use by Their Employees

Answer these questions to determine if you meet an exception to completing Section B for vehicles used by employees who **are not** more than 5% owners or related persons (see instructions).

		Yes	No
37	Do you maintain a written policy statement that prohibits all personal use of vehicles, including commuting, by your employees?		
38	Do you maintain a written policy statement that prohibits personal use of vehicles, except commuting, by your employees? See the instructions for vehicles used by corporate officers, directors, or 1% or more owners		
39	Do you treat all use of vehicles by employees as personal use?		
40	Do you provide more than five vehicles to your employees, obtain information from your employees about the use of the vehicles, and retain the information received?		
41	Do you meet the requirements concerning qualified automobile demonstration use? (See instructions.)		

Note: *If your answer to 37, 38, 39, 40, or 41 is "Yes," do not complete Section B for the covered vehicles.*

Part VI **Amortization**

(a) Description of costs	(b) Date amortization begins	(c) Amortizable amount	(d) Code section	(e) Amortization period or percentage	(f) Amortization for this year
42 Amortization of costs that begins during your 2008 tax year (see instructions):					
43 Amortization of costs that began before your 2008 tax year			43		
44 **Total.** Add amounts in column (f). See the instructions for where to report			44		

Form **4562** (2008)

Form 941 for 2009: Employer's **QUARTERLY** Federal Tax Return

950109

(Rev. January 2009)   Department of the Treasury — Internal Revenue Service

OMB No. 1545-0029

(EIN)
Employer identification number ☐☐ – ☐☐☐☐☐☐☐

Name (not your trade name)

Trade name (if any)

Address
Number   Street   Suite or room number

City   State   ZIP code

Report for this Quarter of 2009
(Check one.)

☐ **1:** January, February, March

☐ **2:** April, May, June

☐ **3:** July, August, September

☐ **4:** October, November, December

Read the separate instructions before you complete Form 941. Type or print within the boxes.

Part 1: Answer these questions for this quarter.

1 Number of employees who received wages, tips, or other compensation for the pay period including: *Mar. 12* (Quarter 1), *June 12* (Quarter 2), *Sept. 12* (Quarter 3), *Dec. 12* (Quarter 4) **1**

2 Wages, tips, and other compensation **2**

3 Income tax withheld from wages, tips, and other compensation **3**

4 If no wages, tips, and other compensation are subject to social security or Medicare tax ☐ Check and go to line 6.

5 Taxable social security and Medicare wages and tips:

	Column 1		Column 2
5a Taxable social security wages		× .124 =	
5b Taxable social security tips		× .124 =	
5c Taxable Medicare wages & tips		× .029 =	

5d Total social security and Medicare taxes (Column 2, lines 5a + 5b + 5c = line 5d) . **5d**

6 Total taxes before adjustments (lines 3 + 5d = line 6) **6**

7 **CURRENT QUARTER'S ADJUSTMENTS,** for example, a fractions of cents adjustment. See the instructions.

7a Current quarter's fractions of cents . . . .

7b Current quarter's sick pay . . . .

7c Current quarter's adjustments for tips and group-term life insurance

7d **TOTAL ADJUSTMENTS.** Combine all amounts on lines 7a through 7c **7d**

8 Total taxes after adjustments. Combine lines 6 and 7d **8**

9 Advance earned income credit (EIC) payments made to employees **9**

10 Total taxes after adjustment for advance EIC (line 8 – line 9 = line 10) **10**

11 Total deposits for this quarter, including overpayment applied from a prior quarter and overpayment applied from Form 941-X or Form 944-X . . . .

12a COBRA premium assistance payments (see instructions) . . . . .

12b Number of individuals provided COBRA premium assistance reported on line 12a . . . .

13 Add lines 11 and 12a **13**

14 **Balance due.** If line 10 is more than line 13, write the difference here **14**
For information on how to pay, see the instructions.

15 **Overpayment.** If line 13 is more than line 10, write the difference here   Check one ☐ Apply to next return. ☐ Send a refund.

▶ You **MUST** complete both pages of Form 941 and **SIGN** it.   Next ➡

For Privacy Act and Paperwork Reduction Act Notice, see the back of the Payment Voucher.   Cat. No. 17001Z   Form **941** (Rev. 1-2009)

IRS Form 941 Employer's Quarterly Federal Tax Return (For Employment Taxes)

9 5 0 2 0 9

Name *(not your trade name)*	Employer identification number (EIN)

Part 2: Tell us about your deposit schedule and tax liability for this quarter.

If you are unsure about whether you are a monthly schedule depositor or a semiweekly schedule depositor, see *Pub. 15 (Circular E)*, section 11.

16 ☐☐ Write the state abbreviation for the state where you made your deposits OR write "MU" if you made your deposits in *multiple* states.

17 Check one: ☐ Line 10 is less than $2,500. Go to Part 3.

☐ You were a monthly schedule depositor for the entire quarter. Enter your tax liability for each month. Then go to Part 3.

Tax liability: Month 1 ☐ .

Month 2 ☐ .

Month 3 ☐ .

Total liability for quarter ☐ . Total must equal line 10.

☐ You were a semiweekly schedule depositor for any part of this quarter. Complete *Schedule B (Form 941): Report of Tax Liability for Semiweekly Schedule Depositors*, and attach it to Form 941.

Part 3: Tell us about your business. If a question does NOT apply to your business, leave it blank.

18 If your business has closed or you stopped paying wages . . . . ☐ Check here, and

enter the final date you paid wages ☐ / /

19 If you are a seasonal employer and you do not have to file a return for every quarter of the year . ☐ Check here.

Part 4: May we speak with your third-party designee?

Do you want to allow an employee, a paid tax preparer, or another person to discuss this return with the IRS? See the instructions for details.

☐ Yes. Designee's name and phone number ☐ ( ) –

Select a 5-digit Personal Identification Number (PIN) to use when talking to the IRS. ☐☐☐☐☐

☐ No.

Part 5: Sign here. You MUST complete both pages of Form 941 and SIGN it.

Under penalties of perjury, I declare that I have examined this return, including accompanying schedules and statements, and to the best of my knowledge and belief, it is true, correct, and complete. Declaration of preparer (other than taxpayer) is based on all information of wh ich preparer has any knowledge.

X Sign your name here ☐

Print your name here ☐

Print your title here ☐

Date / /

Best daytime phone ( ) –

Paid preparer's use only

Check if you are self-employed . . . . ☐

Preparer's name		Preparer's SSN/PTIN	
Preparer's signature		Date	/ /
Firm's name (or yours if self-employed)		EIN	
Address		Phone	( ) –
City	State	ZIP code	

Page **2**

Form **941** (Rev. 1-2009)

Form 941-V,
Payment Voucher

Purpose of Form

Complete Form 941-V, Payment Voucher, if you are making a payment with Form 941, Employer's QUARTERLY Federal Tax Return. We will use the completed voucher to credit your payment more promptly and accurately, and to improve our service to you.

If you have your return prepared by a third party and make a payment with that return, please provide this payment voucher to the return preparer.

Making Payments With Form 941

To avoid a penalty, make your payment with Form 941 **only if:**

● Your net taxes for the quarter (line 10 on Form 941) are less than $2,500 and you are paying in full with a timely filed return or

● You are a monthly schedule depositor making a payment in accordance with the Accuracy of Deposits Rule. See section 11 of Pub. 15 (Circular E), Employer's Tax Guide, for details. In this case, the amount of your payment may be $2,500 or more.

Otherwise, you must deposit your payment at an authorized financial institution or by using the Electronic Federal Tax Payment System (EFTPS). See section 11 of Pub. 15 (Circular E) for deposit instructions. Do not use Form 941-V to make federal tax deposits.

Caution. *Use Form 941-V when making any payment with Form 941. However, if you pay an amount with Form 941 that should have been deposited, you may be subject to a penalty. See* Deposit Penalties *in section 11 of Pub. 15 (Circular E).*

Specific Instructions

Box 1—Employer identification number (EIN). If you do not have an EIN, apply for one on Form SS-4, Application for Employer Identification Number, and write "Applied For" and the date you applied in this entry space.

Box 2—Amount paid. Enter the amount paid with Form 941.

Box 3—Tax period. Darken the capsule identifying the quarter for which the payment is made. Darken only one capsule.

Box 4—Name and address. Enter your name and address as shown on Form 941.

● Enclose your check or money order made payable to the "United States Treasury." Be sure to enter your EIN, "Form 941," and the tax period on your check or money order. Do not send cash. Do not staple Form 941-V or your payment to Form 941 (or to each other).

● Detach Form 941-V and send it with your payment and Form 941 to the address in the Instructions for Form 941.

Note. You must also complete the entity information above Part 1 on Form 941.

▼ **Detach Here and Mail With Your Payment and Form 941.** ▼

Form **941-V**	Payment Voucher	OMB No. 1545-0029
Department of the Treasury Internal Revenue Service	▶ Do not staple this voucher or your payment to Form 941.	20**09**

1 Enter your employer identification number (EIN).	2 **Enter the amount of your payment.** ▶	Dollars	Cents

3 Tax period		4 Enter your business name (individual name if sole proprietor).
⬭ 1st Quarter	⬭ 3rd Quarter	Enter your address.
⬭ 2nd Quarter	⬭ 4th Quarter	Enter your city, state, and ZIP code.

Form 941 (Rev. 1-2009)

Privacy Act and Paperwork Reduction Act Notice.
We ask for the information on this form to carry out the Internal Revenue laws of the United States. We need it to figure and collect the right amount of tax. Subtitle C, Employment Taxes, of the Internal Revenue Code imposes employment taxes on wages, including income tax withholding. This form is used to determine the amount of the taxes that you owe. Section 6011 requires you to provide the requested information if the tax is applicable to you. Section 6109 requires you to provide your identifying number. If you fail to provide this information in a timely manner, you may be subject to penalties and interest.

You are not required to provide the information requested on a form that is subject to the Paperwork Reduction Act unless the form displays a valid OMB control number. Books and records relating to a form or instructions must be retained as long as their contents may become material in the administration of any Internal Revenue law.

Generally, tax returns and return information are confidential, as required by section 6103. However, section 6103 allows or requires the IRS to disclose or give the information shown on your tax return to others as described in the Code. For example, we may disclose your tax information to the Department of Justice for civil and criminal litigation, and to cities, states, and the District of Columbia for use in administering their tax laws. We may also disclose this information to other countries under a tax treaty, to federal and state agencies to enforce federal nontax criminal laws, or to federal law enforcement and intelligence agencies to combat terrorism.

The time needed to complete and file Form 941 will vary depending on individual circumstances. The estimated average time is:

Recordkeeping	12 hr., 39 min.
Learning about the law or the form	40 min.
Preparing the form	1 hr., 49 min.
Copying, assembling, and sending the form to the IRS	16 min.

If you have comments concerning the accuracy of these time estimates or suggestions for making Form 941 simpler, we would be happy to hear from you. You can write to: Internal Revenue Service, Tax Products Coordinating Committee, SE:W:CAR:MP:T:T:SP, 1111 Constitution Ave. NW, IR-6526, Washington, DC 20224. **Do not** send Form 941 to this address. Instead, see *Where Should You File?* on page 4 of the Instructions for Form 941.

Form **944 for 2008:** **Employer's ANNUAL Federal Tax Return**
Department of the Treasury — Internal Revenue Service

OMB No. 1545-2007

Employer identification number (EIN) ☐☐ – ☐☐☐☐☐☐☐

Name *(not your trade name)*

Trade name *(if any)*

Address

Number	Street		Suite or room number
City		State	ZIP code

Who Must File Form 944

You must file annual Form 944 instead of filing quarterly Forms 941 **only if the IRS notified you in writing.**

Read the separate instructions before you complete Form 944. Type or print within the boxes.

Part 1: Answer these questions for 2008.

1 Wages, tips, and other compensation **1**

2 Income tax withheld from wages, tips, and other compensation **2**

3 If no wages, tips, and other compensation are subject to social security or Medicare tax . **3** ☐ Check and go to line 5.

4 Taxable social security and Medicare wages and tips:

	Column 1		Column 2
4a Taxable social security wages		× .124 =	
4b Taxable social security tips		× .124 =	
4c Taxable Medicare wages & tips		× .029 =	

4d Total social security and Medicare taxes (*Column 2,* lines 4a + 4b + 4c = line 4d) . . . **4d**

5 Total taxes before adjustments (lines 2 + 4d = line 5) **5**

6 **TAX ADJUSTMENTS.** Read the instructions for line 6 before completing lines 6a through 6e.

6a Current year's adjustments **6a**

6b Prior years' income tax withholding adjustments. Attach Form 941c **6b**

6c Prior years' social security and Medicare tax adjustments. Attach Form 941c **6c**

6d Special additions to federal income tax. Attach Form 941c . **6d**

6e Special additions to social security and Medicare taxes. Attach Form 941c **6e**

6f **TOTAL ADJUSTMENTS.** Combine all amounts on lines 6a through 6e **6f**

7 Total taxes after adjustments. Combine lines 5 and 6f **7**

8 Advance earned income credit (EIC) payments made to employees **8**

9 Total taxes after adjustment for advance EIC (line 7 – line 8 = line 9) **9**

10 Total deposits for this year, including overpayment applied from a prior year **10**

11 **Balance due.** If line 9 is more than line 10, write the difference here. For information on how to pay, see the instructions **11**

12 **Overpayment.** If line 10 is more than line 9, write the difference here . **12** Check one ☐ Apply to next return. ☐ Send a refund.

► You MUST complete both pages of Form 944 and SIGN it.

Next ➡

For Privacy Act and Paperwork Reduction Act Notice, see the back of the Payment Voucher.   Cat. No. 39316N   Form **944** (2008)

IRS Form 944 Employer's Annual Federal Tax Return (For Employment Taxes)

Name *(not your trade name)*

Employer identification number (EIN)

Part 2: Tell us about your tax liability for 2008.

13 Check one: ☐   **Line 9 is less than $2,500. Go to Part 3.**

         ☐   **Line 9 is $2,500 or more. Enter your tax liability for each month. If you are a semiweekly depositor or you accumulate $100,000 or more of liability on any day during a deposit period, you must complete Form 945-A instead of the boxes below.**

	Jan.		Apr.		Jul.		Oct.
13a		13d		13g		13j	
	Feb.		May		Aug.		Nov.
13b		13e		13h		13k	
	Mar.		Jun.		Sep.		Dec.
13c		13f		13i		13l	

Total liability for year. Add lines 13a through 13l. Total must equal line 9.   **13m**

14   **If you made deposits of taxes reported on this form, write the state abbreviation for the state where you made your deposits OR write** *MU* **if you made your deposits in** *multiple* **states.**

Part 3: Tell us about your business. If question 15 does NOT apply to your business, leave it blank.

15   **If your business has closed or you stopped paying wages...**

    ☐   Check here and enter the final date you paid wages.   ⬚ / /

Part 4: May we speak with your third-party designee?

Do you want to allow an employee, a paid tax preparer, or another person to discuss this return with the IRS? See the instructions for details.

☐ Yes.   Designee's name and phone number   ( )   –

       Select a 5-digit Personal Identification Number (PIN) to use when talking to IRS.   ☐ ☐ ☐ ☐ ☐

☐ No.

Part 5: Sign here. You MUST complete both pages of Form 944 and SIGN it.

Under penalties of perjury, I declare that I have examined this return, including accompanying schedules and statements, and to the best of my knowledge and belief, it is true, correct, and complete. Declaration of preparer (other than taxpayer) is based on all information of which preparer has any knowledge.

✗   **Sign your name here**

Print your name here

Print your title here

Date   / /

Best daytime phone   ( )   –

Paid preparer's use only

Check if you are self-employed . . . . ☐

Preparer's name		Preparer's SSN/PTIN
Preparer's signature		Date / /
Firm's name (or yours if self-employed)		EIN
Address		Phone ( ) –
City	State	ZIP code

Form **944** (2008)

Form 944-V, Payment Voucher

Purpose of Form

Complete Form 944-V, Payment Voucher, if you are making a payment with Form 944, Employer's ANNUAL Federal Tax Return. We will use the completed voucher to credit your payment more promptly and accurately, and to improve our service to you.

If you have your return prepared by a third party and make a payment with that return, please provide this payment voucher to the return preparer.

Making Payments With Form 944

To avoid a penalty, make your payment with your 2008 Form 944 **only if** one of the following applies.

● Your net taxes for the year (line 9 on Form 944) are less than $2,500 and you are paying in full with a timely filed return.

● You already deposited the taxes you owed for the first, second, and third quarters of 2008, and the tax you owe for the fourth quarter of 2008 is less than $2,500, and you are paying, in full, the tax you owe for the fourth quarter of 2008 with a timely filed return.

● You are a monthly schedule depositor making a payment in accordance with the Accuracy of Deposits Rule. See section 11 of Pub. 15 (Circular E), Employer's Tax Guide, for details. In this case, the amount of your payment may be $2,500 or more.

Otherwise, you must deposit your payment at an authorized financial institution or by using the Electronic Federal Tax Payment System (EFTPS). See section 11 of Pub. 15 (Circular E) for deposit instructions. Do not use Form 944-V to make federal tax deposits.

Caution. *Use Form 944-V when making any payment with Form 944. However, if you pay an amount with Form 944 that should have been deposited, you may be subject to a penalty. See* Deposit Penalties *in section 11 of Pub. 15 (Circular E).*

Specific Instructions

Box 1—Employer identification number (EIN). If you do not have an EIN, apply for one on Form SS-4, Application for Employer Identification Number, and write "Applied For" and the date you applied in this entry space.

Box 2—Amount paid. Enter the amount paid with Form 944.

Box 3—Name and address. Enter your name and address as shown on Form 944.

● Enclose your check or money order made payable to the "United States Treasury" and write your EIN, "Form 944," and "2008" on your check or money order. Do not send cash. Do not staple Form 944-V or your payment to Form 944 (or to each other).

● Detach Form 944-V and send it with your payment and Form 944 to the address provided in the Instructions for Form 944.

Note. You must also complete the entity information above Part 1 on Form 944.

Detach Here and Mail With Your Payment and Form 944.

Form **944-V**	**Payment Voucher**	OMB No. 1545-2007
Department of the Treasury Internal Revenue Service (77)	► **Do not staple this voucher or your payment to Form 944.**	2008

1 Enter your employer identification number (EIN).	2 **Enter the amount of your payment.** ►	Dollars	Cents
	3 Enter your business name (individual name if sole proprietor).		
	Enter your address.		
	Enter your city, state, and ZIP code.		

Privacy Act and Paperwork Reduction Act Notice.
We ask for the information on this form to carry out the Internal Revenue laws of the United States. We need it to figure and collect the right amount of tax. Subtitle C, Employment Taxes, of the Internal Revenue Code imposes employment taxes on wages, including income tax withholding. This form is used to determine the amount of the taxes that you owe. Section 6011 requires you to provide the requested information if the tax is applicable to you. Section 6109 requires filers and paid prepareres to provide their identification numbers. If you fail to provide this information in a timely manner, you may be subject to penalties and interest.

You are not required to provide the information requested on a form that is subject to the Paperwork Reduction Act unless the form displays a valid OMB control number. Books and records relating to a form or instructions must be retained as long as their contents may become material in the administration of any Internal Revenue law.

Generally, tax returns and return information are confidential, as required by section 6103. However, section 6103 allows or requires the IRS to disclose or give the information shown on your tax return to others as described in the Code. For example, we may disclose your tax information to the Department of Justice for civil and criminal litigation, and to cities, states, and the District of Columbia, and U.S. commonwealths and possessions for use in administering their tax laws. We may also disclose this information to other countries under a tax treaty, to federal and state agencies to enforce federal nontax criminal laws, or to federal law enforcement and intelligence agencies to combat terrorism.

The time needed to complete and file Form 944 will vary depending on individual circumstances. The estimated average time is:

Recordkeeping . . . . 12 hrs., 12 min.

Learning about the law or the form .   40 min.

Preparing the form . . . .   1 hr., 49 min.

Copying, assembling, and sending
the form to the IRS . . . .   16 min.

If you have comments concerning the accuracy of these time estimates or suggestions for making Form 944 simpler, we would be happy to hear from you. You can write to: Internal Revenue Service, Tax Products Coordinating Committee, SE:W:CAR:MP:T:T:SP, 1111 Constitution Ave. NW, IR-6526, Washington, DC 20224. **Do not** send Form 944 to this address. Instead, see *Where Should You File?* on page 4 of the Instructions for Form 944.

Chapter 11

ST. VINCENT DE PAUL SOCIETY
829 S. SIXTH AVE.
TUCSON, ARIZONA 85702

Date: _____

Received of: _____

List of Items:

_____

_____

_____

_____

Received by: _____

Nonprofit Tax ID # 54-779999

THE VALUE OF YOUR DONATION IS TAX DEDUCTIBLE

THANK YOU!!

Sample Donor's Receipt

Chapter 13

Form **940 for 2008:** Employer's Annual Federal Unemployment (FUTA) Tax Return   850108

Department of the Treasury — Internal Revenue Service

OMB No. 1545-0028

(EIN)
Employer identification number ☐☐ – ☐☐☐☐☐☐☐

Name (not your trade name)

Trade name (if any)

Address
Number   Street   Suite or room number

City   State   ZIP code

Type of Return
(Check all that apply.)

☐ a. Amended

☐ b. Successor employer

☐ c. No payments to employees in 2008

☐ d. Final: Business closed or stopped paying wages

Read the separate instructions before you fill out this form. Please type or print within the boxes.

Part 1: Tell us about your return. If any line does NOT apply, leave it blank.

1   If you were required to pay your state unemployment tax in ...

1a   **One state only,** write the state abbreviation . . . . **1a** ☐☐

- OR -

1b   **More than one state** (You are a multi-state employer) . . . . **1b** ☐ Check here. Fill out Schedule A.

Skip line 2 for 2008 and go to line 3.

2   If you paid wages in a state that is subject to CREDIT REDUCTION . . . . **2** ☐ Check here. Fill out Schedule A (Form 940), Part 2.

Part 2: Determine your FUTA tax before adjustments for 2008. If any line does NOT apply, leave it blank.

3   Total payments to all employees . . . . **3** ☐ ▪

4   Payments exempt from FUTA tax . . . . . . **4** ☐ ▪

Check all that apply: **4a** ☐ Fringe benefits   **4c** ☐ Retirement/Pension   **4e** ☐ Other
4b ☐ Group-term life insurance   **4d** ☐ Dependent care

5   Total of payments made to each employee in excess of
$7,000 . . . . **5** ☐ ▪

6   Subtotal (line 4 + line 5 = line 6) . . . . **6** ☐ ▪

7   Total taxable FUTA wages (line 3 – line 6 = line 7) . . . . **7** ☐ ▪

8   FUTA tax before adjustments (line 7 × .008 = line 8) . . . . **8** ☐ ▪

Part 3: Determine your adjustments. If any line does NOT apply, leave it blank.

9   If ALL of the taxable FUTA wages you paid were excluded from state unemployment tax,
multiply line 7 by .054 (line 7 × .054 = line 9). Then go to line 12 . . . . **9** ☐ ▪

10   If SOME of the taxable FUTA wages you paid were excluded from state unemployment tax,
OR you paid ANY state unemployment tax late (after the due date for filing Form 940), fill out
the worksheet in the instructions. Enter the amount from line 7 of the worksheet onto line 10 . **10** ☐ ▪

Skip line 11 for 2008 and go to line 12.

11   If credit reduction applies, enter the amount from line 3 of Schedule A (Form 940) . . . . . **11** ☐ ▪

Part 4: Determine your FUTA tax and balance due or overpayment for 2008. If any line does NOT apply, leave it blank.

12   Total FUTA tax after adjustments (lines 8 + 9 + 10 + 11 = line 12) . . . . **12** ☐ ▪

13   FUTA tax deposited for the year, including any payment applied from a prior year . . . . **13** ☐ ▪

14   Balance due (If line 12 is more than line 13, enter the difference on line 14.)
  • If line 14 is more than $500, you must deposit your tax.
  • If line 14 is $500 or less, you may pay with this return. For more information on how to pay, see
the separate instructions . . . . **14** ☐ ▪

15   Overpayment (If line 13 is more than line 12, enter the difference on line 15 and check a box
below.) . . . . **15** ☐ ▪

Check one: ☐ Apply to next return.
☐ Send a refund.

▶ You **MUST** fill out both pages of this form and **SIGN** it.

Next ➡

For Privacy Act and Paperwork Reduction Act Notice, see the back of Form 940-V, Payment Voucher.   Cat. No. 11234O   Form **940** (2008)

IRS Form 940 Employer's Annual Federal Unemployment (FUTA) Tax Return

850208

Name *(not your trade name)*   Employer identification number (EIN)

Part 5: Report your FUTA tax liability by quarter only if line 12 is more than $500. If not, go to Part 6.

16   Report the amount of your FUTA tax liability for each quarter; do NOT enter the amount you deposited. If you had no liability for a quarter, leave the line blank.

     16a   **1st quarter** (January 1 – March 31)   . . . . **16a**   .

     16b   **2nd quarter** (April 1 – June 30) . . . . **16b**   .

     16c   **3rd quarter** (July 1 – September 30)   . . . . **16c**   .

     16d   **4th quarter** (October 1 – December 31)   . . . . **16d**   .

17   **Total tax liability for the year** (lines 16a + 16b + 16c + 16d = line 17) **17**   .   **Total must equal line 12.**

Part 6: May we speak with your third-party designee?

Do you want to allow an employee, a paid tax preparer, or another person to discuss this return with the IRS? See the instructions for details.

☐   **Yes.**   Designee's name and phone number   (   )   –

               Select a 5-digit Personal Identification Number (PIN) to use when talking to IRS   ☐ ☐ ☐ ☐ ☐

☐   **No.**

Part 7: Sign here. You MUST fill out both pages of this form and SIGN it.

Under penalties of perjury, I declare that I have examined this return, including accompanying schedules and statements, and to the best of my knowledge and belief, it is true, correct, and complete, and that no part of any payment made to a state unemployment fund claimed as a credit was, or is to be, deducted from the payments made to employees. Declaration of preparer (other than taxpayer) is based on all information of which preparer has any knowledge.

☒ **Sign your name here**   Print your name here

                                               Print your title here

           Date   /   /   Best daytime phone   (   )   –

Paid preparer's use only   Check if you are self-employed   . . . ☐

Preparer's name   Preparer's SSN/PTIN

Preparer's signature   Date   /   /

Firm's name (or yours if self-employed)   EIN

Address   Phone   (   )   –

City   State   ZIP code

Form 940-V,
Payment Voucher

What Is Form 940-V?

Form 940-V is a transmittal form for your check or money order. Using Form 940-V allows us to process your payment more accurately and efficiently. If you have any balance due of $500 or less on your 2008 Form 940, fill out Form 940-V and send it with your check or money order.

Note. If your balance is more than $500, see *When Must You Deposit Your FUTA Tax?* in the Instructions for Form 940.

How Do You Fill Out Form 940-V?

Type or print clearly.

Box 1. Enter your employer identification number (EIN). Do not enter your social security number (SSN).

Box 2. Enter the amount of your payment. Be sure to put dollars and cents in the appropriate spaces.

Box 3. Enter your business name and complete address exactly as they appear on your Form 940.

How Should You Prepare Your Payment?

- Make your check or money order payable to the *United States Treasury.* Do not send cash.
- On the memo line of your check or money order, write:
  - your EIN,
  - Form 940, and
  - 2008.
- Carefully detach Form 940-V along the dotted line.
- Do not staple your payment to the voucher.
- Mail your 2008 Form 940, your payment, and Form 940-V in the envelope that came with your 2008 Form 940 instruction booklet. If you do not have that envelope, use the table in the Instructions for Form 940 to find the mailing address.

▼ **Detach Here and Mail With Your Payment and Form 940.** ▼

Form **940-V**		**Payment Voucher**		OMB No. 1545-0028
Department of the Treasury Internal Revenue Service		▶ Do not staple or attach this voucher to your payment.		2008

1 Enter your employer identification number (EIN).	2 Enter the amount of your payment. ▶	Dollars	Cents
	3 Enter your business name (individual name if sole proprietor).		
	Enter your address.		
	Enter your city, state, and ZIP code.		

Form 940 (2008)

Privacy Act and Paperwork Reduction Act Notice. We ask for the information on this form to carry out the Internal Revenue laws of the United States. We need it to figure and collect the right amount of tax. Chapter 23, Federal Unemployment Tax Act, of Subtitle C, Employment Taxes, of the Internal Revenue Code imposes a tax on employers with respect to employees. This form is used to determine the amount of the tax that you owe. Section 6011 requires you to provide the requested information if you are liable for FUTA tax under section 3301. Section 6109 requires taxpayers and paid preparers to provide their idenification numbers. If you fail to provide this information in a timely manner, you may be subject to penalties and interest.

You are not required to provide the information requested on a form that is subject to the Paperwork Reduction Act unless the form displays a valid OMB control number. Books and records relating to a form or instructions must be retained as long as their contents may become material in the administration of any Internal Revenue law.

Generally, tax returns and return information are confidential, as required by section 6103. However, section 6103 allows or requires the IRS to disclose or give the information shown on your tax return to others as described in the Code. For example, we may disclose your tax information to the Department of Justice for civil and criminal litigation, and to cities, states, the District of Columbia, and U.S. commonwealths and possessions to administer their tax laws. We may also disclose this information to other countries under a tax treaty, to federal and state agencies to enforce federal non-tax criminal laws, or to federal law enforcement and intelligence agencies to combat terrorism.

The time needed to complete and file this form will vary depending on individual circumstances. The estimated average time is: Recordkeeping, 23 hr., 39 min.; Learning about the law or the form, 1 hr., 23 min.; Preparing and sending the form to the IRS, 2 hr., 17 min.

If you have comments concerning the accuracy of these time estimates or suggestions for making Form 940 simpler, we would be happy to hear from you. You can write to: Internal Revenue Service, Tax Products Coordinating Committee, SE:W:CAR:MP:T:SP, 1111 Constitution Avenue, NW, IR-6526, Washington, DC 20224. **Do not** send Form 940 to this address. Instead, see *Where Do You File?* on page 2 of the Instructions for Form 940.

Index

The *Complete* Business Toolkit

ISBN: 978-1-59257-889-4

ISBN: 978-1-59257-920-4

ISBN: 978-1-59257-896-2

ISBN: 978-1-59257-903-7

ISBN: 978-1-59257-870-2

ISBN: 978-1-59257-885-6

ISBN: 978-1-59257-935-8

ISBN: 978-1-59257-944-0

Check out these and more than 30 other business titles in *The Complete Idiot's Guide®* series.

ALPHA